An Arts in Education Source Book

Source Book

A View from the JDR 3rd Fund

An Arts in Education Source Book

A View from the JDR 3rd Fund

Kathryn Bloom
and
Junius Eddy
Charles Fowler
Jane Remer
Nancy Shuker

Edited by Charles Fowler

The JDR 3rd Fund, 30 Rockefeller Plaza, New York, New York 10020

Copyright 1980 by the JDR 3rd Fund, Inc.
Distributed by the American Council for the Arts,
570 Seventh Avenue, New York City, New York 10018.

Library of Congress Catalog Card Number: 79-93012
ISBN 0-9604224-0-4

Designed by Kenneth Dresser
Printed by Corporate Press, Washington, D.C.
The typeface is Palatino

Photo Credits: Page 2, Karl F. Stewart, Imaginarium, Pittsburgh, Pennsylvania; page 11, Related Arts in Education Project, Carbon-Lehigh (Pennsylvania) Intermediate Unit; page 12, Jefferson Primary School, Little Rock, Arkansas; page 23, CEMREL, Inc., St. Louis; page 24, Rob Rhees, Columbus (Ohio) *Dispatch*; page 54, Jim Allison, Jefferson County Public Schools, Lakewood, Colorado; page 86, Pennsylvania Creative Music Workshop; page 94, Montclair (New Jersey) Public Schools; page 120, Kramer School, Little Rock, Arkansas; page 144, Central Susquehanna Intermediate Unit, Lewisburg, Pennsylvania; page 151, Imaginarium, Pittsburgh, Pennsylvania; page 152, Pennsylvania Governor's School for the Arts; page 180, Oklahoma State Department of Education; pages 202 and 214, Jim Allison, Jefferson County Public Schools, Lakewood, Colorado; page 236, Charles Fowler, Overcoming Learning Difficulties Through Music, Cordova School, Alhambra School District No. 68, Phoenix, Arizona; page 240, CEMREL, Inc., St. Louis; and page 244, Central Susquehanna Intermediate Unit, Shamokin, Pennsylvania.

CONTENTS

ABOUT THE AUTHORS

Kathryn Bloom. For her entire professional life, Kathryn Bloom has served the cause of the arts and arts education. A graduate with distinction from the University of Minnesota, she has held the position of Consultant on the Arts for the Association of Junior Leagues, has taught art, and was supervisor of art education at the Toledo Museum of Art. She was Director of the Arts and Humanities Program of the U.S. Office of Education from 1963 to '68 and, at the same time, Special Advisor to the Commissioner of Education representing him in working with the National Endowment for the Arts and Humanities and other government agencies and professional organizations. From September 1978 through August 1979, she was Director of the Arts in Education Program of the JDR 3rd Fund, and it is this 12-year program that is the subject of this book. At the present time, she is Director Emeritus of that program.

Junius Eddy. A former university theater professor, television playwright, film writer, and education journalist, Junius Eddy has been an arts education advisor for both the Ford and Rockefeller Foundations. In the late 1960's, he was an arts education specialist with the Arts and Humanities Program of the U.S. Office of Education. Since 1975, he has provided consulting and writing services to a number of government agencies, including the Department of Health, Education and Welfare and the National Endowment for the Arts, as well as to foundations, arts councils, school systems, and institutions of higher education. At present, he is an independent consultant in the fields of education and the arts residing in Rhode Island.

Charles Fowler. A Washington, D.C. free lance writer, Charles Fowler has been Education Editor of *Musical America* since 1974. He has written widely on the subject of arts education—in book form, pamphlets, scripts for video and film presentations, and in scores of articles. As Consultant in the Arts, he has worked for such diverse organizations as The National Symphony Orchestra and Walt Disney Productions, and for numerous projects, including the National Endowment for the Arts' Task Force on Education and the Rockefeller Panel Study of the Arts in Education. Fowler's degrees include a Doctor of Musical Arts from Boston University. He has taught at every level, and from 1965 to 1971 was Editor of the *Music Educators Journal* for the Music Educators National Conference.

Jane Remer. Even though she holds an M.A. in Teaching with a major in French from Yale Graduate School, Jane Remer has spent most of her professional life in arts education. Early on, she was Assistant Director of Harkness House for Ballet Arts, Assistant Director of Young Audiences, Inc., and, from 1967 to 1972, Assistant Director of Education at Lincoln Center for the

Performing Arts. This was followed by a year as Special Assistant to the Director of New York City's Learning Cooperative, a unit of the Board of Education. For six years, she was on the staff of the Arts in Education Program of the JDR 3rd Fund, most recently in the capacity of Associate Director. At present, she is writing a book based on the experience of the League of Cities for the Arts in Education.

Nancy Shuker. In her previous work with the Fund, Nancy Shuker served as Editor of the book, *Arts in Education Partners: Schools and their Communities*. She holds a degree in journalism from Northwestern University. Among her positions, she has been Director of Research for Corporate Affairs for CBS and has worked in the same capacity for Senator Jacob Javits. From 1969 to present, she has worked for Time Incorporated, chiefly as director of research for various publications, including the *Time-Life Library of Photography*, and as picture editor of the *Time-Life Library of Boating*. Currently, she is a free lance consultant for Time-Life Books in Alexandria, Virginia.

INTRODUCTION

From September 1, 1967 to August 31, 1979, the Arts in Education Program of the JDR 3rd Fund has pursued one major goal: to discover and refine a process for making all the arts integral to the general, or basic, education of all children in entire schools and school systems. During this twelve-year period, a framework was devised for exploring several approaches, and much time, effort, and a considerable amount of money were invested in giving form and substance to the idea.

In a publication of this kind, it is not practical to include detailed information regarding all of the projects and programs with which the Arts in Education Program has been associated. Further, it seemed that descriptions-in-depth of selected programs would be of greater interest and value to the reader than summary information concerning a much larger number of efforts. Therefore, case studies were commissioned in three categories: (1) The earlier programs initiated during the first six years: University City, Missouri and Jefferson County, Colorado; (2) School districts in the League of Cities for the Arts in Education: New York City and Winston-Salem; (3) State education departments in the Ad Hoc Coalition of States for the Arts in Education: the Pennsylvania Department of Education and the Oklahoma State Department of Education.

The case study approach represents an attempt to achieve   xi some objectivity by having independent writers—though ones admittedly knowledgeable about and sympathetic to the overall goals of the Fund—document these programs through on-site interviews and observations. The writers probed the human interactions, problems to be overcome, and the dynamics of change—some traumatic, some triumphant—that have characterized these programs. The intent is to share these experiences with those who may aspire to move in a similar direction and, at the same time, to document the Fund's work over its 12-year history. The case studies were commissioned in 1978 and are updated through 1979.

The several Appendices are compilations of information and understandings gleaned from the Fund's involvement with various arts projects and work with the League of Cities and the Ad Hoc Coalition of States. Appendix A includes brief summaries of all the projects the Fund has been associated with along with a list of the grants the Fund has made. Appendix B summarizes the processes and strategies school districts in the League used to organize comprehensive arts in general education programs and provides addresses for individual districts as a source of further information about specific programs. Addresses for the states in the Coalition are also provided.

Appendix C defines frequently used terminology in an attempt to establish a common language to facilitate more accurate communication. Appendix D presents a rationale for the arts in education—ten specific ways that the arts can contribute to the basic education of every person. Appendix E lists ten characteristics of school systems that have developed effective arts in general education programs, features that ensure an improved educational program. Appendix F characterizes collaborative community/school arts efforts on various levels of educational effectiveness.

A book that attempts to promulgate the accumulated wisdom of 12 years of effort is necessarily the work of many people. Chief among these are the several writers who have set into words the story of the Fund's work and done so with deft eye and keen insight. A special word of thanks is extended to Jane Remer in recognition of her invaluable editorial and organizational advice. Dorothy O'Hara was unfailingly patient and persistent in compiling a variety of presentation styles into a consistent manuscript. I am particularly grateful to Charles Fowler for his expertise and care in editing the entire volume.

In essence, the exposition that follows is a tribute to all the people who have labored diligently to bring the arts—all of them—to all the students in their schools—the chief state school officers, state education department personnel, school superintendents, school board members, principals, artists, arts education specialists, classroom teachers, and parents who had the vision to see the lion in the stone. Without the risks they took, there would be no story, nor could education and the arts have arrived at the collaborative and complementary state they have attained.

Kathryn Bloom

PART I
The First Six Years

CHAPTER ONE
Defining the Task

Kathryn Bloom

In 1963, the Rockefeller Brothers Fund asked a group of prominent citizens from all parts of the country to join in a study of the future development and support of the performing arts in the United States. The study was conducted as a Rockefeller Panel Report on the future of theater, dance, and music in America under the chairmanship of John D. Rockefeller 3rd. The report that resulted, *The Performing Arts: Problems and Prospects*, was published in 1965.

The purpose of the study was to present a thoughtful assessment of the place of the performing arts in our national life and to identify the impediments to their greater welfare and to their wider enjoyment. As such, it was not intended to address specifically the issue of the arts in education. However, as testimony was presented, education and its role in making the arts central to American life was emphasized time after time. As a result, the Report contained a chapter regarding the importance of schools, families, and arts institutions in helping young people develop an understanding and enjoyment of the   3

I am convinced that the quality of our individual lives and the quality of our society are directly related to the quality of our artistic life. We need the arts as the key to the higher order of things—our cultural heritage, our gift of expression, our creative faculty, our sense of beauty.

performing arts.

A remark made by one panel member caught Mr. Rockefeller's attention. It was that perhaps no more than one or two percent of the total population nationally was actively involved and interested in the arts. Four years later, in a major address given in 1969, he expressed his reasons for concern:

> I am convinced that the quality of our individual lives and the quality of our society are directly related to the quality of our artistic life. I cannot prove this to you mathematically or in a test tube, but I know it as an article of faith and I know it through experience— and I believe that you know it too.
>
> If we think seriously about the quality of life, we are forced back to the fundamental questions. What is it all about? What are the end objectives of life? What does it profit us if we solve the great problems, but lose our humanism in the process?
>
> If we really care about the dignity of the individual, about his potential for self-fulfillment, then we must have a deep and rich sense of the place of the arts in our individual lives. We need the arts if we are to be whole human beings—fully alive and vital and in control of ourselves and our environment. We need the arts as the key to the higher order of things—our cultural heritage, our gift of expression, our creative faculty, our sense of beauty. We need the arts if we are to have discriminating taste, the ability to judge levels of quality in all the works of man. And we need them if we are to have the truth—if we are to understand the problems that beset us and if we are to understand ourselves.

During 1966, following the publication of The Panel Report, Mr. Rockefeller convened three exploratory meetings to discuss the feasibility of establishing several pilot projects to determine whether or not the arts could be made a part of the education of every child in entire school systems. The number of participants attending each meeting was not large, but they represented a wide range of interests, experience, and commitment—school administrators and teachers, concerned citizens, persons associated with public and private agencies, and representatives of professional organizations.

The discussions focussed, almost predictably, upon all of the problems that would have to be confronted. To cite several examples:

• Opinion polls showed that even though parents felt the arts were desirable in the education of their children, they also ranked these areas of study at the lowest level of importance in the total educational program.

• How, conceivably, could time be found to offer sequential courses in all of the arts throughout the grades and high school, considering the length of the school day and week, and the number of "solid," or required courses which had to be taught?

4

• Many teachers in grade schools have had little or no

training and experience in the arts and felt uncertain and uncomfortable at the prospect of teaching these subjects. Besides, it was generally accepted that the arts should be taught by highly qualified specialists, and no school system could possibly afford to employ the number of specialists needed.

- In the high schools, art and music were elective subjects. Since the art and music courses, almost without exception, were structured for students with special interests and abilities, only a minority of students were attracted to them. Nationally, about ten percent of the high school population took one or more courses in the visual arts; about twenty percent elected music instruction.

- At that time, student competition for admission to colleges and universities was keen. Since admission standards were based essentially on academic achievement, students who had taken art and music courses were penalized since these courses were considered less important than academic subjects as preparation for higher education.

- Even though community arts institutions had a long history of offering educational programs for school systems, the working relationship between these two types of institutions was often an uneasy one. Professionals in museums and performing arts organizations frequently had little understanding of educational goals and practice and how to relate to them. Many educators lacked an awareness of ways in which cultural organizations operated, and what could (and could not) be expected of them.

- In times of financial retrenchment or crisis in school systems, one fact which could be depended upon absolutely was that specialist positions and programs in art and music would be among the first to go.

- There was no real constituency for art and music in the schools at the community level. For example, if it was necessary to trim the budget for the marching band, parents of youngsters in the band might appear at a board meeting to register their protests. If the total number of art and music specialists in a school system was reduced, meaning that students received substantially less instruction in these subjects, parents might find this a regrettable but necessary decision. However, concerted action was seldom taken at the community level to convince decision-makers in school systems that these instructional services were desirable and important, and that it was necessary to find financial resources to maintain them.

In brief, the arts in education were regarded as superficially respectable but of little practical importance. Traditional art and music programs mainly addressed the interests and needs of talented youngsters, although those with special abilities in the arts have been, over time, an invisible minority in the schools. Persons in school systems at every level of responsibility were, and are, the products of the kinds of schooling that seemed to

Opinion polls showed that even though parents felt the arts were desirable in the education of their children, they also ranked these areas of study at the lowest level of importance in the total educational program.

5

call for change. With little or no exposure to the arts and only a vague understanding of their value in education, there was little, if any, public motivation to address a problem that would be complex and would be uncertain as to outcomes. To attempt to move the idea forward would certainly mean a high risk venture.

In 1965, a year before the three meetings were convened, the Elementary and Secondary Education Act (ESEA) had authorized the largest federal education appropriation ever in the nation's history raising hopes and expectations for improving the performance of elementary and secondary schools. Under ESEA, a large number of grants were being made to school districts nationally for projects in the arts.

The fact that these grants were awarded was encouraging, but as a result some questions were raised about the staying power of the projects. Long before ESEA was passed, experience had shown that school districts were willing to administer cultural enrichment projects that were supported by outside grants. However, these special projects were often considered even more peripheral to educational goals than art and music programs within school systems. Once the grant period expired, so did the project.

There was an awareness among the participants in the Rockefeller meetings that the climate seemed to be right for changing the role of the arts in the schools, but that federally funded "special projects" was not the definitive answer. What was needed was an examination of root causes of the situation that existed, and the development of a systematic, carefully thought-out approach calculated to elicit new solutions to old problems.

Origin of the Idea

In considering ways to devise a program that would make the arts accessible to a much larger segment of our population, Mr. Rockefeller felt it was desirable to begin with children and young people at the elementary and secondary school levels. The question he asked was masterful in its simplicity: "Can we make all the arts part of the education of all of the children in our schools?"

In September 1967, I took a partial leave from my position in the U.S. Office of Education to work four-fifths time as a consultant to the JDR 3rd Fund and its president, Mr. Rockefeller. My assignment was to explore the feasibility of establishing three or four pilot projects to test the idea that the arts could be made part of every student's general education. Through a series of discussions, we agreed on a framework for this exploratory work:

1. We would operate from the premise that the arts *are* important in the education and lives of young people and adults, rather than trying to prove that they should be.

6

2. Rather than concentrating only on art and music, which were the art forms ordinarily taught in the schools, the definition of the arts would be broadened to include theater, dance, and other disciplines.

3. Artists and community arts organizations would be involved in pilot projects and would be regarded as major resources for teaching and learning about the arts.

4. Pilot projects might be new efforts, or they might build upon promising beginnings already under way.

5. Pilot projects would be located in sites that gave promise of success, but they should be sites from which generalizations could be made to other schools and school systems. For example, in the suburban school system where the first pilot was located, the yearly cost of educating each pupil was the average cost for suburban school districts of the same size nationally.

6. Rather than operating from the assumption that the status of the arts in the schools should be improved, meaning larger budgets and more specialists, we believed that the arts could contribute as much to the general education of every child as science, social studies, and language arts. We did not wish to make a quantum leap from "peripheral" to "central" in the curriculum, but we felt the arts should be given parity with other required subjects.

7. It was agreed that grant monies would be appropriated by the JDR 3rd Fund to support pilot projects. Such action would be taken only where there was evidence of a high level of interest on the part of school decision-makers, a willingness to make local financial commitments including in-kind services, and a desire to incorporate new and effective practices into the educational program of the school or school system.

8. Finally, and by no means least in importance, we knew that we could not anticipate equal gains in all projects with which we worked and, in fact, that some might fail. Mr. Rockefeller cautioned particularly that we should not expect results too quickly and that during the developmental stages of any undertaking, it was a mistake "to pull up the plant to see whether the roots were growing."

During the fall of 1967, I began visiting several school districts which had excellent programs in art and music, one district that had a well-developed theater program, and another that offered extensive instruction in movement and dance in the elementary grades. These efforts were not productive. One reason is, regardless of the quality of individual programs in the arts, the persons who administer them generally do not make policy decisions affecting the larger operation of school systems. Power resides elsewhere.

The approach I then pursued was to locate sites in which the arts in the schools were valued at the community level and where it would be possible to gain the support of school boards and superintendents in testing pilot projects. The first potential location identified was University City, Missouri, which is described at length in the case study written by Junius Eddy later in this publication.

We believed that the arts could contribute as much to the general education of every child as science, social studies, and language arts.

7

Procedures designed to develop staff capabilities were used to expand personal and professional interest and competency in the arts among teachers at all elementary grade levels.

Establishment of the Arts in Education Program and the First Pilot Projects

Early in 1968, Mr. Rockefeller and I had several discussions about the establishment of an Arts in Education Program within the JDR 3rd Fund based on the exploratory work and information gained during the first five months of my consultancy. At the April 15, 1968 Trustees meeting, the Arts in Education Program was established as part of the Fund with an annual appropriation of $500,000 a year and, at Mr. Rockefeller's request, I became the Program's Director on September 1, 1968.

At this same meeting, the Trustees of the JDR 3rd Fund appropriated an initial grant in the amount of $232,500 to the School District of University City for a three year period. On May 1 of that year, the first arts in education pilot project began.

Early in 1968, Dr. Gordon J. Klopf, then Dean of Faculties (now Provost and Dean of Faculties) at the Bank Street College of Education, was seeking support for a project that would study ways to integrate the arts and humanities into the curriculum of an elementary school. This proposal was discussed with persons in the U.S. Office of Education. For various reasons it could not be supported by the Office of Education, and I began to think about it in relation to the JDR 3rd Fund.

The intent of the proposal was consistent with the Fund's interests. After a number of discussions to clarify objectives and procedures, it became the second pilot project to be supported by the JDR 3rd Fund. The Arts and the School—A Program for Integrating the Arts in an Elementary School—was carried on during a three year period in Public School 51 in New York City.

Procedures designed to develop staff capabilities were used to expand personal and professional interest and competency in the arts among teachers at all elementary grade levels. These procedures were directed toward reaching several goals:

1. To help school staff identify resources and obtain support materials that could be used to bring all the arts to all the children.

2. To extend the character of arts activity in the school by including creative use of language, dance, and drama, in addition to new thrusts in the visual arts and music.

3. To explore the possibilities for cooperation between schools and outside arts agencies, such as museums and cultural groups, which could extend the scope of the arts for children beyond the school and into the district and the larger community.

4. To build leadership—a people-support system—in the school to design and carry out an on-going integrated arts program.

The pilot project at Public School 51 had a high level of success in affecting administrators, teachers, and students in the school. As a result of the work done, clearer ideas and strategies were formulated for the installation of a total arts program in an elementary school.

During the three years of the project's duration, Bank Street College found that the school principal was the most critical person in the development of the program. As a result, a second project was designed by the Bank Street College, Developing Arts Leadership Teams. It focussed on teams in five elementary schools in the New York City area. Each team included the principal, a teacher, and a staff person from a cultural institution in the area. It was a first and major step in leadership training, both within schools and at the community level, for the arts in education.

The second proposal which developed into a pilot project came from the Mineola Union Free School District in Mineola, Long Island. Even though traditional programs in several art forms were taught in the seven elementary and secondary schools, a group of administrators and teachers felt that the arts were being seriously neglected. In 1965, three years prior to association with the Fund, the superintendent, Dr. Benjamin Wallace, issued a statement supporting the concept of the arts as complementary to the district's goals and stating that they should be an integral part of the total school environment. Conventional programs in music, art, and drama were to be reinforced by a series of artistic experiences and events designed to affect all students, kindergarten through twelfth grade. These experiences would be provided by artists and arts institutions working in collaboration with school faculty members. The budget set by the school district in 1965 was one thousand dollars which, by 1969, had increased to ten thousand dollars.

By 1968, the Fund and the district started to consider a more comprehensive effort. The Mineola staff felt that there was great educational potential in its program, but recognized that they needed to involve more children, to integrate the arts into the total curriculum, and to increase staff and community understanding and acceptance of the arts as an essential part of instructional content.

We recognized that even though many of the schools had taken advantage of performances, exhibitions, and other cultural opportunities, little had been done in an organized fashion to develop related services to the schools such as workshops for students by artists in residence. Nor had systematic efforts been made to explore the relationship of activities of this type to general educational objectives and practices.

At the end of the five year grant period, the Integrated Arts Program which emerged became the focal point of all arts activities and experiences in the schools, and it continues to be totally supported by the Mineola School District. It is comprised of three separate but interrelated components: (1) The Integrated Arts Curriculum for Classroom Teachers; (2) The Arts Events Program with professional performances and experiences for bringing all the arts to all the children; and (3) The Studio Arts Program which provides for regular instruction in music, art, and drama.

Conventional programs in music, art, and drama were to be reinforced by a series of artistic experiences and events designed to affect all students, kindergarten through twelfth grade.

9

The Integrated Arts Program continues to pursue three major objectives:

- to demonstrate the feasibility and value of exposing all children to a variety of arts experiences;
- to reaffirm the place of the arts in the school curriculum, not as segregated activities but as an integral part of the children's learning environment; and
- to provide opportunities for children that will make it possible for them to draw upon the arts for pleasure, and for information about the range of possibilities open to them as human beings.

Overall, then, these early projects were as valuable in terms of sorting out the problems that had to be dealt with as they were in beginning to establish new goals for the arts in education and, accordingly, new modes of operation.

CHAPTER TWO
Extending the Concept

Kathryn Bloom

In retrospect, the fact that the Fund's efforts were exerted simultaneously in several directions, accounts for the accumulation of expertise in the deployment of a variety of strategies to solve the multitude of problems plaguing arts education. For example, several grants were made concurrently with those awarded to the pilot projects. These projects were less ambitious in scope, since they concentrated on one art form such as the visual arts, or on several grade levels rather than on all the arts for all grades from kindergarten through high school. In some instances, they used a different approach to try to solve one or more of the wide range of problems with which the pilot projects were concerned, such as the best means for establishing connections between the arts and other subjects.

As a result of these efforts, an increasingly useful body of knowledge was accumulated regarding the essential ingredients of an arts in general education program, and a variety of procedures that could be used by school systems in developing and implementing such programs.   13

Beginning in 1970, an opportunity presented itself to determine whether this body of knowledge could be applied in a different and much larger school system. Intensive work began with representatives of the Jefferson County (Colorado) School District, and the planning process was expedited by the fact that people from Jeffco, as the District is known locally, visited programs under way, talked with project people, and profited from their experience. The program which grew out of this planning process is described in one of the case studies that follow.

A similar approach was used, starting in 1971, with faculty members of the Ridgewood (New Jersey) Public Schools. Limited financial support and technical assistance was provided by the Fund for developmental purposes. This assistance enabled several faculty members to visit and observe selected arts in education projects supported by the Fund, and to use what they learned in planning and implementing their own program mainly using their own district's resources.

Cumulative experience also was a major factor in the planning and initiation of the Creative Education Program in Oklahoma City in 1972. The Creative Education Program was designed to offer a broad range of services at the community level. A major emphasis, however, was Opening Doors, a cooperative project of the Oklahoma City Public Schools and the Arts Council of Oklahoma City, assisted by the Junior League of Oklahoma City. The Arts Council coordinated the efforts of ten cultural and educational institutions in their development of educational programs based on curriculum needs.[1]

Projects that Support Arts in Education Programs in School Systems

As an alternate approach to refining the concept of "all the arts for all the children," grants were made for projects that were directly related to the Fund's goal, but which did not take place in school systems.

Under this heading, grants were made for two projects designed to develop teaching resources in the arts. The first, matched with funds from the National Endowment for the Arts, was a grant to the College Entrance Examination Board. The Advanced Placement Program of the College Board encourages capable students to do post-secondary level work while in high school and to receive college credit for it. These matching grants supported the establishment of Advanced Placement courses in music, studio art, and the history of art which are now offered in high schools nationally.

---

[1]Opening Doors is described at length, together with a number of other programs that involve cooperative relationships between school districts and community organizations, in *Arts in Education Partners—Schools and Their Communities* published by the JDR 3rd Fund in 1977 and available from the American Council for the Arts.

Traditionally, there have been many teaching resources available for use in specialized courses in art and music, but only limited materials that can be used effectively in classrooms by teachers who have little or no background in the arts. The Aesthetic Education Program at CEMREL (the Central Midwestern Regional Educational Laboratory), which was established the same year that the University City pilot project began, carried out the only comprehensive curriculum work related to the arts in education. These instructional materials were tested in schools in University City as well as other locations, and a number of other projects with which the Fund worked adopted these materials as a component of their arts in education programs.

In 1973, a grant was made jointly to CEMREL and the Asia Society. This was a first step in developing curriculum materials based upon Asian arts and culture for use in American schools.

Traditionally, there have been many teaching resources available for use in specialized courses in art and music, but only limited materials that can be used effectively in classrooms by teachers who have little or no background in the arts.

Research and Evaluation

Some aspects of evaluation of arts in education projects can be done easily. Documentation of projects is not difficult and quantitative elements can be measured, such as how many children, how many teachers, or how many grade levels are being affected. The central issue—evaluating what actually happens to children—remains elusive.

As a first step in developing more effective approaches, the Fund, in 1972, provided support for planning and training conferences and for the development of a *Bibliography for Evaluation of Arts in Education Programs*. This bibliography became part of a new book, *Evaluation in the Arts: A Responsive Approach*, edited by Dr. Robert E. Stake and published by Charles E. Merrill, Inc. in 1975.

The Study of the Arts in Pre-collegiate Education

Closely related to evaluation, although somewhat different in application, is the gathering of basic data on the arts in the schools. In 1973 a grant was made to support A Study of the Arts in Pre-collegiate Education, directed by Dr. John I. Goodlad, Research Director of the Institute for Development of Educational Activities and Dean of the Graduate School of Education, UCLA. This is one of several sub-studies on the school and its community that is part of a much larger research effort, "A Study of Schooling," which is assessing pre-collegiate education. The arts sub-study received joint support from the Fund and the Rockefeller Foundation and will result in the publication of books, reports, monographs, and research data of interest to policy-makers and practitioners in the fields of education and the arts. One result is a book, *Arts and the Schools*,

We are once more searching for the substance of a viable humanism to rescue us from the excesses of our technology; and we just might find the means to infect ourselves with the true contagion of the arts so that they would cease to be something for the very few and become the experience of all.

published by McGraw-Hill, Inc. in the fall of 1979.

Lessons Learned and Used as Building Blocks for Future Development

In July 1973, at a special meeting of the Trustees, Dr. Joseph C. Sloane presented a "Report to the Trustees of the JDR 3rd Fund on the Arts in Education Program." Prepared by Dr. Sloane with the assistance of Dr. Robert Barnard, the report evaluated the growth and development of the program over a six-year period.

In the process of doing the report, Sloane and Barnard visited most of the schools, school districts, and state education departments with which we were working. The assessment of accomplishments and problems encountered as well as suggestions for the future helped to put the work of the Program in clear perspective for the Trustees, and was a valuable resource in charting future directions.

In briefest summary, the report set the stage by observing, "We are in an age of change; education, which is so central to any healthy society, is woefully out-of-date and inadequate; we are once more searching for the substance of a viable humanism to rescue us from the excesses of our technology; and we just might find the means to infect ourselves with the true contagion of the arts so that they would cease to be something for the very few and become the experience of all." It then went on to state: "Something [the JDR 3rd endeavor] strikingly effective over a broad range of educational, and thus social, needs is apparently being discovered, fashioned, or whatever word one many choose to describe the harnessing of an old potency to new ways in unusual places." This statement was placed in a larger context: "The target of these operations was the nearly insurmountable mass of indifference, lack of understanding, antipathy on the part of practical folk, shortage of funds, lack of tradition, cheap substitutes for beauty, and sheer ignorance which have for so long clogged the channels leading from art to people, young and old . . . Is it not pure folly to try to do anything significant in the face of such inertia and active disbelief? We believe not."

The report then described the general plan of attack and went on to analyze Program staff functions—essentially guidance, consultation, and review—as helpful to making each project as autonomous as possible. The use of grant funds was characterized as catalytic: "Since, in most cases, the sums of money involved were not enormous, it was clear that the purpose was to supply the leverage, the missing ingredient, the agent by which change could be brought about . . ."

The section of the report, entitled "Conclusion," reads as follows:

If one is to ask what has been accomplished, the simple reply would be that an exciting and highly

16

promising approach to the teaching of the arts in primary and secondary schools has been started in a number of districts and schools around the country. It is also clear that whole state systems have been influenced to adopt broad programs the result of which will be to achieve these ends.

Both evaluators are convinced that something genuinely valuable is under way there, and both of us feel it would be disastrous to stop when so promising a beginning has been made. The stated goals have been closely adhered to, but they were so huge that the current estimate cannot really speak of *final* success because that would, in effect, imply the conversion of an entire nation. In so far as whole districts have been successfully altered, very real progress has been made. Nor have there been any very significant failures. Over all, success was written in the faces and actions of nearly everyone we met. It may be that young people will not really 'decide' what role 'art will play in his or her life' because *that role will simply be accepted as a natural thing in life,* and the choice will only be which arts and how much.

Here and there programs and projects did not come off as well or as soon as may have been hoped for, but this was sporadic. Both evaluators had a strong sensation of surprise and pleasure at the scope, force, and quality of the educational results we witnessed in New York, Mineola, University City, and Jefferson County. None of these schools will ever be the same again. A significant beginning has been achieved.

We learned that given an acceptable rationale and a plan that provides for orderly change in the educational program, parents, boards of education, and school administrators would continue to endorse, support, and strengthen arts in education programs.

By the time the Sloane report was completed, several basic facts regarding arts in education programs had begun to emerge: For example, we learned that given an acceptable rationale and a plan that provides for orderly change in the educational program, parents, boards of education, and school administrators would continue to endorse, support, and strengthen arts in education programs. This was demonstrated explicitly by the fact that these programs were beginning to be regarded as important as other subjects of study such as language arts, mathematics, and science. Most significantly, school districts and several state education departments with which we were beginning to work had taken some first steps to provide for major operating costs out of their own budgets rather than relying solely on "outside" funds.

It became evident that the willingness of school districts to continue supporting arts in education programs was a direct outcome of certain phenomena observed in the schools: Student achievement levels in basic skills did not decline; rather, they remained constant or tended to rise. Teachers discovered new and more interesting ways of structuring traditional instruction which seemed to result in more effective approaches to learning for children. Attitudes toward and motivation for learning as well as attendance improved among both children and teachers. Individual schools became more exciting and attractive environments.

Over time we have also learned that comprehensive arts   17 in education programs have certain characteristics, or objectives, in common. They:

- Relate the arts to each other and to other subjects of study;
- Strengthen existing art and music programs while expanding to other arts like theater, dance, environmental design, photography, filmmaking, and the literary arts;
- Draw more fully on community resources—artists as well as arts and cultural organizations;
- Meet the special needs of special children—both the gifted and the handicapped; and
- Help reduce personal and racial isolation.

A major question still remained: What procedures could be identified or developed by which schools and school districts could plan and implement arts in education programs most effectively and efficiently, so that they would become solidly institutionalized?

Networks of School Districts and State Education Departments

The Arts in Education Program has always considered the educational needs of large urban school systems to be of major importance. The formal announcement of "All the Arts for All the Children," a joint venture of the New York City Public Schools and the JDR 3rd Fund in May 1974 bore witness to this concern and proved to have far-reaching impact and significance.

My associate, Ms. Jane Remer, was responsible for working with representatives of the New York City Board of Education in planning and developing their Arts in General Education (AGE) Program. She was also responsible for subsequent programmatic developments in five other school districts, and the coordination of the League of Cities for the Arts in Education, a national network formed by these school systems. An excerpt from a paper she wrote recently defines more specifically the unique characteristics of the New York City/JDR 3rd Fund partnership:

> While a review of the original position papers, working documents, and rationale for New York City's AGE program reveals the important legacy the program inherited from six years of the Fund's experience, the New York City program marked a turning point because it was unique in several significant ways:
> 1. For the first time, the Fund and a major urban school system officially agreed to become partners in the planning and development of a comprehensive arts in general education program. This partnership was established through an exchange of correspondence that clearly defined commitments, roles, and functions.
> 2. Defying philanthropic tradition and establish-

18

ing a precedent for the Fund's future work, no major grant was awarded to the school district. Instead, we provided technical and consulting assistance and participated actively in every phase of the program from conceptualization to the design of plans and strategies for management, implementation, documentation, and disssemination. This was also the first time that a staff member of the Fund was involved in the day-to-day operation of a program from the beginning.

3. The arts and the AGE program in particular were to be used to test whether or not and in what ways schools could develop and improve themselves by working in concert with other schools and with the support of an array of agencies, organizations, and people within and outside the system. The hypothesis to be tested was: How can an AGE program and the AGE approach to change—where the arts are used as content, tools for interdisciplinary teaching and learning, and as vehicles and catalysts for innovation—galvanize the process of total school development and result in better schooling for children and youth?

4. In the Fund's earlier projects, the development of programs placed primary emphasis on teacher training, curriculum development, and the involvement of artists and artist-teachers. In AGE, these elements were considered important as program components and as support systems, but *the goal was and is school development through the arts.* The idea was to integrate the arts into the teaching and learning process and thereby alter the entire climate and operation of the school.

5. The emphasis on an organized approach to school change was perhaps the most unique aspect of New York City's AGE program. Through networking and collaboration, basic and cost-effective strategies, the goal was to develop prototypes that would be available for inspection and generate documentary evidence of a model process for other schools and school districts to study and adopt if they wished.

The plan developed for the New York City AGE program established the framework and guidelines for individual programs in five additional school districts with which the Fund joined forces: Seattle, Minneapolis, Little Rock, Winston-Salem, and Hartford. In April 1976 teams comprised of key administrators and other staff members from these six school districts met to exchange information and learn in detail what was taking place in other locations. At this meeting the school districts decided to form the League of Cities for the Arts in Education with the Fund acting as Coordinator.

A second geographically diverse network which has been coordinated by the Arts in Education Program is the Ad Hoc Coalition of States for the Arts in Education. Like the League of Cities, the Ad Hoc Coalition developed from work being done individually with state education departments that had declared their commitment to the idea of all the arts for all the children. Established in May 1975, the Ad Hoc Coalition is comprised of state education departments in Arizona, Califor-

The idea was to integrate the arts into the teaching and learning process and thereby alter the entire climate and operation of the school.

19

These programs illustrate an approach that appears to show promise in its ability to survive even the most dire fiscal and social crises as well as school system overhauls and shifts in administrative and instructional leadership.

nia, Indiana, Massachusetts, Michigan, New York, Oklahoma, Pennsylvania, and Washington. My former associate, Mr. Gene Wenner, was responsible for work with the individual state education departments and for the coordination of the Coalition until he left the Fund in April 1978. Since then, I have assumed this responsibility.

The Fund's associations with state education departments began in 1972 in New York State when Project SEARCH was initiated in six public school districts and one parochial school. The Division of Humanities and the Arts of the New York State Education Department had overall responsibilities for coordinating the project. Major operating costs came from Title III of the Elementary and Secondary Education Act. The Fund made grants over a several year period to assist with the development of teaching materials and evaluation.

The purpose of Project SEARCH was to develop and test learning experiences of an exemplary nature in humanities-arts programs. In addition, it was expected that these sites would serve as demonstrations to other school districts in the state, which has proved to be the case. At present the New York State Department of Education is in the process of implementing a comprehensive statewide plan to integrate the arts into general education.

Also in 1972, a series of discussions between JDR 3rd Fund staff members and representatives from the Pennsylvania Department of Education resulted in a developmental grant to the Department. Subsequently, the arts were declared a priority in basic education in the Commonwealth. The background, the process which was used, and the outcomes are described in Dr. Charles Fowler's case study.

During the next several years the Fund established working relationships with seven other state education departments. In some instances this involved joint agreements with chief state school officers to provide technical and consulting services that were considered in the nature of grants. With other state departments, the responsibilities of the Fund have been informal.

Both networks have accomplished much in a relatively short time. For example, League programs are providing a working definition of the concept and philosophy of the arts in general education in six diverse urban school districts from different geographic areas. These programs illustrate an approach that appears to show promise in its ability to survive even the most dire fiscal and social crises as well as school system overhauls and shifts in administrative and instructional leadership. Not least, given the national educational climate in which the current cry is "back to basics" with no clear understanding of what is basic, this network is proceeding in an organized fashion to develop authentic and tangible demonstrations of how the arts *can* serve the basic educational, social, and emotional needs of children and youth.

The Coalition has proceeded in a more diverse fashion than the League, since the individual state departments were not using a mutually-agreed upon plan. Rather, planning and program implementation have been more spontaneous, and it has taken the state department representatives longer to arrive at a consensus regarding effective practices and procedures. However, priorities for statewide arts in education programs have been established as the basis for program development, and in several states boards of education have approved programs for implementation state-wide.

Authentic and tangible demonstrations are being developed to show how the arts can serve the basic educational, social, and emotional needs of children and youth.

These two networks are mutual support systems and function as powerful multipliers on several levels. First, they accelerate the gains being made within the individual school systems and state departments and provide reality checks through the exchange of ideas and information among individuals with similar goals and objectives. Second, both networks have reached a stage of capability and sophistication that enables them to deal with issues, consolidate their gains, and undertake special projects, with their efforts coordinated by the staff of the Arts in Education Program.

The members of the two networks have taken an active role in disseminating information and materials about their programs. They contribute to professional publications and participate in state, regional, and national conferences concerned with education, the arts, and arts in education. They provide technical and consulting assistance to the Office of Education, the National Endowment for the Arts, foundations, professional arts associations, other school districts, and state education departments and, frequently, to one another.

The significance of the technical and consulting work being done by network representatives should be kept in perspective. Due to the nature of their day-to-day responsibilities the amount of work that can be done by any one individual is limited. Nevertheless, the experience and knowledge acquired by those participating in the two networks, as well as the effectiveness of the JDR 3rd Fund Administrative Fellowship Training Program, is resulting in the emergence of a consultant bank of informed and capable persons.

The Administrative Fellowship Training Program

In the fall of 1977, my associates and I recognized the urgent need for leadership training in the arts in education and established the JDR 3rd Fund Administrative Fellowship Training Program. It was initiated for a half-year period with grants of $5,000 to each of the six school districts and nine state departments in the League of Cities and the Ad Hoc Coalition. In May a second appropriation was made to provide grants of $6,000 to each of these educational agencies to continue the fellowship program during the 1978-79 year.

That year, one state department committed matching funds of $5,000 and five contributed $6,000 so the fellows could work for most or all of the year. Most of the League districts 21 have done likewise.

From observation and the reports of the participants, it is clear that the Fellowship Program has been of major value in providing on-the-job training to fledgling administrators of arts in education programs. It is also clear that school districts and state education departments have been strengthened by the capabilities the fellows bring to these programs and that fellowships of this kind help to spread the word about the arts in education nationally.

CHAPTER THREE
Case Study: University City— Ten Years of AGE

Junius Eddy

In the winter of 1973, there appeared on the educational scene a seminal evaluative document entitled, *All the Arts for Every Child*. It was published by the JDR 3rd Fund, and it reported on the outcomes of a school-based educational change project which this small national foundation had been supporting for nearly five years. In essence, it traced the genesis and initial testing of a unique educational idea: the possibility that the arts could become a fundamental part of the education of every child at every grade level in an entire school system.

The site at which this developmental work took place was the School District of University City, Missouri, a suburban system of about 8,000 students on the western border of St. Louis. Some of the factors that led to its selection by the Director of the Fund's Arts in Education Program, Kathryn Bloom, were its relatively manageable size, its location near an urban center, its growing racial complexity, its commitment to educational change and innovation, and the potential for generalizations applicable to other school systems.

Suffice to say, here, that University City in 1968 seemed to the Fund to be a system—and a community—with a challenging mix of real-world characteristics, more typical than "ideal," and certainly no neat, uncontaminated push-over as an experimental site. With replication possibilities in the background, however, it was an appropriate setting in which to explore an "arts in general education" philosophy, to examine its operational manifestations closely, and find out whether such an idea could be made to work in an entire school system of moderate size.

Genesis of An Idea

As the first of the JDR 3rd Fund's experimental approaches to system-wide arts in education development, the University City Project became the crucible for shaping much of what came later. For it was in the schools of University City that the Fund's subsequent developmental work in this field was originally modeled, sharpened, and clarified. Thus any true account of that work must begin here.

The University City Project got under way with two in-service workshop sessions for teachers in the summer of 1968, and it ended three years later with the board of education voting unanimously to approve a new organizational plan—the Comprehensive Arts Program—to sustain its continuing development. By the time the grant period had officially ended in mid-1971, the JDR 3rd Fund had expended about $232,000 to develop and test the idea, and U-City (as it's known in the area) had contributed almost as much—$215,000.

In addition, the Fund supported a major evaluation component beginning with the second year of the project. This was carried out under a separate $110,000 grant to CEMREL, the Central Midwestern Regional Educational Laboratory located nearby in St. Louis, which had, by then, achieved an impressive record in arts education research and evaluation. In all, CEMREL's U-City evaluation activities were written up in six volumes of detailed studies, the last of which analyzes what it terms "The Transitional Year, 1971-72," covering the project's difficult fourth year, when the school system assumed the major share of project costs.

In actuality, the project phase, viewed in terms of the Fund's continuing involvement, can be said to have lasted *five* years because a two-year extension grant in much smaller amounts was ultimately awarded by the Fund to help see the project through its fourth and fifth years.

All the Arts for Every Child, although appearing during the project's fifth year, focuses almost exclusively on the initial three-year pilot phase. It was prepared and largely written by Dr. Stanley S. Madeja, a former university teacher and U.S. Office of Education art specialist who became the project's first director.

Because it drew heavily on CEMREL's studies and evaluation materials, and because of its thorough-going honesty in dealing with that crucial time, Madeja's account remains the most reliable source of information we have about those early developmental years. The present writer has depended on it substantially, therefore, in the brief summary of those years that follows.

The Setting

When Madeja began visiting University City with Bloom during the pre-project planning period in the winter and spring of 1968, he found an upper middle-class residential community of some 55,000 people. They included college professors, other professionals, white- and blue-collar workers, and persons holding managerial positions in business and industry.

Essentially, it was a city with a strong tradition of community support for education and of parental participation in school affairs. It was also a community in the process of transition, socially and educationally. The city had, five years earlier, placed itself in the vanguard of suburban communities in terms of race relations by passing an Open Housing Resolution which, shortly, would bring about major changes in its population mix and in school enrollment patterns.

In fact, by 1968, as the project began, the percentage of minority students in the schools had already doubled, rising from 7 to 15 percent as increasing numbers of black families, living in desperately overcrowded conditions in St. Louis, began to move into the community. And the school system was already beginning to grapple with "the educational changes required by the needs and demands of the community's new, non-white residents."[1]

It was also grappling with other aspects of educational change. The Ford Foundation's three-year Comprehensive School Improvement Project (CSIP) had just run its course, and the system was deeply involved in all kinds of innovative ideas—team teaching, flexible scheduling, the involvement of teachers in planning and policy level decisions, and so on. In particular, the CSIP project had spurred the system to develop "conceptual approaches to teaching through the integration of subject areas."[2]

Planning and Staffing

It was this emphasis on "the integration of subject areas" that seemed most appealing to Bloom and Madeja as they began their pre-project planning in earnest during the winter

University City was a challenging mix of real-world characteristics and an appropriate setting in which to explore an "arts in general education" philosophy.

---

[1]Stanley S. Madeja, *All the Arts for Every Child* (New York: the JDR 3rd Fund, 1973), p. 9.
[2]*Ibid.*, p. 5.

It was an approach directed to nothing less than the total school curriculum and designed to involve every child in the system.

and spring of 1968, because the project's central thesis was itself integrative in its approach. The Arts in General Education (AGE) Project posited that learning in and through the arts would not be limited to existing art and music programs or to those few students with special talents or a strong interest in the arts. It was an approach directed toward nothing less than the total school curriculum and designed to involve every child in the system.

These concepts were discussed fully with key U-City administrators and faculty members throughout the planning process and, once basic agreement was reached about them, they were translated into specific project goals. The essential tasks and strategies for reaching these goals were outlined, and the staffing needs were clarified.

It was determined at these sessions, moreover, that if the new program was eventually going to be assimilated into the system and continued on an economically feasible basis, the project staff should attempt to operate within the district's existing organizational structure.

In terms of arts staffing, that structure was comprised of one visual arts specialist and six music specialists (three instrumental and three general) serving the district's eleven elementary schools. The two junior high buildings, housing grades seven to nine, were staffed by a total of ten specialists (six in visual art and four in music) who were providing arts experiences in one-semester, required classes in art and music. At the senior high level, art and music were elective subjects and thus a smaller staff of specialists (two in art and two in music, the latter mainly handling band, chorus, and orchestra activities) was needed because the classes were taken by a limited number of students. Opportunities for work in dance or theater were virtually non-existent, except for what could be done with drama in the English classes and by the specialists responsible for physical education. System-wide leadership and coordination was provided by two supervisors, one in art and one in music. Thus, at this time, the total U-City arts specialist faculty—exclusive of the new project staff—came to 23.4 full-time equivalents (FTEs).

In staffing special projects of this kind, however, the basic problem, as Madeja saw it, was "whether to utilize existing staff, reallocating their time to the project, or to bring in outside staff, supposedly objective and innovative, to implement project goals."[3] The decision here was to do a little of both.

Madeja, as Project Director, and two staff members came from outside the system, while two other specialists were appointed from the district. The latter included Diane Davenport, from the general music faculty, and Rose Marie Banks, a social science teacher whose project responsibilities were mainly in environmental studies. The "outsiders" were Jim Allison, an art educator from the Jefferson County Public Schools, Lake-

[3]*Ibid.*, p. 19.

wood, Colorado, who joined the staff in 1969 to coordinate visual arts activities, and Judie Contrucci, a theater arts specialist who had formerly taught in the Pennsylvania schools.

Goal-Setting

Other artists, teachers, and arts educators were engaged from time to time, during the project, to conduct workshops and/or take on various other assignments, but it was these five professionals, serving as the so-called permanent staff, whose job it was to press forward with the primary project goals that had emerged from the planning process. These goals were to be the basis of all subsequent project activities:

- To provide experiences in all the arts for all students at every level of the school system;
- To permeate the general education program with arts concepts in order to improve the level of arts instruction;
- To develop instructional units to provide a sequential learning experience for students;
- To develop generalizable plans which might be used to implement similar projects in other settings; and
- To involve regular classroom teachers in the process of curriculum development.

This final goal ultimately became one of the cornerstones of the project. It was the chief instrumentality used by the staff for getting at most of the other "general education" goals—beginning with the first summer's workshop when seventy-five teachers took part in sessions aimed at helping them formulate specific instructional units. It was, indeed, the primary process by which teachers and, through them, students would be helped to recognize "that there is a body of knowledge in the literary, performing, and visual arts that is relevant to general education and which can be used as content in other subject areas."[4]

By the time the grant monies started flowing to the project and the staff had set to work, these fundamental goals, principles, and strategies had been thoroughly discussed with the then-Superintendent of Schools, Dr. Martin Garrison, his Assistant Superintendent for Curriculum and Instruction, Dr. Glenys Unruh, and with members of the U-City Board of Education. A basic overall commitment to the project's goals had been established—a commitment strong enough, incidentally, to survive the tenure of four successive superintendents and six out of seven new faces on the school board during the initial three-year period.

Thus, as the project began to move forward that first year, two major developmental prongs of an "arts in general edu-

There is a body of knowledge in the literary, performing, and visual arts which is relevant to general education and which can be used as content in other subject areas.

---

[4]*Ibid.*, p. 14.

cation" program had been clearly established: (1) that existing specialized arts programs were to be strengthen *and expanded*, wherever possible, to include all the arts; and (2) that interdisciplinary approaches to learning that drew on and utilized various arts disciplines were to be initiated. A third element—making more regular and effective use of community arts resources of all kinds (agencies, organizations, institutions, and individual artists)—would come more fully into play as the project developed. (It might be added that, although these three elements were subjected to all manner of "reality situations" during the course of the project and were indeed battered somewhat in the process, they ultimately emerged from the pilot crucible largely intact and established themselves as fundamental tenets of the Fund's later work in other settings.)

Moving Ahead

In order to achieve better system-wide understanding of the project, a major effort was made early on to establish a sound rapport with the principals and administrative staffs in each school building. This was the genesis of another tenet that was subsequently built solidly into the core of the Fund's work with later projects: a recognition of the crucial role of the building leader, without whose understanding and support very few curriculum ideas (old or new) are ever implemented in any district's schools. The purposeful orientation of building principals to program goals and strategies became then, another cornerstone of the project; these, after all, were the leaders closest to the firing-line and could, if their cooperation were cultivated, be a moving force in disseminating information and implementing programs in each of the schools.

But principals, like superintendents, board members, and teachers, and even project staff members themselves, don't generally stay put very long. They move (onward and, one must assume, upward), and this matter of the continuing turnover of school personnel of all kinds and at all levels was one of the problems that plagued the project throughout its three-year existence. Furthermore—and this will be re-emphasized later—it has remained a problem ever since, as the "project" shifted to "program" status and was gradually absorbed into the system.

But these were obstacles yet to be encountered as that first year progressed. The responsibilities of the staff, during this period, were about equally divided between working with teachers and giving demonstration lessons in the classrooms, working on the development of new instructional units, and organizing and conducting inservice and summer workshops.

On this basis, Madeja and his colleagues moved through the first year of the project and on into the next two years with considerable success at closing in on the major tasks they had set for themselves and for the district as a whole: developing, with broad teacher involvement, a series of instructional units that tied the arts to other academic areas; creating a number of complementary arts resources in the district; and making more extensive use of the artistic and cultural resources of the greater St. Louis community.

Moreover, as the third year of the project began, efforts were devoted to strengthening its staffing complement. DeWitt Zuse came to University City to serve as Associate Director of the project; he was assigned the task of coordinating the activities of all the arts in the district and of assisting in the transition from project status to an ongoing arts program.

This matter of the continuing turnover of school personnel is a problem that has plagued the project throughout its existence.

Developing Units of Instruction

The major project emphasis throughout the three experimental years was on the development of individual units of instruction which, based in the arts, could be utilized by classroom teachers when and as they wished in the course of their regular academic teaching. Indeed, this is the essence of the AGE idea.

Early on, the decision was made not to attempt to devise new semester- or year-long *courses* in the arts, but rather to provide effective teaching and learning opportunities that drew on the arts within the variables of the regular classroom situation—people, resources, and school organization. The language arts and social studies, for obvious reasons, became the focus of much of this curriculum development activity.

Otherwise, the premises on which this entire effort rested were several. The units were to be designed with a base in one or more of the arts; they would consist of perhaps ten or a dozen "lessons" per unit; they would use a variety of instructional media and materials; and they would not require formal training in the arts to teach them effectively.

In order for these units to serve as bridges between the arts and learning content in required subject areas, the project staff devised a development process whereby classroom (and other subject-matter teachers) worked cooperatively with specialists in the arts to formulate the *substance* of the units and the methods to be used in teaching them.

Madeja's final report lists some 14 separate arts-related instructional units that had been completed by project's end—seven at the elementary level, four at the junior high level, two at the senior high level, plus a "Theater Game File" which could be used by teachers throughout the kindergarden through twelfth grade continuum. Their interdisciplinary nature can be discerned from some of the titles: "The Circus," "Folktale," "Communication of Mood," "The Nature Scroll," and "Gateway to the West" (elementary); "Redesigning the Community," and "Themes and Moods in Spanish Art" (junior high); and "Editing: A Way of Life," and "The Packaged Soul," a media/popular arts/advertising unit (senior high). 31

In a separate development, five "Aesthetic Education Program Packages" were created independently by CEMREL during that same three-year period. Two U-City elementary schools—Greensfelder Park and Daniel Boone—were utilized to field-test and refine these units, and teachers who taught the units experimentally in those schools were consistently involved in the feed-back and refinement process. When finally published by CEMREL, these units were purchased with project funds and introduced to classroom teachers throughout the elementary grades. Their titles—"Constructing Dramatic Plot," "Creating Word Pictures," "Relating Sound and Movement," "Creating Characterization," and "Investigating the Elements: Meter"—reflect their central aesthetic focus and their attempt, when appropriate, to relate one or more art forms.

Of the fourteen AGE units that were ultimately completed, a note in the final report makes this perceptive and down-to-earth observation: "It is unrealistic to suggest that all units are of equal value, but it is even more unrealistic to expect that any individual unit works well every time it is taught." The human factor, indeed, seems consistently to affect even the best of plans, including those which result in producing sound educational materials.

Utilizing and Creating Complementary Resources

While all of this was going on, the project staff also managed to establish a number of other arts-related events and subprojects within the University City school system, among them, a Central Media Laboratory, a manipulative child's environment called, The Space Place, an Experimental Kindergarten, and a student-designed playground structure. And they strengthened a process already under way to some extent—that of enlisting the assistance of artists and performing groups throughout the greater St. Louis metropolitan area in programs and projects aimed at providing a wide range of experiences in the arts for U-City students and their teachers.

Foremost, perhaps, among the internal school-based developments was the establishment, in the University City high school, of a Central Media Laboratory. Initiated during the first year of the project, with major assistance from Harris Jackoway and other members of the U-City faculty, the new Media Laboratory centralized all of the school system's media hardware (equipment) and software (materials) in one place. It served, among other things, as a teaching and learning center in production techniques, a place where students and teachers could learn how to use the available equipment and produce original software of their own, in projects growing out of classroom media study.

Much of the infusion of *outside* artistic and cultural resources which took place during the project period seems somewhat commonplace today, when it is almost standard practice for schools concerned with comprehensive arts education programs to make more effective use of such community resources. Ten years ago, however, these practices were only beginning to evolve—aided, in no small degree, by the federal funds available through titles of the Elementary and Secondary Education Act of 1965 and, more modestly, by the education program of the National Endowment for the Arts.

It is unrealistic to expect that any individual instructional unit works well every time it is taught.

The St. Louis Symphony and the St. Louis Art Museum were, of course, paramount among the cultural institutions brought into more direct association with the U-City schools. By 1970, the staff had managed to transform the traditional, somewhat "elitist" symphony experience (in which only those students who could pay full price got to attend the regular children's concerts) into special concerts open to *all* U-City students. The district contracted with the Symphony for two concerts yearly—one for kindergarten through third grade youngsters, another for those in grades four through twelve—which were planned jointly by the conductor, the orchestra management, and school personnel. The programs were built around a central theme, such as "Sounds from Nature," "Part/Whole," or "Sound and Movement," and new teaching materials were developed for pre- and post-concert use. Each child attending was asked to pay a small, nominal amount, and the school board and the Missouri Arts Council provided the difference.

The St. Louis Art Museum, under a separate JDR 3rd Fund grant, developed a number of new school services and relationships, investigating in depth its existing educational program and redefining the role of its education department. It developed supplementary instructional materials based on the content of the museum's collections which could be correlated with non-art subject areas, particularly social studies. An in-service course for U-City teachers on the museum's resources was also developed and staffed by the museum.

Area performing groups—chiefly those operating within a major area-wide ESEA Title III project called MECA (Metropolitan Educational Center on the Arts)—were also factored into the U-City arts program on a continuing basis. The MECA theater group provided some fourteen performances for U-City students based on improvisational theater techniques and related directly to work teachers were doing in their classrooms using the "Theater Game File."

Beyond this, frequent use was made of the St. Louis Jazz Quartet and other Young Audiences ensembles as part of the project; in each case, the concerts included the history and conceptual explanations of the works these groups were performing.

And finally, U-City served as one of six sites selected by the Arts Endowment to pilot the use of artists-in-residence in the public schools; a metals sculptor from the area worked for a year in the high school, as part of a project that later developed into NEA's Artists-in-Schools Program.

33

Teachers will allot time and energy to introducing arts concepts into their courses, if the arts people make the effort to apply themselves to the problem of defining the content and instructional strategies.

An Interim Assessment

These, then, were the fundamental components of this germinal arts in education pilot project, and CEMREL's evaluation of the final two years analyzed and assessed the project along a number of relevant dimensions.

Directed by Donald Jack Davis, CEMREL's work was designed, in part, to be "formative" in nature, providing the project staff with systematic feedback about the perceptions of school personnel regarding the project's strengths and weaknesses. This was accomplished through a continuing series of interviews with students, teachers, administrators, and the project staff itself.

Madeja acknowledges that these initial feedback interviews underlined some key weaknesses in the original planning and administration of the project: poor communication between some school personnel and the staff; weak working relationships between the staff and the district's existing arts faculty; and a general uncertainty among the faculty about the place of the arts in the total curriculum. Neither group, in effect, seemed to fully understand the needs and aims of the other at this point.

Beyond all this, it is apparent from the final report that Madeja and his staff assigned major importance to the lesson learned about the role that teachers can play in curriculum development. In essence, this lesson was simply that *classroom teachers do not generally have the necessary arts background to develop instructional units in the arts on their own, so that a team approach should be employed when such processes are undertaken*. The language arts and social studies areas are obviously most amenable to this process. "Teachers will allot time and energy to introducing arts concepts into their courses," the report says, "*if the arts people make the effort to apply themselves to the problem of defining the content and instructional strategies.*"[5]

A second major lesson—with direct application to similar developmental projects—is that "when a project has the broad goal of . . . permeating the total curriculum with the idea of all the arts for all the children, it must deal not only with the problems related to the teaching of the arts but with problems concerning the general education of every child. This means that *the educational, social, political, and organizational problems of the total school system*"[6] *will undoubtedly have a moderating impact on developmental aspects of the project*.

And a third major lesson in all this would seem to be that a project of this kind must gain support not only from the faculty and students within a school system but from those people who are the decision-makers—the principals, the superintendent, the school board, and the community at large, as well as the students and faculty. "If one thing that has appli-

---

[5]*Ibid.*, p. 92.
[6]*Ibid.*, p. 99.

cability to other arts programs was learned from the project," Madeja writes, "it is that *a broad base of support must be generated—a base built not around individuals but around an organizational structure and a conceptual framework that can be continued whether or not the initiators still remain.*"[7]

And yet, by the time the project's original three years were up, it was possible for Madeja to suggest that substantial progress had been made. Among other things, he noted that:

- A steady increase had occurred in the numbers of high school students taking arts courses. By 1972, figures indicated that enrollment in regular high school art classes had risen 30 percent, and in music 40 percent, since the beginning of the project;
- Some 45 percent of the elementary students were now involved in arts activities beyond the scope of existing art and music programs—and almost half the elementary teachers over the three years found more time in the school day to teach the arts;
- A "general awareness" had been established within the district that the arts can be "general education" for all students rather than "specialized education" for a few students, thus broadening substantially the base for teaching the arts in the schools;
- A durable and extensive resource of materials for interdisciplinary instruction in the arts had been developed and an overall plan for a comprehensive arts curriculum initiated;
- Complementary resources had been created within and beyond the district which exemplified imaginative ways of using arts-related programs, projects, and events to broaden the arts initiative within an existing educational program.

Madeja concludes *All the Arts for Every Child* with this obvious but always necessary caveat: "The ultimate goal of the Arts in General Education Project is to reach all of the students with all of the arts, and the success of the project will be more easily measured a few years from now on the basis of whether or not the momentum it has generated can be maintained in the University City school system. The project has at least set the conditions for meeting that goal."[8]

"Project" Becomes "Program"

As the arts in general education activities at University City moved from project to program status in the summer of 1971, it received assurances from the JDR 3rd Fund that modest funds would be available to assist with the transition process over the following two years. The total amount under this two-year

A "general awareness" had been established within the district that the arts can be "general education" for all students rather than "specialized education" for a few students, thus broadening substantially the base for teaching the arts in the schools.

---

[7]*Ibid.*, p. 101.
[8]*Ibid.*, p. 92.

extension grant came to $36,900, with $21,300 budgeted for 1971-72 and $15,600 for 1972-73. These funds were utilized for such items as professional salaries and consultants, as well as for continuing the teacher training and curriculum development work initiated during the original project.

Madeja had been dividing his time, following Zuse's arrival the previous year, between his assignment as Project Director and work with CEMREL's developing Aesthetic Education Program. (He became Director of that program in 1971 and ultimately a CEMREL Vice President in 1973, positions he still holds at this writing.) With the adoption by the school board of the plan for a Comprehensive Arts Program, Zuse was appointed Director of the Arts for the district with responsibilities for overall coordination of the arts and carrying out the comprehensive plan which had been developed.

During this initial transition year, the former project staff members—Diane Davenport, Rose Marie Banks, Jim Allison, and Judie Contrucci—were retained by the school system to function as a school-wide "arts resource team," working primarily at the elementary level as initiators of programs and as teacher trainers.

These new staffing arrangements were accompanied, according to Madeja, by some fear among the system's existing arts staff members that the project was taking over their domain and was not supportive of the existing program—yet another sign that not enough emphasis had been placed early in the project on involving the existing arts staff. "Consequently," as the report put it, "the most traumatic year . . . was the one in which the new staffing plans were finalized and carried out."

The leadership traumas, such as they were, received additional fuel in March of 1972 when Zuse resigned. Leadership of the Arts in General Education Program became, at this point, more or less a team function under the general direction of Assistant Superintendent Unruh, who had been closely associated with the project (and highly supportive of it) since the early planning stages in 1968. (Dr. Unruh, in fact, has continued to provide overall direction for the program up to the present time, as part of her district-wide responsibilities for Curriculum and Instruction.)

Now, however, factors over which the Arts in General Education Program really had no control were also bringing changes to the district that, in one way or another, could not help but affect the program's development. Operating costs continued to rise, enrollments declined, and the percentage of blacks in the student body rose to 50 percent (from 15 percent in 1968).

Despite the personnel changes, organizational dislocations, and leadership problems affecting the program, Unruh's report to the Fund covering the two-year extension grant period lists the following accomplishments:

- New art and music electives at the junior high level, and an increase of enrollment in *all* ninth grade arts courses, reversing the trend of previous years;

- A dramatic increase in enrollments in the high school's specialized arts courses, with 70 percent of all students now taking one or more courses compared to 30 percent five years before;
- Continued demand within the elementary faculty for the project-developed instructional units and the CEMREL packages, and regular inservice training in their use;
- Systematic efforts to expand student participation in arts programs provided by the arts resources within the St. Louis community; and
- A reaffirmation by the board of education in 1973 of support for the aims and purposes of the Arts in General Education Program.

Perhaps the most notable development to occur during this period involved the preparation of a proposal for a High School for the Arts, designed as a school-within-a-school (the U-City senior high), which would have the arts at the core of its curriculum. The proposal was developed during the spring of 1973 and successfully funded under a three-year ESEA Title III grant that would begin in the fall of that year.

The proposal envisioned a greatly expanded curriculum in the arts; new interdisciplinary courses tied in with English, science, and social studies; extensive work in projects using a variety of audio-visual media; special arts-oriented field trips; expanded use of community artists as in-class resource persons; and a major involvement of students in redecoration and expansion of the high school's arts facilities. Although the program would be offered to all interested high school students, it was expected that at least 200 students with a strong interest in the arts would be involved daily the first semester in a three-hour interdisciplinary block of time, either in the mornings or the afternoons.

The project was to be carried out under the direction of Tom Lawless, then chairman of the high school's art department, with a budget that enabled three additional full-time faculty members to be hired. An Arts Awareness Curriculum Council had been formed to serve as an advisory body to the project.

It was clear that this significant development had its roots firmly in the groundwork laid during the previous five years of the AGE Project. In fact, one of the principal motivations behind it seemed to be the growing demands being made on the high school for more intensive work in the arts by students who had been influenced during their elementary years by aspects of the original project. The fact that the new proposal placed considerable emphasis on making connections with other academic areas, suggests that the interdisciplinary concerns of that project, though originally having only minor influence at the secondary level, had not been lost on the senior high school faculty.

A further sign of growth was the dramatic increase in the schoolwide staff of arts specialists—up to a high of 37.4 FTE's

There has been a dramatic increase in enrollments in the high school's specialized arts courses with 70 percent of all students now taking one or more courses as against 30 percent five years before.

Clearly, University City is now a radically different place from what it was when the project began ten years ago.

by 1973-74, the year following the two-year extension, as compared with 23.4 FTE's in 1968 when the project planning was begun.

Thus, as the five years of declining JDR 3rd Fund support for the project were officially ending and the program's continuation costs were, for the most part, being picked up by the U-City schools, it was clear that an auspicious beginning had been made, even through the sometimes traumatic transition years. It could not yet be said (after five years, anymore than at the end of the first three) that the ultimate goal of providing "experiences in all of the arts for all students at every level of the school system" had indeed been achieved. But certainly, sound developmental work was still going on, and the gap, in terms of the numbers of students being reached, was steadily being closed.

A Decade of Change

"Coming out of that initial JDR 3rd funding period, when everybody was pretty euphoric about what we had under way—it was like having a new car with everybody on the block looking at you enviously." This is how Diane Davenport, the music supervisor, characterizes the U-City climate following the five years of Fund support. Davenport has been involved since the project began; for the last few years, she served (with art supervisor, Margaret Peeno) as co-coordinator of the Comprehensive Arts Program. She resigned from the system in 1978, but her "insider's" view of the program's ten-year growth and development is remarkably candid.

"We were getting all that attention from around the country, and locally, too—visitors galore," she observes. "And then we kind of slowed down and got into the doldrums, you might say. We went on trying to teach people all these concepts without really having a valid plan or an updated set of system-wide goals. It seems to me we lost our leadership about the time we were ready to consolidate our gains." When Zuse left, Davenport points out, the position of Director for the Arts was never continued and the program was forced to "limp along" under three successive sets of co-coordinators. She says, "They (myself included) were never free enough from teaching to provide the full-time direction we needed."

If she is perhaps a bit too hard on herself in this analysis, Davenport has nonetheless touched on a number of key factors which, over the next five years, appear to have influenced the general shape of U-City's Comprehensive Arts Program today. Some of the other factors are certainly not indigenous to U-City alone: the inexorable series of changes—organizational, financial, and demographic—to which the city and the school district have been subjected in recent years.

Some of these changes are immediately visible; others lie hidden under the surface. But clearly, University City is now a radically different place from what it was when the project began ten years ago and even when it ended five years ago.[9]

One of the first things to strike a visitor to the U-City schools these days is that the major restructuring of grade levels and building units that was adopted five years earlier, has caused substantial organizational changes within the district. Instead of ten elementary schools, a 6th grade center, two junior high schools and a senior high school—in operation during the first five years—there are now eight elementary schools (kindergarden-5), a middle school (grades 6-7), a junior high school (grades 8-9) and the senior high school, housing a High School of the Arts and an alternative unit for career education that function as "schools within a school."

The arts specialist staff, which mans the Comprehensive Arts Program within this new structure, consists today of about 40 persons filling some 33 full-time slots, an increase of nearly ten full-time positions over the 1968 arts staff. To U-City's credit, this increase has taken place during a ten-year period, when the system has lost about 1,050 students (or 13 percent), and when its total faculty has declined by over 70 full-time positions, or nearly 20 percent.

System-wide, U-City's total budget for the arts, *per se*, has risen steadily over these ten years to just over $611,000 during 1977-78 (about six percent of the annual operating budget). Of this, the visual arts receives about $283,000, music about $297,000, and dance and drama (largely at the senior high level) about $30,000.

To keep pace with programmatic increases of this nature during the highly inflationary 1970's, the system's annual operating budget has nearly doubled over the ten-year period, reaching $10.8 million in 1977-78. This has happened despite a recent series of levy failures and the consequent budget-trimming this entails.

Perhaps the most striking change to occur, however, is that affecting the racial make-up of the student body itself, as the non-white (and mainly black) enrollment rose from 15 percent in 1968 to 50 percent five years later, and finally to just over 72 percent in 1978. Richard Palmer, a former U-City school board member, believes that this shift within the student body has helped to sustain the district's commitment to the arts and perhaps given it an even more compelling rationale than was evident when the project began.

Furthermore, there appears (to a casual observer at any rate) to be an unusual degree of harmony today within U-City's racially-mixed student body, whatever incidents and dislocations may have marked these changes. Significantly, too, through all these ups and downs, U-City finds that some 80 percent of its high school graduates consistently go on to attend higher education institutions, many on substantial scholarships.

The arts specialist staff consists today of about 40 persons, an increase of nearly ten full-time positions over the 1968 arts staff. To U-City's credit, this increase has taken place during a ten-year period, when the system has lost about 1,050 students, and when its total faculty has declined by over 70.

---

[9]This narrative was completed during the summer of 1978, and the statistical data encompassed within this "ten-year look" does not extend beyond that point.

A Contradictory Picture

Where, then, amidst all these changes and developments, does one find the arts in the University City schools today? And more particularly, how has the system fared recently with respect to the original goals of the AGE Project and the steady movement toward them that characterized the first five developmental years?

There are no easy answers to these questions, and the picture that emerges is often contradictory. There can be little doubt, on the one hand, that the momentum toward those original project goals has been dampened considerably. At the same time, it is also clear that Univeristy City remains a community committed to the belief that "the arts should be an integral part of the total curriculum," in the language of a recent school bulletin. The school board and administration have, once again in 1978, reaffirmed U-City's long-standing commitment to the district's arts program as a fundamental element of what is called its "Basic and Enriched Educational Program."

Indeed, a visitor finds the schools themselves to be pleasant, busy, and friendly places. The halls in most of the elementary schools are boldly and colorfully painted (one, it seems, by the new principal during the previous summer). There are handsome and often whimsical murals on cafeteria walls done by local artists with student help. And displays of student work abound—African masks, woven fabrics, geometric designs, block printing, colorful cutouts (a follow-up to a Matisse exhibit at the St. Louis Museum), and a wide range of mobiles.

Though much of this work seems clearly to be related to language arts and social studies, apparently it has not been accomplished in the general classrooms. Mainly it has emerged from the art rooms, under the guidance of what is unquestionably an imaginative and dedicated group of visual arts specialists. And one has only to drop in on classes in these rooms to sense what an outstanding group of teachers they are.

The high quality of the specialists on U-City's art staff today is, in fact, one of the fundamental reasons why the program remains a strong one within the conventional arts disciplines themselves. With few exceptions, this generalization can be applied across-the-board; at every level of the system one finds professionals of remarkably high calibre engaged in vivid, essential, and exacting work with students—praising them, demanding, lecturing, exhorting, showing, cajoling, humoring, exemplifying, in short, *teaching*.

Nonetheless, there are those puzzling contradictions. For example: since more specialists are serving fewer schools at the elementary level than was so ten years ago, and since elementary enrollments have been reduced sharply, it's a bit startling to find that—by the school's own estimates—the average per pupil instructional time for both art and music comes only to about 70 minutes a week. This differs very little from school systems which, in contrast to U-City, place only a peripheral emphasis on the arts.

40

To take another example: in a system where the phrase "all the arts for every child" first gained currency, it's a surprise to find most of this masterful teaching by specialist staff still confined to the conventional art forms—the visual arts, and general and instrumental music. Of the 33 full-time arts positions mentioned earlier, about 27 are almost evenly divided between art and music, while perhaps three (all at the secondary level) are largely made up of the part-time services of several dance and theater specialists. (The remaining staff positions are divided between media personnel, leadership and coordination tasks, the "interdisciplinary arts," and several elementary specialists who spend a fifth-time on aesthetic education.)

For several years, two performing artists had been employed half-time as elementary theater-dance specialists, but these positions were eliminated a year ago. "We couldn't justify them," a board member says, "in terms of student contact hours."

Thus, while all of U-City's elementary and middle school students are undoubtedly being "reached" by *all* of the arts, lack of specialists in either theater or dance at these levels would seem to suggest that the substance is minimal in these important art forms. When students reach eighth and ninth grade at Hanley Junior High, where two part-time dance and theater people teach several elective courses, the situation improves somewhat. But with an enrollment of 1,100, these offerings do not penetrate very deeply into the student body.

A full year of either art or music (or a term of each) is required for high school graduation in University City, and this requirement, in full or in part, can be satisfied either at the senior high level or in the ninth grade at Hanley. Many students, indeed, appear to have taken this ninth grade option in recent years, and school officials believe it's a result of the long-term arts in general education emphasis at the elementary level. There is evidence, moreover, that at least 40 percent of Hanley's students are involved in these arts courses annually.

In addition, perhaps another hundred Hanley students yearly are taking a team-taught related arts course called the "A.R.T.S. Program." It's described in the "Hanley Course Booklet" as a program "for those students who have a commitment to the creative arts and who truly want advanced experience in this field." It represents a major attempt at this level to offer a program in "all of the arts," although not "all of the students" can yet avail themselves of this opportunity.

At every level of the system one finds professionals of remarkably high calibre engaged in vivid, essential, and exacting work with students— praising them, demanding, lecturing, exhorting, showing, cajoling, humoring, exemplifying, in short, teaching.

The Senior High Program

For those students who gravitate seriously toward the arts at the senior high school level, the climate improves markedly. About a quarter of the system's arts staff—nearly eight full-time people—work at this level. Virtually all of the arts instruction offered at this level, whether in the specialized disciplines or through integrative tie-ins with other fields, is provided by the 41 faculty of the High School of the Arts (HSA) and the faculty of the district's music department. Curiously, it was not until 1978-79 that the music program finally became a regular part of the HSA.

The visual arts staff consists of five persons representing approximately four full-time faculty positions. Their course offerings range across the board, including ceramics, painting and drawing, sculpture (in a variety of media), textiles, photography and graphics, and art history (both European and American). In addition, the HSA faculty includes two dance specialists (one nearly full-time and the other nearly half-time) and an English teacher who spends virtually all of his time in theater and drama work. (Incidently, drama and theater are taught as after-school credit courses, an advantage to students who wish a longer practice period and a less congested schedule.) There are, moreover, at least two other faculty members—one a practicing poet who teaches in the English department, the other teaching American studies in the social studies department—who have, in the past five years, been providing most of the regular high school's commitment to the arts in general education idea for HSA students.

The senior high music faculty consists of three persons, one of whom is full-time in general/vocal music (primarily as director of the choral program), and the other two instrumental music specialists (one full time, the other one-fifth time), whose major responsibilities are directing the senior high bands, choruses, and orchestra.

As with the music faculty, the dance and drama staff devote a considerable portion of their time to performance activities—dance concerts and the all-school dramatic and musical productions—as well as teaching specific courses in their fields. (This last year, for example, 21 youngsters enrolled in improvisational theater.)

School officials estimate that some 568 students (or about 36 percent of the high school enrollment) have had at least one "arts experience" this past year, including those involved in courses of an integrative nature in social studies and English. Obviously, those involved in the music program represent a good share of this, since the indications are that about 200 to 250 students are taking HSA courses any given year.

Integrative Work in Elementary Classrooms

With respect to the centerpiece of the original project—the goal of permeating the general education program with arts concepts and developing instructional units to provide a sequential learning experience for students—there is no discernable common pattern within U-City's elementary schools today.

Certainly, it cannot yet be said, ten years later, that arts concepts *permeate* the general education curriculum, nor that the instructional units that were developed yet provide the

42

sequential learning experience for students that was originally envisioned.

However, in addition to a set of the major CEMREL packages now available in nearly every building and at the Arts Resource Center, each elementary classroom contains a copy of the "Theater Game File," every one of which is "well used," according to Davenport. Furthermore, over the past few years, three more AGE instructional units have been developed (mainly by specialists but with considerable classroom teacher in-put): "Sea Magic," a unit for grades three to five on the underwater environment; for grades four to six, units on "The Eskimo" and "The Northwest Coast Indians."

Overall, it would appear that the utilization of these instructional resources (and of the AGE packages in particular) varies considerably from school to school. In at least two of the schools, there seems to be an unusually high level of experience and familiarity with approaches based on this kind of integrative work and aimed at giving the arts a more fundamental role in the daily learning lives of youngsters in the classroom.

One of these schools, Daniel Boone, with a predominantly black enrollment, has been used over the years as a testing and demonstration site for CEMREL's aesthetic education packages. Here, it is apparent that aesthetic education has become a vital part of the curriculum; at least 10 of the 20 teachers were said to be using CEMREL units on a regular basis, and from all one could observe, using them with genuine skill and enjoyment. New teachers are constantly offered (and accepting) opportunities to become familiar with new CEMREL units of which there are nearly 20 in all geared to various elementary levels. On the other hand, many teachers indicated that they weren't too familiar with the various AGE packages; their use, in fact, appeared to be more random in nature.

Daniel Boone School seems, in a sense, to have developed a kind of vertical design for its Comprehensive Arts Program; that is, there is somewhat less interest in the integrative model (tying in the arts "horizontally" at each grade level with other subject matter areas) and a greater concern for aesthetic education as something of a separate vertical track. Aesthetic education simply takes its place in the curriculum along with the other academic subjects. Tie-ins are accomplished largely through the contributions that familiarity with aesthetic concepts can make to individual teaching styles and practices.

Just the opposite situation seems to prevail in Flynn Park, the second of the two elementary schools in which the arts appear to have a firm foothold. There is, at Flynn Park, what might be regarded as more of a horizontal approach—more regular use of the AGE units that make direct links to other areas of the curriculum at all levels. Although the CEMREL units have a modest following among the teachers here, there is somewhat less stress or dependence on them as a separate body of aesthetic learning. This, incidentally, is a school with a mainly white enrollment, almost the reverse of Daniel Boone. However, both schools, each in their own way, suggest in 43

With respect to the centerpiece of the original project— permeating the general program with arts concepts—there is no discernible common pattern within U-City's elementary schools today.

rather exemplary fashion what ought to be going on in school systems with a commitment to this work.

In both schools, the specialists from the Arts Resource Center continue to work quite closely with classroom teachers, assisting with arts-oriented projects in the classroom, creating direct links to the academic work in their own art or music classes, providing resource materials and ideas when asked (and that happens often), and attempting constantly to introduce new instructional units to an expanding group of teachers. And in both schools, the principals, each in *his* own way, are strongly supportive of faculty members who teach in this fashion, without insisting that the approach be adopted by those teachers who don't feel committed to it or comfortable with it.

It appears, however, that the other six elementary schools range up and down the scale on these matters. In some, there seems to be a moderate commitment to the idea, while in others, it appears that very little is going on that could be termed truly integrative. To be sure, one can find classrooms where obviously skilled teachers are doing sound and purposeful work, but not necessarily involving the arts to any real extent.

Such impressions about the range and extent of integrative arts developments in these six schools are generally substantiated by teachers, principals, and supervisors across the district. When teachers are asked for their opinions about the AGE or CEMREL units, their responses range from, "They really do help in getting social studies [or language arts] concepts across," to, "Well, I use the 'Theater Game File' once in awhile, but I haven't done much with the rest of them lately."

The principals—four of whom were assigned to their schools in the last five years, and only one of whom has been in his school since the project began—are highly supportive of the arts in general education concept and give great credit to the project for opening their eyes to its scope and purposes. But they seem to agree that, although every elementary child in the system is being "reached" by art and music at least on a weekly basis, "probably only 20 to 30 percent get a real involvement in terms of the total umbrella concept."

There is a general feeling among these principals that some of the instructional units "are too complicated to be used much; teachers try them and don't get very far; and the expectations for some of the units are too high for the grade levels where they're being used." The root of the problem, as one principal put it, is that "the newer teachers haven't had a hand in developing the units, and we don't have enough specialists or resource teachers to train them to do it, or *sometimes* even enough to provide guidance for teaching them. There's really no time, anymore, for specialists to get together with teachers (or with one another) on a regular basis."

The two co-coordinators of the Comprehensive Arts Program, Davenport and Peeno, hold generally similar views about the extent of the integrative arts processes at the elementary level. Requested at one point, to try (if they could) to make a percentage estimate of each school in terms of the degree to which the arts were consistently integrated into general class-room learning, they were in reasonably close agreement in their estimates. Their percentages, respectively, ranged all the way from 2 to 5 percent in one school to 70 to 80 percent in another. (They both agreed, incidentally, on the two schools referred to earlier as outstanding in this respect). When both sets of re-sponses for all eight elementary schools were averaged out, they came to about 32 percent overall.

Among the more positive developments just getting under way in the elementary schools, was a new visual arts project for all fifth grade classes sponsored and developed jointly by the U-City Schools and the St. Louis Art Museum. Entitled "Arts and the Basic Curriculum," the project is focused on ways in which the museum's resources and personnel can contribute directly to the language arts and social studies curriculum. All fifth graders in the system will have spent 12 half-days in the museum during the spring (1978) term. The program is being team-taught by homeroom teachers (following three days of museum orientation) and by specially trained museum person-nel. It's possible that this effort to involve a specific level of classroom teachers in what seems an exemplary approach to the arts in general education idea may serve to reinstitute the integrative approach with a new generation of U-City's ele-mentary teachers and provide the basis for a fresh commitment to the process.

The High School of the Arts

Because of the specialized subject-matter context that is customary in most secondary schools, there has been only limited opportunity to involve senior high non-arts faculty in solid integrative work. This is a factor that Madeja and his colleagues took into account early in the original project and which soon caused them to focus their integrative efforts on the elementary schools.

A visitor is soon made aware that the integrative purposes of the High School of the Arts have been considerably blunted of late.

A visitor to the system is soon made aware, therefore, that the integrative purposes of the HSA have been considerably blunted of late. Although it has managed to continue as a specific entity over the past few years (following the end of the Title III grant), it has not had particularly easy sledding.

Keith Shahan, formerly Assistant Principal at the HSA and subsequently U-City's Director of Personnel, foreshadowed some of the reasons for this in his 1976 Harvard doctoral dis-sertation, completed the year the three-year grant period ended. Shahan's work describes HSA's initial attempts to in-tegrate the various art forms with one another and its subse-quent moves toward integrating the arts generally with the other disciplines: dance tied in with the study of foreign lan-guages, math with aspects of physical education, ceramics with chemistry, physics with photography, and various art forms with English and social studies. 45

Shahan explains some of the problems in communications, scheduling, and course-credit that arose in connection with the program. Because much of the HSA program involved such things as regular field trips (to arts events and institutions), longer classes extending beyond the normal school day, and even some evening sessions with community artists, the "increased demands on the staff rose to almost intolerable levels," Shahan notes, since the staff were all carrying full teaching loads as well.

One way in which students in the HSA were initially identified was through an arrangement which enabled them to select their own faculty advisors. Although this idea soon began to spread to other academic departments, it ultimately foundered because of what Shahan describes as "territoriality"; that is, the fact that some regular faculty members felt threatened when students failed, on occasion, to choose them as advisors. "But advisories are the key concept," Shahan says, "and unfortunately they haven't proved popular in the larger school, where they're seen as a bureaucratic nuisance."

Shahan believes that, measured in terms of "student satisfaction," the program has been a success. "All objective measures have shown this to be true," he points out. He also believes that *varying* degrees of progress have been made, when measured against interdisciplinary program goals, "all without lessening the quality of advanced arts experiences."[10] And he concludes by stating what would appear to be the bedrock problem, namely, that "there has been a successful adaptation on HSA's part to the regular school, but that the regular school still has much to learn from the HSA."

The very fact that the program still exists and continues to engage nearly 250 students each year in its single-disciplined and interdisciplinary work is a considerable testament to the commitment and dedication of the faculty. But many of the same problems Shahan identified continue to plague the program today; bit by bit, it seems, valuable chunks of the original idea are gradually being chipped away, mainly by systemic factors beyond the staff's control.

Tom Lawless, the visual arts teacher who directed the HSA during its Title III years, sums it up this way: "What we're really losing, I guess, is our flexibility, when we're faced with these problems of scheduling, money, procedures, and the like. Take our outside activities, for example—visits to studios, museums, and historic sites; it just about killed us to keep that kind of schedule and carry a full teaching load, too. But the kids got so much out of it, we were glad to do it. Well, that's all been curtailed now, because of legal problems. We now need to carry a million dollars of insurance and have no more than four kids in a car whenever we go anywhere. And that's just about done it in."

---

[10]Keith Shahan, "The Administrative Role in Developing Innovations" (unpublished doctoral dissertation, Harvard University, 1976), p. 58.

Lawless believes that one major setback was the procedural problem of senior high students not being able to choose their own advisors. "That was what got us started, really, as an identifiable subsystem in the school, but as other faculty members began to feel threatened by it, we've been under the gun to abandon that, too."

Albert Salsich, a poet and English teacher, points out that "the problem mainly is the schedule. I'd love to go visit an HSA art class and talk about Whitman, for example, but I've got five English classes every day, and there's just no time for these kinds of interdisciplinary things anymore."

"Interest among our teachers in American studies was intense with respect to arts involvement when the program began," says Dennis Lubeck, a member of the social studies faculty who has worked closely with the HSA. "But it's getting harder and harder to maintain now, I'm afraid."

Despite such frustrations, however, Carol Ray (who presently chairs the art department and heads the HSA), Lawless, and their colleagues are proud of what has been accomplished and believe the HSA will continue to hold its own somehow. They seem determined, moreover, to keep working in these interdisciplinary directions as best they can.

Finally, they point with great pride to an after-school event—"Cabaret Voltaire"—that has by now become something of a monthly institution at University City. It was established early in the HSA's existence as an occasion when students, faculty, parents, artists from the community, and former students can come together and perform in whatever manner or art form they wish. In its way, it's a kind of community celebration of the arts that continues to have a substantial following. "You have anywhere from 50 to 200 students and adults all sitting around and sharing," says Lawless. "It's a very warm and moving time, and we intend to keep it going."

Much of the high school arts program is expressed, of course, in the concerts, dance performances, and theater productions that seem to occur with regularity throughout the year and in other workshops arranged for periodically. An example of the latter is the recent winter afternoon when a principal dancer in the professional touring company of *The Wiz* came out, at the invitation of dance specialist Andrea Lebovitz, and conducted a master class on the high school stage for perhaps fifty of her dance students. Many of these same students, together with their counterparts in art, music, and drama, combined their talents the following week in a generally rousing production of the old Broadway musical, *Anthing Goes*.

On balance, the HSA has proved, until the setbacks of the past few years at least, that solid interdisciplinary work involving the arts *can* indeed be done at the secondary level, when an innovative environment for it exists. The school has clearly expanded the opportunities for students in the arts beyond the conventional art and music program. As Lawless points out, "we've *always* had darned good music and art departments, but what's resulted from our work these past five years is a

On balance, the High School of the Arts has proved that solid interdisciplinary work involving the arts can indeed be done at the secondary level when an innovative environment for it exists.

47

new interest by students in dance, theater, and poetry. That can be traced back, I think, to the original AGE Project and its emphasis on *all* of the arts."

Other Developments

There continues to be a steady if not overwhelming use of community arts resources by the U-City schools, particularly the elementary schools. The spring symphony concerts at Powell Hall are attended by all elementary students; there are visits to Shaw's Gardens for nature study; and performances by professional theater and music groups take place throughout the year.

The Media Center, too, has taken firm root in the system. Teachers have expanded their use of its new facilities in the district's central office building for development of materials and the production of a wide range of instructional aides.

And finally, during the summers and the intervening school years, the arts staff and the Media Center staff have continued to provide opportunities through workshops and seminars for staff development and inservice training in the arts, mainly at CEMREL-sponsored sessions.

Up Against the System

Although the University City schools provide the basis for these highly subjective concluding observations, no exclusive connotation is intended. It is the writer's opinion that the systemic factors, which over a ten-year span seem to have contributed to a loss of momentum for the AGE idea in U-City, are largely endemic to school systems anywhere, regardless of size, type, or location.

The problem of teacher turnover in University City, for example, and similar changes in the administrative staff and the school board itself, appear to present major developmental problems for innovative projects of this sort. Generally, because it happens gradually, the effect is largely imperceptible; but looked at over a ten-year period, the cumulative impact can be profound, indeed.

In University City, there have been six different superintendents since 1968, when the original AGE Project began. School board membership has changed completely once and, in some positions, twice. Only one of the present elementary principals has held his post since the project began, while four others have come to their schools, though not necessarily to the district, in the last five years.

With respect to the teaching faculty, it's more difficult to obtain specific figures. In one elementary school, however, the principal (now in her third year there) indicated that "nine out of 20 teachers who were here when I came are not here anymore." It seems safe to say that a teacher turnover figure approaching 60-70 percent could have been the case in University City over the past ten years, and even that may be conservative. On the other hand, of course, as job security becomes more important in this era of "reductions in force," such severe turnover rates as these might not be maintained.

When it comes to U-City's art specialist faculty, however, the ten-year turnover picture is even more dramatic. As the arts staff expanded over this period from perhaps 25 to 30 part- and full-time positions to its roster of 40 in 1977-78, a total of 102 individuals have moved into and out of those jobs! Only seven people (4 in the senior high school and three in general music), who were on the arts staff when the AGE Project began, are still employed as specialists today.

The turnover of personnel may, therefore, be one of those crucial systemic issues that arts projects in particular must come to grips with in the long run, because the arts have far less of a foothold in education than do most other disciplines. Continued developmental work must build on the gains of each teacher and/or administrator who has come to recognize their value. Retraining and gradual osmosis can be the building blocks, but the inexorable departure and transfer of trained arts-aware personnel often turns that training process into something of a squirrel cage. As the developmental momentum inevitably slows down, those responsible for staff development find themselves working twice as hard merely to hold the ground they've gained. It's not that educators aren't perfectly aware of this syndrome; rather, it's seldom borne in mind when projects are in the planning stages, at a time when countervailing strategies, if squarely faced, might be factored in.

It's interesting to speculate whether the high rates of faculty turnover in University City could be an indirect result of that city's progressive racial policies and the consequent shift from 15 to 72 percent non-white enrollment these past ten years. This may be part of the price suburban systems have to pay when they are courageous enough to take a human-rights stand that provides greater housing and educational opportunities for nearby urban non-white populations. Since 80 percent of U-City's high school graduates are now going on to higher educational institutions, such a stand seems to have paid off handsomely in this instance, and it is a tribute to U-City's strong overall educational program.

The administrative changes, especially those among elementary principals, may have also hampered the steady progress toward project goals. Although each new administrator who came into a principalship position seemed sympathetic to these goals, changes in the leadership of individual school buildings generally mean that innovative approaches begun under previous leadership will be marking time, so to speak, until the new leader has emerged from his or her shake-down period. By that time, moreover, new educational priorities will have emerged—the "basics" are a current example—and it is often difficult to recharge the original innovative batteries. Proj-

As the developmental momentum inevitably slows down, those responsible for staff development find themselves working twice as hard merely to hold the ground they've gained.

ects like those involving the arts in general education, which depend heavily on the sustained support of the building leader, seem bound to suffer from such changes, over time.

And finally, the leadership changes occurring in the AGE Project itself—and in the Comprehensive Arts Program which followed it—have also taken their toll with respect to steady and continued movement toward some of the original project goals. Following Madeja and Zuse as directors of the project, there were three successive sets of co-coordinators providing leadership for the Comprehensive Arts Program under Unruh's overall supervision. Because her supervisory duties as Assistant Superintendent of Curriculum and Instruction were spread all across the district's educational program, Unruh's advocacy role with respect to the Comprehensive Arts Program could never be strongly unilateral in nature, regardless of the depth of her commitment to the program over the years. That commitment has been very deep indeed but, as Richard Palmer put it, "She simply couldn't push the arts at the expense of everything else."

And Palmer, a former school board member, points to other elements of the development problem as well. "Looking back," he says, "the constant organizational reshuffling of the arts staff (project and program) seems to stem from the fact that we've really had two separate kinds of arts approaches in the district. One was focused on the arts *specialists* and another was focused on the arts in general education idea, and we've always been searching for ways to bring about an effective meeting of the two." (Unruh has subsequently pointed out that, during the 1978-79 school year, an effort was initiated to help bridge this specialists/AGE gap by setting aside part of each elementary specialist's teaching time for inservice demonstrations on aesthetic education.)

Palmer believes the failure fully to integrate the existing or newly-hired specialists into the project was one of its real shortcomings (and he is echoing, here, some of the assessments made by Madeja in his final report five years ago). "In a sense," Palmer observes, "that first summer workshop, which relied so heavily on new people from outside the district, may have played a greater part in all this than we knew at the time, simply because it didn't take full advantage of the specialists' strengths that were here."

This question receives retrospective elaboration from Madeja today. "The U-City system was hoping at the time to move forward on a major differentiated staffing pattern model," he commented recently. "And our idea was aimed at getting a group of 22-25 FTEs into that pattern as arts people, some on school-wide resource teams and some doing regular instructional work with kids."

"We had a good core group beginning to form," Madeja went on. "They believed in the idea and *started*, at least, to work as a team. But, like a good ball club or a good business, the team ultimately got broken up as time went on. People left and new people came in, and when this happened, it was hard to sustain the idea because the money, human resources, and the time required couldn't continue quite long enough to get the idea fully established."

It is remarkable, in retrospect, how perceptive Madeja and his evaluators were back in 1972-73 concerning the problems of a systemic nature that were only incipient then but later emerged to compromise particular aspects of the project's subsequent development.

Madeja speaks (in *All the Arts for Every Child*) of the necessity for "re-laying much of the groundwork that had been laid earlier *without interrupting the flow* of the project" as new personnel came into leadership positions. This, clearly, is a problem that has haunted both the project and the program from the beginning, and its root cause, of course, can be traced to the turnover syndrome.

As the original project entered its third year, Madeja noted the need for trained arts specialists to spend more time, not on instructional activities but working directly with the classroom teachers in each building; he noted the need for training "arts facilitators" among the faculties of each school to serve as catalysts and coordinators; and he noted the need for more "administrative help with the project and for improving the working relationships between existing arts specialists and the project." These matters also were never solved completely then, and they remain as continuing needs today.

In the conclusion of his final report, Madeja observed that "a broad case of support must be generated—a base not built around individuals but around an organizational structure and a conceptual framework that can be continued whether or not the initiators (of the project) still remain."

Coming full circle, it is perhaps Madeja who has stated the problem most succinctly with respect to the systemic issues touched on here. "In the last analysis," Madeja said recently, "you can only do so much to get ideas like this started—in the arts or anything else. At some point, early on, you (the innovator) have to deal with that phenomena called 'The School System'—the way it typically behaves, the way it allocates its resources, deals with its staff, sets its priorities, and is affected by personnel changes and by other new educational ideas that come along. And the sooner this happens the better, really, because it forces you to face the realities of your situation."

A Look Ahead

It would be a grave mistake to assume from any of the foregoing that University City's arts program is, in any sense, in the midst of an irreversible decline. To be "treading water" for a time does not imply "going under."

The wonder of it is, in fact, that the process has managed to lodge itself as firmly as it has within the district, given the systemic forces ranged against it. These, of course, include not only the turnover and demographic issues already noted, but 51

The wonder of it is that the process has managed to lodge itself as firmly as it has within the district given the systemic forces ranged against it.

also the decreasing enrollment and the increasing requirements of the operating budget, the changes in organizational structure, the social and political factors affecting tax levy submissions (with many defeats in the process), the personnel changes having nothing to do with turnover, and the inevitable shift in educational priorities over the ten-year period.

If all of U-City's elementary students are not yet regularly involved in all of the arts, staff efforts and the district's continued commitment to the idea have at least made it possible to maintain that estimated 32 percent overall interdisciplinary involvement that Davenport and Peeno have so pragmatically acknowledged. (And this, after all, is merely an educated guess, not a hard and fast figure.)

If the interdisciplinary effort at Hanley has not been greatly expanded since the foothold was first secured, at least it has in no way been dislodged, and there is a very strong program there in art and music, as well. And while the HSA may have suffered some temporary setbacks in its long-term interdisciplinary plans, there can be little question about the greater breadth and continued excellence of its existing programs in the arts *per se*.

There are, moreover, signs that a watershed may have been reached in University City and a re-energizing process now seems likely to occur. Following on the heels of several district operating levy defeats in the fall of 1977, the measure was re-submitted again in the spring of 1978 and ultimately won voter approval. Additional if modest resources may flow to the arts program from this action; but even if the measure had been defeated, Dr. Irene Lober, the new Superintendent of Schools and a staunch supporter of U-City's arts programs, stated that no *selective* cuts affecting the arts were planned.

Furthermore, two recent administrative changes seem likely to give a stronger impetus to the re-energizing process. First, the role of Coordinator of Comprehensive Arts was reinstated as a full-time administrative position beginning in the fall of 1978, and Dr. Robert Hutcheson was named to fill that position. Second, Keith Shahan, long regarded as a firm friend of the HSA, has moved to the Senior High School as Principal. Perhaps both of these moves will, in Davenport's words, "help University City return to the original first principles of the project and develop a system-wide plan, a new conceptualization of the process that recognizes the pros and cons of our whole experience with this idea up to now."

Finally, as suggested earlier, one of last year's developments at the elementary level—the fifth grade "Arts and Basic Curriculum" Project with the St. Louis Art Museum—holds the promise of sparking a new interest in the arts in general learning among a major segment of elementary teachers.

Even if these developments[11] did not bode well for the

---

[11]With respect to the section titled "A Look Ahead," Dr. Unruh, whose current title is Deputy Superintendent, observes that "several advances have been made . . . under Dr. Hutchesons's leadership" during the 1978-

future of this idea in University City, there remains the deeper fact of "The Crucible" itself—the invaluable chance it provided to test out some of these heretofore largely *un*-tested approaches bearing on the place of the arts in a total curriculum and the design of a truly comprehensive arts program.

This was the first instance, one is compelled to emphasize, in which the concept of a general education mission for the arts was given any substantial trial in an entire school system. It is also the only major project-become-program which has been susceptible to the cumulative effect on its development of "the realities of schooling" over a ten-year span.

But somebody, to be sure, had to go through it all *first*. Somebody had to design the full-range of project-to-program developmental processes, try them out, and make the initial gains and the learning mistakes, so that others could set about such work later with better planning, fresh insights, and a greater understanding of all that's involved. It will be interesting to see, as subsequent projects elsewhere attain similar longevity, whether U-City's kind of staying power can be duplicated.

So, it is in this testing, refinement, sharpening, and clarification of *the idea* that one discovers, perhaps, the ultimate value of the U-City experience. Not that, in University City itself, this idea either "succeeded" or "failed," but rather that it paved the way and proved that the basic idea was educationally valuable and worthy of *further* refinement.

This, University City has done, against the same kind of odds every such project can expect to face as, year by year, it finds itself "up against the system." Now, as U-City involves itself in the continuing battle with these systemic forces, it seems to be proving something else as well: namely, that projects like this can learn from their *own* experience and be better prepared to reenter "The Crucible" once again.

It is this testing, refinement, sharpening, and clarification of the idea that would seem to be the ultimate value of the U-City experience.

79 academic year. Among other things, she notes that the "single directorship has brought the comprehensive arts staff into a cohesive, cooperating unit"; that the District has "again added theater arts and dance to the elementary schools" (one full-time person and one fifth-time person); that "new visual arts/music curriculum guides have been completed and are in use"; that "the Fifth Grade Art Museum Program is flourishing in its second year and expects further continuation"; that "Music has been incorporated into the High School of the Arts"; that the "ties with CEMREL's aesthetic education program continue to be strengthened"; and that an inservice program for aesthetic education has been initiated, as noted earlier.

CHAPTER FOUR
Case Study:
The Inservice Factor–Jeffco's Arts in Education Program

Junius Eddy

During the winter and spring of 1970-71, the staff of the Arts in Education Program at the JDR 3rd Fund began to consider strategies for expanding its work in the arts in education field beyond the "pilot-testing" stage to a new (and perhaps more challenging) level of development. Could the processes for effecting fundamental educational change through interdisciplinary approaches involving the arts—ideas then being piloted in University City and in several other small districts—be equally effective in larger and more complex school systems? Processes that seemed to be working well in, and having a genuine impact on, systems with 6-8,000 students might have little chance of effecting such changes, at least on a short-term basis, in systems with enrollments of, say, 60-80,000 students.

It seemed to the staff that, if the idea couldn't hold up in valid ways on a larger scale, its ultimate merit as an educational change process with national implications would be severely compromised, and it was time to find out. Accordingly, the search for an appropriate school system in which to try it out was begun.

Through a series of somewhat serendipitous circumstances, involving people then working in the University City project and at CEMREL, the educational laboratory in nearby St. Louis, the attention of the Fund's staff was drawn to the Jefferson County School System, a large suburban district in Colorado just west of Denver.

Exploratory talks were initiated with officials in the Jefferson County schools, a proposal was submitted, and ultimately—in the summer of 1971 as the University City project was ending its initial three-year period—the Colorado district received a $51,200 grant for planning purposes during the following school year. The narrative that follows is an attempt to describe what has happened since.

The Setting

Jefferson County sprawls across nearly 800 square miles of Colorado countryside. You enter the county where Denver merges indistinguishably with suburbia at Sheridan Boulevard, and you are still in it as you pass through Golden, in the foothills of the Rockies, 12 miles to the west; and you *continue* to be in it as you follow US 6 through Clear Creek Canyon another 40 miles into the mountains. Going the other way, Jefferson County stretches for fifty miles, nearly to Boulder on the north, and south almost a quarter of the way to Colorado Springs.

Until 1950, some 39 separate school districts were encompassed within its boundaries, but following consolidation that year the boundaries of the county are today the boundaries of a single school district that the state has designated as R-1, the Jefferson County School System. With a current (1977-78) enrollment of 82,000, it is the largest school district in Colorado and 34th in the nation in number of students enrolled.

Over the past several decades, the county and the schools have experienced unusually rapid growth. School enrollment has increased by about 25 percent (20,000 students) during the last ten years, and the district-wide population has grown from about 127,000 in 1960 to an estimated 353,000 today. And, although the rate of growth has slowed somewhat in recent years, the northern and southern extremities of the county are still experiencing a population influx. A few schools in those areas are even on double sessions.

In a more concerted effort to deal with the expanding enrollment in these areas, the district initiated in 1974 an unusual year-round school program called "Concept 6" (because it divided the year into 6 largely equal terms). Seventeen of the 115 schools in the district went on the Concept 6 Plan in 1974, and twenty-seven more were added in 1977 so that, today, somewhere over a third of the students are involved in year-around schooling.

Clearly, if scale and complexity were among the Fund's
essential criteria in selecting a site for this next stage of devel-

opment, the school system in Jeffco (as it's known in those parts) met the test. Its size dictates that it be divided into 12 geographic areas, one for each high school attendance area. Many of these areas are either comparable to, or larger than, the University City school system in its entirety. Area enrollments range from those sparsely-settled populations like Golden (in the foothills) and Evergreen (deeper in the mountains), with perhaps 5-6,000 students, to those in the more compact, densely-populated areas like Lakewood, Wheatridge, and Arvada where area enrollments reach 12-15,000 students.

Generally, Jefferson County residents appear to be reasonably well-off economically, reasonably well-educated as a whole, and rather conservative politically. The 1970 Census showed that the county was in the top two percent among all counties in the nation in *median* family income; at least half its adult residents have completed high school and one in every five has completed at least four years of college.

One element of complexity missing from Jefferson County, but which complicated the University City picture during the project development years there, is the factor of racial change or diversity. Almost 95 percent of Jeffco's students are white, with Hispanic students (at 3.6 percent) accounting for most of the non-white enrollment. This situation has remained relatively stable over the past seven years.

Apart from its sheer size, then, it is the growth factor which has given the school system its chief element of complexity over this period. To keep pace with the enrollment increase of about 10,000 students during this 1971-78 period, the district's annual operating budget has more than doubled, rising from just over $60 million to nearly $145 million today; its capital budget has increased from $2.7 million to $6.8 million; and its district-wide instructional staff has grown from 2,634 to 3,227. (This increase of nearly *600 new teachers* in seven years is in striking contrast to U-City's *loss* of 71 teachers in ten years and its *present* faculty complement of 323.) Moreover, the cost-per-student in Jeffco more than doubled, jumping from $629 to $1,563 since 1971.

The Fund was also looking for a school system committed to processes of educational change, and Jeffco had a history of encouraging such practices. It was, furthermore, a district in which the traditional kindergarden through twelfth grade programs in art and music were exceptionally strong and functioning well, from all the Fund could determine, and this was a prime Fund requirement as well.

Directed by Larry Schultz, the visual arts coordinator, and Alex Campbell, the music coordinator, these programs appeared to be adequately (but certainly not lavishly) staffed for a system of its size. There were faculty complements of 95 visual arts specialists, 96 in general music, and 47 in instrumental music. Students in the elementary schools were receiving from 70 to 90 minutes of instruction each week in art and in music, and instrumental music instruction began at the fourth grade level.

Could the processes for effecting fundamental educational change through interdisciplinary approaches involving the arts be equally effective in larger and more complex school systems?

This district is very cautious about accepting new practices. You don't get anything into the system unless it's been carefully looked at, thought about, worked with awhile, assessed, and ultimately trusted.

At the secondary level, beginning in the junior high schools, (serving grades 7-9), studio approaches to the visual arts and performance experiences in music were a high priority. Although neither music or art were required for graduation in Jeffco, there appeared to be a very high level of student participation in arts activities and elective courses.

The Catalyst

Developments such as Jeffco's Arts in Education Program usually can be traced back to someone who played a key role in their genesis, and Schultz appears to have served in that capacity in this instance. "At about that time," he says, "I began to feel something was missing. I just felt we had to have another dimension if we were going to keep on growing educationally, but I didn't know what that dimension was. I thought it was probably something of an interdisciplinary approach, but with a hundred teachers each for Alex and me to supervise there was no way we could find the time to develop such an approach."

It was Schultz's pursuit of that "other dimension," however, that led him, partly by way of CEMREL, to University City, where Jim Allison, a friend and former colleague in Colorado, was then working as a visual arts consultant with U-City's Arts in General Education (AGE) Project. CEMREL, moreover, had recently placed a professional visual artist in residence in the Jeffco system, as part of a pilot "artist-in-residence" program it was administering and evaluating for the National Endowment for the Arts; this brought Schultz in contact with Stanley Madeja, the director of the U-City project, who was then devoting half-time to the development of what would become CEMREL's wide-ranging Aesthetic Education Program. The exchange of ideas began between Schultz and Madeja and Allison, and it was they who brought Schultz and his Jeffco colleagues to the attention of Kathryn Bloom and Jack Morrison at the JDR 3rd Fund.

These, then, were the roundabout (and somewhat serendipitous) chain of events which led to the Fund's preliminary discussions with Jeffco officials and which, in turn, ultimately brought Kathryn Bloom to the Jefferson County School System for personal visits.

The Planning Stage

"This district," said Jefferson County's Superintendent of Schools Arthur Ohanian recently, "is very cautious about accepting new practices. You don't get anything into the system unless it's been carefully looked at, thought about, worked with awhile, assessed, and ultimately trusted. The district is very selective about what it 'takes in' and harbors . . . and that goes for people and for programs."

58

Ohanian's observations underline the fact that Jeffco's encouragement of experimentation and its record of adopting sound new ideas is laced with an unusual degree of pragmatism. It has a rigorous, step-by-step procedure, in fact, for its planning and development cycles when promising curricular programs and innovative projects are being piloted.

When the Arts in Education planning grant was received from the JDR 3rd Fund, in the summer of 1971, the project's goals and objectives had largely been determined during the proposal development and grant negotiation stage. Still, it generally followed the pragmatic Jeffco development cycle.

In addition, the Fund made it possible, during this time, for a number of Jefferson County people to take advantage of the fact that a prototype for the idea already existed in University City. Visits were arranged to U-City (and to CEMREL) for Jeffco administrators, teachers, and parents, to enable them to observe that project firsthand.

These visits provided Jeffco's art and music coordinators, in particular, with a chance to observe not only the *substance* of the program there, but the *processes* U-City was going through to develop its program. As Schultz points out, "These observations and discussions with U-City people helped us sidestep many of the problems the U-City staff had to struggle with as they learned through trial and error."

Schultz believes that, among other things, they learned that sound and consistent leadership is absolutely essential; that the teachers who will be participating must be fully informed and involved during the planning stage; that the CEMREL materials could be used successfully, if placed with teachers who were well-trained and sympathetic to the arts; and that it was wise to begin with a small segment of the school district and not to tackle the entire district right off the bat.

These were crucial lessons, and the Jeffco people made the most of them as they moved into that initial planning year. For one thing, the point about beginning with "a small segment of the school district" forced them to consider, early on, which segment of the Jeffco system might make the most effective site for experimenting with the concept.

Actually, the Golden area was selected for the pilot test prior to receipt of the planning grant. In a way, it almost selected itself. First of all, it was considered to be of manageable size. The city of Golden, once the territorial capital and now the county seat, had a population of about 11,000 in 1971 and—drawing students from the ranches, farms, and mountain dwellings surrounding it—a school enrollment within its attendance area numbering over 5,600. With one high school, two junior highs, and eight elementary schools (including an Outdoor Lab School for sixth graders), the Golden Area was, as a 1973 Evaluation Report put it, "typical of more districts in the nation than the huge Jefferson County R-1 system of which it is a part."

It was, nonetheless, something of a cultural center in and of itself. Artists and writers of national repute had come there

Observations and discussions with U-City people helped us learn that sound and consistent leadership is absolutely essential; that participating teachers must be fully informed and involved during the planning stage; that the CEMREL materials can be used successfully if placed with teachers who are well-trained and sympathetic to the arts; and that it is wise to begin with a small segment of the school district.

The financial parameters were not well-specified, and the schools had unrealistically high expectations of the amount of money that might be available.

to live, and it has probably been their presence that accounts for the emergence, in Golden, of two homegrown cultural institutions: The Foothills Art Center and Heritage Square. For the project planners, they provided one of the essential components of the arts in education matrix—opportunities for more effective use of community arts resources—without having to depend solely on what was available in metropolitan Denver, 12 miles to the east.

Thus, the matter of a site for the pilot virtually solved itself. Golden was an obvious choice. In addition to its manageable size, its relative isolation, and its local cultural attractions, there was a clear desire for involvement in the project coming from within the Golden Area schools themselves, or at least from the Area Superintendent, Gene Cosby.

To make sure that the interest and commitment went beyond that and embraced building administrators, teachers, and parents deeper within the area schools, Schultz and Campbell took pains to involve the art, music, drama, and physical education specialists throughout the district, as well as the Golden Area principals and teachers. Thus, in addition to arranging a series of orientation sessions for the Golden contingent, the planning staff conducted a three-day orientation for all district specialists. It attracted nearly 300 participants and was led by knowledgeable arts educators from CEMREL, U-City, and the Fund itself, as well as the Jeffco planning group.

Out of these preliminary efforts at "awareness building," the fundamental work of the planning year began in earnest: namely, to develop an *operational* proposal for submission to the JDR 3rd Fund that would support developmental work on Jeffco's Arts in Education Program over a three-year period.

It was decided that this would be done by having each school in the Golden Area develop its own proposal detailing how it intended to implement the various program components based on its own individual needs and resources. These eleven individual proposals would then be integrated into an overall area-wide proposal.

Planning Year Lessons

As it happened, the Golden schools went at this assignment with such enthusiasm that the outcome produced the first homegrown lesson the Jeffco planning group had to learn about these developmental processes. Douglas Sjogren, on whom Jeffco has relied heavily over the years for formative assessments of the program, highlights the essence of this problem in an informal evaluation paper he completed at the end of the third year.

Sjogren, who at the time was Director of the Human Factors Research Laboratory at Colorado State University, writes that "the financial parameters were not well-specified, and the schools had unrealistically high expectations of the amount of money that might be available. Their individual

60

proposals were rather 'blue-sky' in nature and, as a consequence, the integrated proposal totaled something over $300,-000!" After considerable negotiation, the operational grant was finally approved by the Fund for $107,000—about a third of what the schools had proposed. "Obviously," Sjogren observes, "the schools had to reduce greatly their proposed activities, and this created considerable negative effect toward the project at the start."

It is to Jeffco's credit that, despite these misunderstandings and the temporary dampening of enthusiasm they produced, the energy of the staff and the truly *basic* interest of the schools managed to keep the project's momentum going. At least, as Sjogren puts it, these and other factors were "sufficient to overcome the inertia, and the work did start [in Golden] without too much lag time."

The original intention was for development work to continue there for a longer period so that sound, working models of varied school-based arts in education programs could be designed for the district to draw on and replicate in other areas.

The Golden Area Pilot

Jeffco's Arts in Education Program (or the "AIE," as it became known around the district) actually was confined specifically to the Golden schools for only about eighteen months after the project became operational with the start of the 1972-73 school year. One gathers that the original intention was for developmental work to continue there for a longer period (perhaps up to three years) so that sound, working models of varied school-based arts in education programs could be designed for the district to draw on and replicate in other areas.

The decision to move to other areas on an earlier time-frame is still debated by many in the Jeffco schools. The final decision was something of a compromise of viewpoints, arrived at largely for strategic internal reasons. Whatever the merits of that decision, the Golden Area pilot emerged as an unusually effective trial run for processes later solidified in the expansion to other attendance areas and in the ultimate district-wide operation now in existence. It seems, in fact, to have served more as a "training base"—a time in which to develop an enormously gifted cadre of arts resource people for subsequent work—than as a specific model for other areas or individual schools elsewhere in the district.

Up to now, Schultz had, for all intents and purposes, served as director of the planning phase. However, as the implementation phase began, he and the planning group—with the backing of the central office and notably Art Ohanian, who was at the time Jeffco's Assistant Superintendent—had assembled an initial "arts team" staff of three persons to direct this work. Two, Bill Thompson and Joyce Johnson, were from within the district and had been working together for three years at Bear Creek Elementary School in another Jeffco attendance area.

Thompson, after 19 years as an elementary teacher in the Denver schools, came to Bear Creek as its principal in 1969 and activated an arts program there that placed particular emphasis 61

To a larger degree, this "involvement" of 60 percent or more of the Golden Area's instructional staff was achieved by utilizing the inservice workshop mechanism.

on drama and the theater arts. He had depended heavily in this work on Johnson, an experienced classroom teacher with a strong specialization in creative drama, whom Thompson had recruited as a full-time theater arts teacher when he came to Bear Creek. Together, these two committed and arts-oriented educators were persuaded to join the Golden Area program, Thompson as community resource specialist and Johnson as theater arts specialist.

Serving as Coordinator of the AIE activities in the Golden pilot was Jim Allison, who had decided to leave his post as the visual arts consultant with the University City project and return to Colorado. Previously, Allison had spent six years as an art teacher at elementary and junior high school levels prior to his U-City post and had received his Master's Degree in Art Education from the University of Northern Colorado. Over and above these credentials, of course, was his firsthand involvement in the early years of the AGE Project at U-City, where he had seen the impact of interdisciplinary activities in the arts on that school system and had become firmly committed to that educational philosophy.

With leadership of the project in the hands of this three-member "arts team," the work in the Golden Area began. For the most part, developmental activities during this first operational year were geared primarily to establishing an effective and recognizable Arts in Education Program in these eight elementary and three secondary schools.

Since each of these schools had described its goals (and how it hoped to set about achieving them) in the "proposals" submitted for the grant application, the staff wisely decided to use these proposals as the entry point in its work with individual schools. Sjogren states in his report that the emphasis was on building a close helping and instructive relationship with the teachers to implement the philosophy and skills that lay at the core of the program. His data indicate that, by year's end, over 140 of the 220 teachers in the Golden schools had been involved in project activities of one kind or another; included were 97 of the 111 elementary teachers, but only 46 of the 109 secondary teachers.

To a large degree, this "involvement" of 60 percent or more of the Golden Area's instructional staff was achieved by utilizing the inservice workshop mechanism. A wide-ranging series of workshops, in a variety of differing art forms, was planned by the AIE Program staff and conducted, by and large, by the staff members themselves. Several were open to teachers throughout the district, and these district-wide ventures seemed essential to the staff for developing an awareness about the AIE Program that would lay the groundwork for later developmental work elsewhere in the county.

The major workshop effort was, of course, confined to Golden Area teachers (and principals) alone. Most of these sessions were offered to all Golden teachers, though several were designed to serve the faculties of individual school buildings. Six elementary schools, for example, were sites for training

teachers in the use of CEMREL's Aesthetic Education units—
"Creating Word Pictures," "Constructing Dramatic Plot," and
"Characterization"—in sessions that reached some 75 elementary teachers in all. These same schools also participated in a
series of workshops, led by Allison, that were concerned with
environmental design.

Johnson's unique talents in the field of theater and drama
in education were also drawn on heavily throughout the year.
Among the workshops she conducted were a series of ten
sessions, drawing some 80 teachers, on a subject she called
"Theater Potpourri" that was aimed at preparing classroom
teachers to use the CEMREL "Theater Game File" and at gen-
erating ideas for theater arts activities based on existing Jeffco
curricula.

Photography also emerged in many school proposals as a
major skill development area, "a vehicle that could be used by
teachers to bring interdisciplinary arts relationships within the
total school curriculum." Allison, a practicing photographer,
responded by offering eight inservice sessions, totaling some
20 hours, for teachers interested in learning more about this
visual medium.

Meanwhile, Thompson, the community resource specialist, and Johnson worked closely with Heritage Square, the
Foothills Art Center, and other local arts groups to make these
resources more fully a part of the educational program. They
arranged field trips to these places, to a children's theater, The
Denver Art Museum, and to other area arts establishments,
and, in turn, artists and historians as well as performing groups
visited the schools on a regular basis, among them, the Denver
Symphony Orchestra, the U.S. Marine Corps Band, the University of Colorado music department (which presented an
opera), and ensembles from Young Audiences. One of the
more intriguing in-school events involved the local Trouping
Children's Theatre whose actors worked with about 40 Golden
High School drama students on ways they might contribute to
theater activities at the elementary level.

Thompson also conducted surveys aimed at identifying
individual artists and resource groups in the community that
could be drawn on more regularly by the schools. The upshot
was an Arts Resource File that was ultimately published and
made available to teachers throughout the Golden Area. And,
in what has since become an annual event for the Jeffco schools,
nearly 700 students, teachers, and parents took part in three
"arts tours," to New York City, Mexico, and Colorado Springs,
that were arranged by Schultz, Allison, and the AIE staff. (To
date more than 4,200 Jeffco folks have participated in these
annual tours.)

To sharpen the focus and to bring all the programmatic
efforts to bear more fully on the development of a process
model for the program, one of the elementary schools, Earle
Johnson, was selected as a kind of demonstration school. In
terms of specialist personnel, staff attention, and the application
of community resources, Earle Johnson was undoubtedly a 63

Photography also emerged as a major skill development area, a vehicle that could be used by teachers to bring interdisciplinary arts relationships within the total school curriculum.

The extraordinary success of Sandcastle seemed to be due equally to its away-from-school setting and to the time it permitted for the development of close interpersonal relationships and for a kind of intense immersion in various arts processes.

Operation Sandcastle

In April of 1973, as the first year was drawing to a close, the project staff inaugurated an event that proved to be so successful that it has now become a tradition in Jeffco's AIE Program. This was a three-day workshop called "Operation Sandcastle" (held in a mountain retreat over a Friday, Saturday, and Sunday), that provided 45 teachers and administrators with a more concentrated and intensive involvement in the arts and interdisciplinary possibilities.

Through demonstrations and participatory activities, the AIE team proposed "to stimulate teachers by opening their eyes and minds to the varied uses of arts in daily classroom activities." The team itself planned the entire event and led most of the sessions, concerned on this first occasion with photography and the creation of multimedia presentations for classroom use, with improvisational theater techniques, and with visual perception.

The extraordinary success of Sandcastle seemed to be due equally to its away-from-school setting and to the time it permitted for the development of close interpersonal relationships and a kind of intense immersion in various arts processes. Its subsequent impact has also depended on the growing confidence of the staff in determining precisely the kinds of arts experiences that teachers and administrators would respond to, on their own growing abilities as leaders of these in-depth sessions, and on their skill in identifying an impressive group of outside resource people to assist them when the occasion arose.

By the end of the 1977-78 school year, 19 Sandcastle Workshops had been conducted for Jeffco personnel—Sandcastle #20 was scheduled but had to be cancelled due to a freak May snowstorm—and the only major problem seemed to be that previous participants tended to sign up in such numbers that first-timers often had trouble being accommodated.

Thus, in all of these ways—but mainly through extensive use of the inservice workshop principle—the AIE project staff not only made unusual progress toward project goals in Golden, but also brought a broader dimension to this achievement: namely, it generated a highly positive response to the arts in education concept on the part of other teachers around the district, as evidenced by their strong participation in workshops and other project activities. So positive was this response, indeed, that administrators in two other Jeffco attendance areas had, by the end of the year, requested that the project be expanded to include them.

Yet, in many ways, its very success, at least in terms of those requests for expansion to other parts of the system, crystalized an issue that is one of the more fascinating procedural elements emerging from the Jeffco arts in education experience.

Growing Pains: When Is a Model Not a Model?

The request for expansion—and the administrative dilemmas associated with it—raised questions both of a financial and a philosophic nature which, as noted earlier, are still being debated in Jeffco today to some extent. Since the decision point itself has long since passed, however, the issue is rather a moot one. It nonetheless illuminates the pulling and hauling among concerned individuals (and institutions) that often takes place in projects of this kind, particularly in very large school systems; and it suggests the compromises that are often made with differing kinds of priorities when major procedural decisions become necessary.

The fundamental question facing all those involved in the Jeffco project toward the end of that first year's pilot in Golden was essentially this: Assuming a valid education model is under development in one segment of a large school system, when (and how) should the attempt be made to transfer that model to other parts of the system?

Pressures favoring "expansion now" were clearly building up within the district. Bill White, Jeffco's Director of Program Planning, points out that "originally this whole development was identified as 'Golden's Project,' but as teachers in other areas got more and more involved, many of them felt they could do it better, and they wanted a chance to prove it. At the same time, as 'the baby' of one area, it was a natural thing for Golden to want to retain exclusive ownership of the project a while longer."

Individuals within both the AIE staff and the staff of the JDR 3rd Fund certainly understood and, to some extent, supported the "expansion-now" rationale, but the majority opinion of both staffs seems to have been against it.

The official position of the Fund stressed the importance of confining the project to the Golden Area awhile longer—for another year at least—in order to flesh out the model more fully before any transfer attempt was made. As the Fund saw it, the development process needed further maturation.

This attitude appears to have been echoed by most of the AIE staff members themselves. As Johnson puts it, "We really didn't *have* a model at that point that could be replicated in other areas. Had we existed for another couple of years in Golden, I'd have been willing to have *anybody* come and judge for themselves whether any given school was a success or a failure as an arts in education model, but not after only one year. For better or worse, though, the decision was really made not on the 'modeling idea' but on other grounds entirely."

These "other grounds" seemed chiefly to revolve around financial issues and the kind of commitment to the idea that the district had to make as it faced the matter of contributing an increasingly greater share of project funds. Despite the apparent success in Golden, there was still, at top levels of the administration, only minimal understanding of what was meant by

The fundamental question toward the end of the first year was this: When (and how) should the attempt be made to transfer an educational model to other parts of the system?

65

If we're going to put over $40,000 into this idea, then the benefits have to be spread around the district to other teachers and students.

"the arts in education" idea and the budgetary commitment required to develop it.

The same could be said of the board of education itself. So long as most of the funds to support that development came from the Fund, there had been little necessity for these levels of authority to do much more than approve the arrangements and receive occasional reports on how things were going. But when the district was called upon to make cost-effective decisions that would, during the second year, budget "line item" funds for as much as a third of the cost of project activities (primarily for staff salaries), justification on grounds other than merely "servicing" the Golden Area appeared to be essential. "If we're going to put over $40,000 into this idea," the argument presumably ran, "and even more in succeeding years, then the benefits have to be spread around the district to other teachers and students, and there's obviously a growing demand for them already."

Limited Expansion

What emerged from these conflicting viewpoints was something of a compromise which, while it didn't fully please everyone concerned, did contain aspects of what everybody wanted. The resolution of the problem, simply put, was to continue the project in the Golden Area for half the second year and, in January 1974, to expand it to two additional attendance areas, Lakewood and Arvada-Pomona.

The total second-year budget was $108,500, slightly larger than the previous year's, with $44,500 provided by the district and $64,000 contributed by the JDR 3rd Fund. *In toto*, these amounts would enable the project both to bulwark the effort in Golden and to gear up for the attempt, in January, to begin serving some 41 individual schools in three attendance areas, instead of only eleven schools in one area. To serve both purposes, the budget made provision for the project to hire two additional staff members in January to assist with this major programmatic change, and it enabled an additional half-time arts resource person to be hired for assistance in Golden. It also supported the continuation of the two resource specialists— Larry Winegar in art and Nancy Pitz in music—who had been helping to supervise those specialized programs, freeing Schultz and Campbell for continued part-time involvement with the project.

Thus, although things remained ostensibly the same during the first half of that year (with work in Golden generally proceeding as an extension of the first-year program), the changes looming ahead altered rather substantially the kinds and amounts of time the staff could devote to that work.

One solution to the Golden problem, as the staff saw it, was to focus its workshop efforts specifically on training a cadre of teachers in those schools that could serve as the staff's "strong right arm" in Golden. As a result, some Golden teachers did

66

indeed develop into valuable resource people who helped the AIE concept to persist in that area after the expansion effort took place. A further boost to Golden was the approval of a one-year ESEA Title III grant of $23,000 to continue and expand the demonstration activities at Earle Johnson Elementary School during 1973-74.

In terms of planning for the expansion to Lakewood and Arvada-Pomona, the staff decided to raise the familiar workshop principle to yet a higher and more concentrated level—in effect, to design a series of all-purpose "awareness workshops" that could be conducted during the spring in each of the 29 new schools. In addition to these orientation sessions, which included information on the kinds of inservice experiences the AIE staff could provide, they scheduled three more Sandcastle Workshops and arranged for one or more "follow-up workshops" in those schools that evinced a strong interest in the program.

When the January 1974 changeover occurred, two additional staff members were hired on a full-time basis with district funds, as planned. Carole Vits, a music specialist with background in creative movement, was already employed by the district; Gail Hynes, a secondary curriculum specialist concerned especially with the field of creativity, came from Chicago and was slated to work largely with the junior and senior high schools.

At this time, the lines of authority were somewhat clarified as well, because responsibility for the project shifted from the Golden Area Superintendent to the Director of Special Projects, Bob Wilson, in the central administration office.

Now the process of orienting the 29 new schools to the AIE Project became a major priority, as the staff geared up to conduct the "awareness workshops" and other inservice programs that had been planned the previous fall. A list of inservice activities compiled by Sjogren indicates that something on the order of 285 separate workshops or demonstrations were conducted during that second operational year, and that over 9,700 students had been involved in one way or another in project-sponsored activities, a truly overwhelming accomplishment!

More importantly perhaps, in the long run, the AIE staff (but principally Allison as Project Coordinator) had begun to solicit the interest of several curriculum coordinators within the central office bureaucracy. Planning was started on the development of resource-material packages for teachers, especially in language arts and social studies, in an effort to overcome what appeared to be some apprehension among the coordinators about the project and its orientation toward interdisciplinary curricula.

Somehow, the AIE Program came through this difficult transition year in much better shape than it went into it—stronger, more influential, more adequately staffed, and more committed to the idea than ever. It had been an enormously energetic and productive period and, riding on the crest of that accomplishment, the staff moved concertedly into the third— 67

Something on the order of 285 separate workshops or demonstrations were conducted during that second operational year, and over 9,700 students were involved in project-sponsored activities.

The AIE team divided its time among three kinds of assignments: (1) school-based workshops, demonstrations, and in-depth work with teachers; (2) development of new instructional units; and (3) inservice workshops.

and last—year of developmental activity as a Fund-supported project. Still working out of offices located in Golden, they nonetheless were able to continue services to all three attendance areas.

The Fund's support was reduced still further the third year, to $53,900, but the district's line-item support—rising to $69,144—was nearly 60 percent of the total project budget of $123,000. This increased evidence of administrative and board of education confidence in the program was crucial to the project's survival, but the Fund's continued assistance was equally so.

As Bill White observed recently, "It's good the JDR 3rd grant didn't run out at the end of the Golden pilot, because that's when the project was having its problems getting its feet firmly planted on new ground."

Diversified Team Tasks

There was a minor staffing change during the third year. Bill Thompson decided to return to administration as an elementary school principal, and Christy Kennett was hired from outside the district to replace him as the community resources specialist. Her work that year was principally with the Denver Art Museum, helping Jeffco teachers and museum personnel to identify better ways in which the museum could contribute to specific educational objectives.

The other four members of the AIE team—Johnson, Vits, Hynes, and Allison (who, as coordinator, continued to spend perhaps half his time on administrative tasks)—divided their time roughly among three general kinds of assignments. First, they offered their services to individual schools or to groups of principals as they had previously, responding to any and all requests for school-based workshops, demonstrations, and in-depth work with individual teachers.

Second, they expanded their work with the language arts and social studies curriculum coordinators, cooperating in the development of new instructional units. These units, unlike those developed in University City, were written into the curriculum guides of *other academic areas,* where they served as arts-oriented supplements rather than separate curriculum packages. This approach, which gave a strong arts focus to kindergarten through sixth grade materials in other content fields, emerged as a primary strategy for moving the arts in education idea to the district as a whole.

The staff also developed a unique curriculum enrichment activity for the fifth grade which it called "The Bicentennial Trunk." Filled with historical materials of all kinds (old books, historical accounts, pictures, Sears Roebuck catalogues, letters), the trunk stimulated all kinds of literary, artistic, and social projects as it circulated through the schools—and was general enough to retain its value after the bicentennial year.

Johnson recounts a particularly moving story about one fifth grade girl who became entranced by a collection of letters in the trunk, letters written by another little girl around the turn of the century. "She followed up on almost every letter," said Johnson, "writing to relatives or friends of the girl's family who might still be living in town, or elsewhere—and she tracked them down, too. She and *her* family even made a special trip there during vacation to talk with the girl's descendants and see the places she wrote about. It was a real labor of love, but somehow her teacher never got a chance to mention it all to me. She thought I knew about it, I guess, but I didn't. And the really sad part is, we had put together *a second trunk* with other letters by that same little girl, and our girl never knew they existed. If she had, just think what a great treasure they'd have been to her at that time. I felt awful when I heard about it."

It can be no surprise that the *third* general assignment the AIE staff set for itself was to continue the practice of offering inservice workshops. More and more, however, they were open to all comers anywhere in the district rather than to the three original attendance areas alone. This was not by chance but was undertaken with the same goal in mind as that underlying their work with the curriculum coordinators—greater district-wide recognition and acceptance—a mandate which, by midyear, began to emerge as a major priority of Jeffco's central administration to assure that the project would become a continuing program.

An instance of this was a special series of workshops that were limited to a group of three elementary schools—one in each of the original project attendance areas—which had been selected for intensive work in connection with an "Aesthetic Education Learning Center" (AELC) that CEMREL had established in the district. These schools, including Earle Johnson in Golden, were known as the AELC Cooperating Schools, and a series of orientation sessions for their teachers were held periodically during the year.

Thus, although some staff attention was devoted to the community resource issue (mainly through the Denver Art Museum project), the principal concern of the staff continued to be the inservice workshop—refining and improving its leadership, expanding its subject matter scope, and depending on its influence to reach farther and deeper into the district.

The modeling process originally envisioned for the Golden schools was essentially abandoned as a dissemination and replication strategy by the end of this year—and, in its place, there emerged almost total reliance on the inservice teacher retraining instrumentality for lodging the AIE Program solidly within the district's curriculum.

Going District-Wide: Another Transition Period

As the JDR 3rd Fund's four-year support was nearing an end in the spring of 1975, it became more obvious than ever

The principal concern of the staff continued to be the inservice workshop—refining and improving its leadership, expanding its subject matter scope, and depending on its influence to reach farther and deeper into the district.

It struck the administrators that, through the AIE program, they had a ready-made mechanism for bringing vitality and stimulation to teaching in all disciplines.

that continuing administrative and board of education support for the AIE Program could only be enlisted if services were made available to all areas of the Jeffco school system. At this time, Roice Horning moved from a high school principalship to Jeffco's central office to become Director of Special Programs. As such, he also became the central office administrator of the AIE Program.

Horning played a significant role in the program's development to district-wide status, initially through his assistance in helping the AIE staff develop a major planning document, a "Prospectus" that outlined the program's goals, justification, budget estimates, evaluation procedures, and strategies for serving the entire school system over the next few years. This document received wide circulation within Jeffco's top administration and policy-making circles that spring, and by the beginning of the next school year, 1975-76, it had been largely approved as a blueprint for the program's plan for "going district-wide."

The administration proposed, and the board of education adopted, a line-item budget of $108,000 for the program, a level of support that slightly *exceeded* that of the first project year when the JDR 3rd Fund provided *all* the funding. This was a remarkable vote of confidence for the fledgling program and its staff, and one of the reasons it occurred emerged from a different and unexpected quarter.

"That transition to full district funding was a difficult time," Horning recalls. "The JDR 3rd grant period was ending, and we suddenly ran into some obstacles we didn't know we had. We found there was considerable citizen-parent confusion about the program, and I must confess that some of *us* were rather uncertain, too. The AIE had been interesting and valuable as a new program several years earlier, but *our* question was: What can it really contribute *now?* I remember spending hours with the team trying to clarify it, asking in essence, "What the hell *is* it?' We had to define it clearly before we could sell it as a permanent and fundamental educational program."

And Planning Director White elaborates on this: "When you say 'arts *in* education,'" he points out, "you have to wonder what the distinction is between that and what we were *already* doing in art and in music, both very strong programs in Jeffco. When you call it 'arts in *general* education,' the distinction gets a bit clearer. But we hadn't been using that phrase here in Jeffco, and it confused a lot of people, including some of us here in the 'head shed.' And then it suddenly came to us— from out in left field, actually—what we were dealing with here."

At that time, White explained, the administration had a charge from the school board to upgrade instruction in *all* content areas. It wasn't seen as a single-discipline approach, in language arts or science or basic skills, or even in music or art; rather, these administrators were looking for something that would be a kind of total catalyst, a different strategy for ways to upgrade teaching in general in the district. At the same time,

70

they were trying to understand the distinction between Jeffco's regular arts programs and the AIE Program. As they gradually realized that the basic distinction lay in the AIE's interdisciplinary connections—and in its teacher-centered strategies—it struck them that, through the AIE Program, they had a ready-made mechanism for bringing vitality and stimulation to teaching in *all* disciplines. And that fit exactly with the board's mandate to upgrade instruction.

"We'd been getting good feedback on the AIE from teachers and administrators," says White, "in terms of the new creativity, imagination, and stimulation teachers were getting from it. So, it all held together as an idea. I can say that this rationale and definition of the Arts in Education Program holds up to this day, and it continues to get strong support in budget hearings."

Most Jeffco administrators agree with White and Horning that it was through this linkage of the arts with teaching in general that board and administrative support for the program finally developed in 1975. But it had tough sledding, even so. "That was a time when we had a real budget crunch," Horning adds, "and when we first began looking at the long-range costs of district-wide development, we were in a real quandary, and, to tell the truth, we almost dumped it!"

In fact, although the program seems to have survived because of its acknowledged contribution to teacher improvement, the budget crisis of 1975 severely reduced *all* elements of Jeffco's educational program, the AIE Program included. District-wide school board policy forced budget reductions that, for the AIE Program and the art and music departments, meant the loss of one full-time staff member in each area. Kennett, Winegar, and Pitz, as the last people hired, were all affected by this reduction-in-force.

At this time, however, the AIE Program had moved from its original headquarters in Golden to more centrally-located quarters in the Columbia Heights Elementary School in Lakewood, a building which, due to decreasing enrollments in that area, had been turned into an administrative and teacher service center. And another way in which the AIE Program survived the budget reductions actually represented a further vote of confidence, but of a different kind. Bob Ferris, the Area Superintendent in Arvada-Pomona, had seen enough value in the team's work to offer to carry two members of the AIE staff, Vits and Hynes, within his own *area* budget ratio as resource people. This, despite the fact that he knew the program's district-wide mandate meant that Vits and Hynes would be working in other attendance areas besides his own. Thus, their salaries were no longer reflected in the program's central office budget.

Meanwhile, the four-member team, which had now been working together for almost two years, continued developing its district-wide teacher inservice effort. And, to provide more of a home base for this work, an Arts Resource Center for Jeffco teachers was established at Columbia Heights that included materials and equipment from the original Aesthetic Education

Most Jeffco administrators agree that it was through the linkage of the arts with teaching in general that board and administrative support for the program finally developed.

Learning Center.

Aid from The Staff Development Academy

A vehicle which now began to give more institutionalized focus to the AIE Program's district-wide effort was a new "Professional Growth Program" that had become operational a year or so earlier following a lengthy period of study and planning. It was effected principally through what was called "The Staff Development Academy," and the entire enterprise was headed by Horning who, by then, had been appointed Director of Staff Development and Supplemental Funding.

The Academy, in effect, formalized and centralized all of Jeffco's inservice activity. Horning had a two-member staff to help with the scheduling, planning, and budgeting of inservice courses and workshops, most of which were built on requests from some 20 program areas, including the AIE Program.

The Academy had its own budget to cover all this inservice work, as well. Requests for courses were written up well in advance by each program area and, if approved by the Academy, its budget provided for all inservice materials, and the cost of hiring substitutes, instructors, consultants, or workshop leaders.

This unique professional growth program for teachers is one of Jefferson County's strongest assets, and it began to be used regularly by the AIE Program beginning with the 1973-74 school year. That year, the Academy budgeted $5,600 for the program's inservice activities. By the 1978 budget year, that amount had been increased to $8,915 with the strong likelihood that a requested increase to $12,300 for 1979 would be approved. It should be pointed out that these amounts are not reflected in the program's regular budget.

Rounding out the 1975-76 program activities of the AIE Program were a series of six full-day arts in education workshops for Jeffco administrators. Modest support for this activity was ultimately received from the JDR 3rd Fund in the amount of $12,500, the Fund's only subsequent contribution to the program following the four years of planning and operational support.

Thus, over those years, and including the administrative workshop support the fifth year, the Fund's developmental assistance totaled $288,600. The district's central office contributions, on the other hand, came to $221,644 during this time. This total half million dollars of funding, which brought the program to what must be considered a high level of development, does not include the district's additional commitment of monies reflected in the Academy's budgets and the salaries of two staff members firmly lodged in Ferris's area budget.

Certainly, these levels of support cannot, by any stretch of the imagination, be considered modest for program development activities of any kind, in any school district in the country.

72   By comparison, the five-year developmental support by the

JDR 3rd Fund to the University City project came to $269,229, while the U-City School System's contribution amounted to $381,080 over that period. This, in a system perhaps one-twelfth the size of Jeffco, is a remarkable commitment, and it is equally remarkable that Jeffco managed to produce such an impressive arts in education impact on roughly similar funds, when applied to a much larger and more complex district. It must be remembered also that these arts monies were committed during a period when school systems everywhere were beginning to feel the impact of taxpayer revolts with their resulting levy failures and financial cutbacks. And they were committed to an idea which, until perhaps ten years earlier, had little if any precedent anywhere in the nation's public schools.

These arts monies were committed during a period when school systems everywhere were beginning to feel the impact of taxpayer revolts with their resulting levy failures and financial cutbacks.

The Arts Resource Team

Operationally, Jeffco's AIE Program works today in much the same way it did two years earlier, only more so. The four-person Arts Resource Team remains as the basic staffing unit and "inservice" is still its primary *modus operandi*.

And, as Johnson put it recently, "Inservice really means *any* service we give to a teacher. It's not just the formal courses we offer through the Academy, but anything we do that brings us into a positive relationship with teachers—a tutorship, a response to a phone call, a demonstration, a trip out to a classroom, a single-school workshop, or whatever."

Allison and his team estimate that today perhaps a third of their time is spent on planning and conducting these single-school workshops or in individual follow-up activities in the schools. Another third is devoted to district-wide inservice programs—Sandcastle weekends, or other courses arranged through the Staff Development Academy. And the remaining third of their time is devoted to the planning and development activities that are necessary to support these efforts and to maintain the other elements of the program: informing schools about the availability of various arts resources and arranging for their use; assisting in the writing of arts components for curriculum guides in other academic areas; and, increasingly, responding to requests for consultant help in school systems elsewhere in the country.

During the 1977-78 school year, nearly 420 Jeffco teachers signed up for the 16 arts in education workshops scheduled through The Staff Development Academy, three of which were Sandcastle weekends. Among the twelve inservice offerings conducted by the AIE team during the fall of 1978 were three on aspects of photography; a Sandcastle variant called "Razzle-dazzle Castle;" a Reader's Theater and a Technical Theater course; courses in Modern Poetry, Creativity in the Classroom, and Movement Activities Related to the General Curriculum; courses in the Arts in Africa and the American Indian; and independent study in The Arts in Education.

73

The Administrative Team

At the administrative level another variation on the "teaming" principle is evident in the way Allison, Schultz, and Campbell function as coordinators. Working out of shared office space in the district headquarters building, these three professionals have worked closely together in recent years to orchestrate the activities of the Arts in Education Program with those of the Art Program and the Music Program. Without in the least shortchanging their fundamental roles as art and music coordinators, Schultz and Campbell have, each in their own ways, "bought into" the arts in education concept, and their advocacy of and support for it bring a special and very important sense of unified purpose to Jeffco's overall arts program.

Thus, in addition to the regular Academy courses offered by the AIE Program, both the Art Program and the Music Program offer a yearly series of inservice opportunities for their own clienteles. And, although most of these courses are discipline-oriented and aimed at professional growth within each specialty area, more than a few each year deal with arts in general education concepts, approaches, and activities.

The Art and Music Program

There are today, in Jeffco, some 158 elementary art specialists, up from 95 in 1971; 78 of these work in the elementary schools and 80 at the secondary level. In music, the specialist complement rose from 143 in 1971 to 185 today. This number includes 103 at the elementary level (75 general music and 28 instrumental music) and 82 at the secondary level (42 general, 40 instrumental).

Clear evidence of the respect and support that Schultz and Campbell have engendered within the administrative hierarchy is the fact that they (and their counterpart in social studies) are the only three Jeffco program coordinators who have been given the opportunity to interview and make recommendations on new applicants for teaching positions in their fields. In all other fields, this process is handled exclusively by the District Personnel Department.

One of the stronger influences on interdisciplinary teaching based in the arts has been the full-scale revision of the elementary music curriculum which, under Campbell's direction, was completed several years ago and is now in use throughout the district. This revision process was launched at about the time that the three arts coordinators initiated their joint efforts to collaborate with the social studies coordinator to develop more arts-oriented teacher's guides in that field. Campbell, who admits to some early uneasiness concerning the integrative aspects of the arts in education approach, has now become one of that program's strongest advocates, as long as, in his words, "the basic skill-and-concept continuum of the art form goes along with it."

"In music," Campbell points out, "we've simply said, 'Okay, we'll use the African unit (or whatever) to *do* it.' In kindergarten through grade two, it's mostly skills and concept development. At the third grade though, we put less *direct* emphasis on this and begin to make use of the integrative units we've developed to tie those skills and concepts to the other academic areas. And, starting with fourth grade, this becomes the *main* emphasis. So, we now have our own *music* curriculum units in all those fields, with teacher's guides for each unit and a plan for fitting them all in at the appropriate times and age levels."

At the third grade level, these integrative approaches are first introduced through a unit called, "Music of the American Indian." In fourth grade, there are units on the "Sounds of Africa" and the "Music of Japan." At the fifth grade level, two units on the folksong have been developed, one geared to folklore in literature and the other related to study of America's westward movement. And in sixth grade, in addition to units concerned with jazz, electronic, and rock music, the curriculum revision provides music units that relate to the study of Mexico and to Greek mythology.

"We figure a kid in the elementary grades will get something in music roughly every other day," says Campbell. "The formal instrumental work, from fourth grade on, is voluntary, but I'd judge we probably have an average of 40 percent of our kids involved on that basis."

As already noted, Jeffco students aren't required to take anything in the way of arts courses after the sixth grade, and the music program at the secondary level, predictably, is much more heavily performance-oriented. Courses in band, chorus, and orchestra are the most popular, of course. Campbell estimates that about 39 percent of the 16,528 junior high and 29 percent of the 21,681 senior high student population were enrolled in music courses of some kind during 1977-78.

Schultz, of course, operates his art program under similar conditions at the secondary level, where nothing is required, but a wide range of elective art classes are offered. And the enrollments are generally comparable to Campbell's. Schultz's figures, for 1977-78, indicate that students signing up for the various art classes were roughly 40 percent of the total junior high enrollment, and 25 percent of the senior high enrollment.

Schultz readily admits that there has been no fundamental revision of the elementary visual arts curriculum similar to that undertaken by Campbell and his music faculty. "Our people have developed some major interdisciplinary units, of course," he says. "They now include units on the arts of Africa, the Eskimo, and the American Indian, and one on pre-Columbian Art. But we haven't felt the need to go beyond that."

Schultz believes that the visual arts specialists are, nonetheless, as firmly committed to skill-and-concept development as their colleagues in music, and that they, too, appear to be finding imaginative ways to weave that sort of instruction into new interdisciplinary units that have been developed. "Our

We now have our own music curriculum units in all those fields with teacher's guides for each unit and a plan for fitting them all in at the appropriate times and age levels.

75

Eskimo Arts unit," he points out, "is essentially a good art history supplement to a social studies topic but, because the Eskimos printed on stone, that unit *also* lends itself to print-making. In the same way," he adds, "the pre-Columbian unit ties in with sculpture and pottery, the Indian unit with wood carving and mask-making, and the African unit with batik and jewelry."

Allison contends that it's mainly through Campbell's and Schultz's programs that a strong measure of "aesthetic quality control" is exerted on the AIE Program.

Elaborating on this point, Campbell says that "when you start getting into aesthetics and skill development, that's where the arts specialists have to come into the picture on a much stronger base than the classroom teacher. Larry and I hope our people can begin training the kids to work with greater skill, and to *listen* and to *see* with greater discrimination than they would ordinarily, and then use the classroom teacher to fulfill the interdisciplinary connections. It's really kind of an inter-locking circle, and this is one of the strongest reasons why you can't really engage in this sort of interdisciplinary program *without* the art and music people."

Schultz offers a unique statistic which is, to him, dramatic evidence of the way in which the growth of the arts in education idea in Jeffco has affected just a single element of the visual arts program. "In 1971 I happen to know—because I had to order it—we used about 3,000 pounds of clay from the warehouse. By 1976, believe it or not, we were using over 94,000 pounds, most of it at the elementary level! It was during those years, you see, that Larry Winegar started introducing our 'pre-Columbian' pottery activities which were aimed heavily at getting kids involved. Some of this increase came from our higher enrollments, but there's no question in my mind that an awful lot of that extra clay went into those kid's pre-Columbian pots!"

Finally, building on the initial collaborative experience with the social studies coordinator, Allison says that recently ar-rangements have been made for a visual area specialist and two other classroom teachers to work full-time, during 1979-80, on curriculum development in the Hispanic arts of the southwest. In addition, the AIE Program is working with the Language Arts Coordinator, Carol Crawford, to develop an interdisciplin-ary unit involving photography and theater arts in the high school language arts program.

In all of these ways, then, it is clear that the purposeful effort these three central-office administrators have made to work and plan together, and to join with the other coordinators for curriculum development in non-arts fields, is beginning to pay off. So, too, are their efforts at fostering more cooperative relationships between the specialist teachers in the arts and the members of the Arts Resource Team. The latter effort has, in fact, served substantially to reduce the misunderstandings that so often arise when the discipline-oriented music or art teacher is confronted by the new breed of arts resource person who's

76

coming at the arts from an *inter*disciplinary point of view. One finds very few specialists in Jefferson County today who resist this approach or see it as a "watering-down" of the arts disciplines.

The arts team members maintain that this attitude has developed mainly because the programs in art and music were strong and well-established when the AIE Program began. "When we started working on the 'all-the-arts' concept here," Vits pointed out, "we were really charged with filling in those art forms that didn't exist in the district then—photography, theater, creative movement, and dance. That helped make 'Arts in Education' look like something different, but also it was clearly no fundamental threat to the art and music people. In fact, when we began getting into integrative work in those fields, we simply asked the art and music people to help us with it, and many of them did!"

When we started working on the "all-the-arts" concept, we were really charged with filling in those art forms that didn't exist in the district—photography, theater, creative movement, and dance.

The Elementary Schools

There are some 75 elementary schools in Jeffco today. In most of these schools, there seems little question that the specialist teachers of art and music are an unusually imaginative and committed group of educators and that students are being reached, therefore, by programs that are far above the average. Concept 6 (the year-around program) and a shifting student population within the district has, in some schools however, resulted in curtailed instructional time, as the cadre of specialists is being spread between more and more schools. Many schools that formerly had specialist teams all to themselves now must share those teachers with at least one other school.

The impact on the elementary schools of the centerpiece of the AIE Program—its integrative philosophy—is somewhat harder to discern. But there is general agreement among Jeffco administrators (who see the district-wide picture) and even some teachers (whose inservice experience has brought them in contact with others across the district) that at least a third of these school faculties have probably accepted that general philosophy and are involved fairly regularly in its practice.

Communications between the resource team and the schools have, in most instances, been established and maintained through small in-school "arts in education teams" set up by supportive principals. These teams may be composed either of the specialists (art, music, and physical education), a group of classroom teachers, or, in most cases, representatives of both groups, and sometimes by working through the Library/Media person.

There are over 70 Library/Media specialists serving K-12 in Jeffco today, with at least one for every two elementary schools. In a few Jeffco schools, indeed, these resource people have taken on major leadership functions on the school-based arts teams—coaching plays, integrating literary study with specific art forms, and using photography and animated film projects 77

A few specialists admit to some uneasiness with respect to the level of artistic work that is accomplished under the AIE Program.

to develop interdisciplinary connections.

There are, of course, problems. Despite all the effort aimed at fostering cooperative specialist-classroom teacher relationships as a means of effecting arts-related interdisciplinary approaches, the "ice still needs to be broken between these two groups in a good many places," as one art teacher put it.

And, perhaps more fundamentally, a few specialists admit to some uneasiness with respect to the level of artistic work that is accomplished under the AIE Program. As one of them said, "It's terribly important that kids have a solid background in art and music, *per se*, when they start getting involved in these arts in education activities. They need to have a deeper level of understanding *in the arts* to engage in it successfully. If we don't somehow bring this 'quality' concern into the AIE Program more fully, I think we're doing the kids a big disfavor. I certainly support the program, but I still have some fears that it may compromise on quality, unless we manage to take it to a deeper level of conceptual thinking."

This attitude doesn't seem to be widespread, but the very fact that several sincere and committed teachers voiced it suggests that it's something the program leadership must keep constantly in mind.

The Secondary Schools

There are 20 junior high schools and 12 senior high schools in Jeffco (as of 1977-78) and, as might be expected, they have not been able to respond as readily as the elementary schools to the integrative and interdisciplinary concepts that lie at the heart of the AIE Program. Here, subject-matter teaching takes over and, no matter from what direction interdisciplinary concepts are emerging, it is never easy to break out of that daily class-after-class, discipline-by-discipline continuum.

In Jeffco—it bears repeating—the regular programs in music and art remain strong and effective in the secondary schools. Beyond this, although dance as an art form is hardly discernible at this level, there does appear to be growing strength, quality, and diversity emerging in many junior and senior high schools with respect to the theater arts. There are seven theater teachers in the Jeffco schools today, and there are growing numbers of English/Language Arts teachers, at the secondary level in particular, who have begun to take on play production projects in recent years and to take the discipline itself seriously.

With respect to interdisciplinary approaches based in the arts, there is evidence that work of this nature has, nonetheless, taken place in one school or another, often against considerable odds. Some of the forms in which it emerged (and the frustrations it often entailed) follow:

- An English teacher (who is also developing a Language Arts Curriculum Guide for the Humanities) teaches a humanities course at Golden High School that now, with the recent addition of dance and theater resource people to the school arts team, deals with *all* the arts;

• Six high school faculty members had been members of an Interdisciplinary Resource Team (created following their attendance at a Sandcastle session) and taught an arts-related course that was allotted one period of released time every day; but, says a spokesman, "politics were working against it within the faculty, and we're having trouble sustaining it. It's now down to two periods a week";

• A junior high music teacher observed that her principal had created a highly supportive climate for interdisciplinary work and she had been, for some years, pulling the social studies, drama (language arts), music, and art teachers together to create a series of school-wide events, many based on historical periods, such as that concerned with the Forties and World War II;

• A junior high school English teacher noted that, until a year or two ago, she was teaching a combination Creative Writing/Visual Arts Class; "I wanted to teach writing through visual literacy," she said, "but the idea foundered on the central office saying, 'If you don't teach what the County Language Arts Curriculum prescribes, we just can't support you.'"

If we don't somehow bring this 'quality' concern into the AIE Program more fully, I think we're doing the kids a big disfavor.

Even the interdisciplinary concept itself is hard to describe accurately. Says a high school chemistry teacher: "People figure that, if you get four specialists of some kind teaching a class together in one room, all of a sudden *It*—the Interdisciplinary Person—will walk out the door. But it doesn't work that way. If only the art specialist does the art part or only the scientist does the science part, the student is forced to conclude that, 'I *can't* be a scientist *and* something of an artist, too.' It's just more specialization, and we've got to go beyond this."

And an art teacher believes that, "Interdisciplinary studies ought to be everybody's bag, not just the arts team's. I hope we never get somebody tagged as being responsible for an 'Interdisciplinary Studies Program'; it should be part of *every* central office coordinator's responsibility at the secondary level."

All in all, one is left with the impression that if professionals of this calibre, with this degree of dedication to interdisciplinary concepts, remain involved, even the secondary education program in Jeffco may one day become susceptible to change and adaptation. It is clear, moreover, that all of the strategies of change won't have to emanate exclusively from the Arts Resource Team; there are non-arts teachers and many administrators now working in the system who will provide their full share of the rationale and the impetus. In truth, they already are.

Some Concluding Observations

Over the past several years Jeffco's AIE Program has elicited continuing high-level administrative and board of education support. Its central office funding level has remained close to the $100,000 level during each of these years, and its financial support from other district programs and areas has been gradually increasing, if only to keep pace with inflation.

In addition, the program has applied for and received a series of small outside grants, largely from federal sources, to augment particular aspects of its work. All of this suggests that Jeffco's AIE Program is doing what's needed to attract national interest, recognition, and funding. It also means that it probably deserves it.

With respect to one of the program's other tenets—regular and more effective use of outside resources—most of those involved in leadership positions admit that this has not been given, nor has it received, the highest priority. In part because the district encompasses so large an area and so many individual schools are involved, it has been difficult to maintain this aspect of the program on a par with its impressive inservice and curriculum-building work. To arrange, for example, for a single performing group (or even one individual artist) to visit every elementary or secondary school in the system would simply be financially prohibitive.

High among the program's priorities over the next few years are the development of a kindergarden through twelfth grade photography curriculum, a theater arts curriculum, and a much greater emphasis on an art-form that has so far been largely left untended, namely, dance. But, building on some pilot work in the Arvada area, the staff is determined to find ways to bring dance into a more central position within its operational structure, beginning perhaps at the junior high level. In this, it has broad backing from key central office administrators as well.

There remains, however, the major question of the Arts Resource Team's continuing ability to serve in the future as effectively as it has up to now. Much of its effectiveness has come about because the program developed *gradually*, from a focus on one area, through a period when it served only three areas, to its current responsibility for the entire district's arts in education concerns. But, as Horning points out, "There's simply no way for four people to have the same impact on 115 school buildings as they had on 11 and then on 40 schools."

Whether this admittedly diluted effort can ever really keep up with the demands in the still-growing system is highly problematical, and although the addition of a dancer to the team would strengthen it in some ways, it seems unlikely that this could really solve the larger problem of district-wide impact. Though it's probably financially untenable, what's really required at this point is *another* two- or three-member team. Already, one hears from the schools and from the team members themselves concerns expressed about the team's inability to give as much concerted attention to individual schools as it previously did, and about the pressures that prevent it from providing as much informal consultative and follow-up work in them. As University City discovered over the years, the "care and feeding" aspects of a program like this (in order simply to maintain what has already been started, let alone reach into new territory) are not only formidable, indeed, but crucial to the program's continued growth and survival.

This problem is, in many ways, inextricably bound up with another one alluded to earlier: teacher and administrative turnover, a factor which also plagued the University City project. In Jeffco, because the system as a whole is still growing and because jobs there are desirable, the "turnover" problem is not one of personnel *leaving* the district but of transfers *within* the district.

The system is presently in rather constant flux. As it continues to expand, experienced teachers can exercise the "transfer right" written into their contracts (at their insistence) and move to schools nearer to their homes, perhaps. Others, new to the system and on one-year Limited Contracts, may be forced to leave when enrollments decline. The result is that some of the best faculty ensembles with genuine *esprit de corps* (for arts in education purposes or otherwise) are gradually being dismantled, year-by-year.

This process makes the "care and feeding" element a virtual necessity. How the Arts Resource Team will meet this challenge in the years just ahead (and how the district will deal with the problem) is one of the crucial tasks Jeffco appears to have before it. And, in a sense, it represents Jeffco's version of the systemic changes endemic to public schooling that were described in the earlier chapter on University City.

It seems appropriate, in conclusion, to point to what is perhaps at the heart of the team's ability to function so effectively in this seven-year development situation. It revolves around its member's status as resource faculty "on assignment" (as Jeffco calls it), rather than instructional faculty with day-to-day classroom teaching responsibilities.

The team's independence, its ability to float within the system, to respond to the growing requests for assistance by the schools, and to plan and conduct its truly massive inservice program—these factors seem to be the real key to the program's growth and survival.

The team's independence, its ability to float within the system, to respond to the growing requests for assistance by the schools, and to plan and conduct its truly massive inservice program—these factors seem, to this observer at least, to be the real key to the program's growth and survival. Obviously, district administrators have continued to find that the program's ultimate value lies in what it is contributing generally to the overall improvement of teaching in the district. That the team has managed, under ever-more-complex circumstances, to make such a strong contribution to Jeffco's educational program is a tribute to the superb professionalism, the imaginative capabilities, and the boundless energies of each of its members.

Clearly, these are qualities not easy to come by when you set out to form a team of this nature. As of this writing, this particular four-person team has now been working together for almost six years, and much of what they are now capable of 81 doing they learned from one another. As Vits says, "For all the years we've been together, we still do plenty of peer teaching, and we all know there are still things we can learn from one another."

The result is that, whatever their respective speciality fields may have been in the beginning, they have by now really become *generalists* across the arts in education field. Beyond this, they genuinely function as a team: they support one another, fill in for one another when needed, build on one another's ideas in staff meetings, minister to one another's frustrations, and feel completely free to disagree with one another at any time—all without any visible evidence of defensiveness or ego problems. Educators use the words "team" and "teamwork" a great deal these days, but it appears to this observer that the members of Jeffco's Arts in Education Team have given true definition and meaning to those words.

PART II

The Second Six Years: School Districts

INTRODUCTION
New York City—Birthplace of the League of Cities' Model Process for School Change and Development through the Arts

Jane Remer

As Kathryn Bloom points out in her introduction, the basic plan for a comprehensive arts in general education program that has as its focus school change and development through the arts was originated in New York City in July 1973. At that time the JDR 3rd Fund and the New York City Public Schools agreed to work as partners in the planning and development of a joint arts in general education venture, "All the Arts for All the Children," known familiarly as AGE.

At the request of Dr. Edythe J. Gaines, then Executive Director of the Division of Educational Planning and Support and its Learning Cooperative, the Fund prepared a position paper and later a blueprint for action in collaboration with key personnel from the central board, local school districts, the schools, and the arts and cultural community.

The New York City plan built on and incorporated the accumulated knowledge and experience of the Fund with pilot projects and Gaines' commitment to educational excellence through individual school development. It took into account 87 the structural organization of the nation's largest and newly decentralized school system and the realities of contemporary urban life: fiscal crises, racial and ethnic diversity, union power, and a complex set of bureaucratic agencies and procedures. Within this context it laid out the goals, characteristics, and processes for school change and development through the arts; it did not prescribe a specific program, a curriculum development or teacher-training effort nor did it promise large amounts of incentive money to potential participants. School programs were to be developed by the participants themselves using existing resources and relying heavily on the strategies of networking and collaboration.

The materials prepared by the Fund for the project included:

- A rationale for the arts in general education;
- A description of the characteristics of effective arts in general education programs at the school and district levels;
- Criteria for elementary and secondary school participation in the program and guidelines for the selection process;
- Strategies for the formation of a network of demonstration, cooperating, and consultative schools;
- A description of the school development process;
- Criteria for the effective use of cultural resources and artists in the schools;
- A definition of the roles, functions, and responsibilities of all participants in the planning and development process; and
- A statement that the main source of funds for the program would come from existing central and local school tax-levy budgets. In lieu of a grant, the Fund's contribution was to provide technical, consulting, and management assistance. (It should be noted that, although the plan operated on the theory of a zero-based budget at the outset, a substantial amount of outside funds for planning, staff development, and artist services was secured.)

Although the program was to be launched in a relatively few schools in largely uncharted waters, it was hoped that in time an arts in general education school development prototype would emerge that could apply to a large number of schools and school districts within New York City and perhaps nationally.

"Design for Change": The AGE Manifesto

The concept of school development and system-wide change has its roots in a relatively little-known four-page document entitled, "Design for Change," a Special Supplement to the New York City Public Schools' *Staff Bulletin,* May 15, 1972.

"Design," although cooperatively authored, was essentially Edythe Gaines' brainchild. A former New York City public school teacher, principal, and community superintendent, she was asked to become the director of the new Learning Cooperative, an arm of Chancellor Harvey Scribner's office. The Cooperative's official function was to assist in the school decentralization process and provide services to the field by bringing together various educational, cultural, municipal, and private groups "to recreate excellence in the city's public schools."

The Co-op had a small, dedicated staff and big ideas which it laid out in "Design." The core of its philosophy may be summed up as follows:

> The new educational system is a network of interrelated and interacting component parts of which the core school is a key part. The core school is one in which a pupil is enrolled and accounted for, where he spends a significant amount of time, where he is assisted with "brokering" the other parts of the education network, and where he is provided with certain foundational learning (e.g., basic literacy).

Key concepts in this document were demonstration ("beacon light") schools, networks, linkages among schools and between schools and the community's resources, an on-going leadership and staff development effort, and an information and feed-back system. Basic to these concepts was a strong belief in individualized and humanized education, choice of teaching and learning style and environment, education as an integrated process, and parent and community involvement in schooling.

"Design" did not attempt to foretell or prescribe specific programs, educational support services, or even a master strategy for system-wide overhaul. It was intended as a credo, and it was hoped that practitioners would convert ideas and beliefs into effective practice. It did, however, spell out one central strategy:

> Change is never comfortable and therefore is rarely welcomed. Quite the contrary. Usually it is resisted either overtly or covertly. Consequently, change will not occur unless it is deliberately planned for. We plan to include in each program or proposal a specific mechanism whose function it is to set in motion a specific set of strategies by which the changes we are aiming for are likely to be brought about . . . That is the revolution we seek!

School programs were to be developed by the participants themselves using existing resources and relying heavily on the strategies of networking and collaboration.

The Concept of School Development through the Arts and the Process for Achieving It as Formulated in AGE

What made the New York City AGE program unique was Gaines' decision to join with the Fund to determine whether and how the arts could become the organizing principle and the instructional framework for overall school improvement. The Co-op's Beacon Light School network left the choice of philosophical goal and the strategies for achieving it up to each 89

In arts in general education programs, the arts are viewed as basic disciplines worthy of study in their own right, as tools for learning other subjects and life skills, and as vehicles for total school reorganization and revitalization.

school. In the AGE program, however, the goal was explicit: "All the arts for all the children," and those principals, staff, union representatives, parents, and student leaders who wished to work towards this purpose were invited to stand up and declare themselves.

In the original plan, the goal of AGE was: "To improve the quality of education for all children by incorporating all the arts into the daily teaching and learning process . . ." In school programs that subscribe to this goal, the arts are viewed as basic disciplines worthy of study in their own right, as tools for learning other subjects and life skills, and as vehicles for total school reorganization and revitalization.

In order to qualify as comprehensive, a school's arts in general education program design was to include all of the following:

- Interdisciplinary teaching and learning in which the arts are related to each other and to other areas of the curriculum;
- High-quality instructional programs in each art form for all students;
- The effective use of the community's arts and cultural resources, in and out of school;
- Special programs in the arts for children with special needs (the gifted and talented, the handicapped, the educationally disadvantaged); and
- The use of the arts, artists, and arts organization services to reduce personal and racial isolation.

The concept of school development and the process by which change through the arts was to be effected were spelled out as follows:

- The individual school is the most efficient, manageable, and logical social unit for educational change.
- The principal is the educational as well as the administrative leader of the school community and can effect fundamental, positive changes in schooling by regularly involving supervisors, teachers, parents, and students in the decision-making process and the implementation of school programs.
- Change is difficult, especially if the alterations proposed deviate substantially from the prevailing norm. Thus, schools cannot and should not go this route alone since they need the support of other schools, the community district, the central board, and other public and private agencies and organizations outside the school system.
- City-wide and district-wide networks of "like-minded" schools are formed for mutual support, problem-solving, and the sharing of information and resources.
- These networks must be coordinated by a "hub" or management team that provides technical and consulting assistance, orchestrates support services, and identifies and secures the human, financial, and physical resources which the schools have determined are essential to progress.
- Over time, these networks serve as tangible demonstrations of a particular idea or concept translated into effective

practice. They provide a talent bank of resource professionals and a source from which information about their experience can be captured and shared with a wider audience.

The individual school is the most efficient, manageable, and logical social unit for educational change.

The process by which schools were to be selected was also defined. All elementary and secondary schools were to be notified of plans for the program, given guidelines and criteria for participation, and asked to submit proposals. A screening committee would review the proposals, visit each school, and gather other relevant information. A determination would be made as to the relative merits of the proposals and the actual potential for the schools to carry them out. Key factors governing the committee's decision-making process were to be evidence of the school's understanding of and commitment to the AGE goals and philosophy; community, district, and teacher union support; and the demonstrated ability of the principal to provide strong and imaginative leadership. Since AGE programs were to be primarily "grass roots" efforts, this last criterion was given a great deal of weight when it came time to make final recommendations.

The goal, the five characteristics, the change theory, and the school selection process outlined above are at the heart of the AGE program. When plans for AGE were officially announced in May 1974, they proved sufficiently appealing to attract proposals from thirty-two schools representing 13 community districts and the senior high school office. As plans went from paper to practice and the strategies for transforming this design into reality were documented, the New York City AGE approach proved persuasive to school superintendents, school boards, and a broader public nationally.

From New York City to the League of Cities in Three Short Years

Planning for the New York City Program began in July 1973. The League of Cities for the Arts in Education was formed in April 1976. In the space of three short years, Minneapolis, Seattle, Little Rock, Hartford, and Winston-Salem entered into partnership with the Fund and, with New York City, voluntarily agreed to form a national network with the Fund acting as coordinator and the main source of support.

When individual partnerships with the Fund were first established, it was New York's experience and the New York City plan that proved instructive to the five other school systems. This is not to say that the New York City approach was taken on faith or followed blindly. Indeed, it was often difficult for some to imagine how anything that occurred in New York City could apply to any other urban setting. However, where experience, processes, and working papers seemed to generalize, they were readily adapted to the local scene; where they did not pertain because of singular local conditions they were set aside, sometimes for future reference.

91

It seems increasingly clear that school systems that opt for this approach are finding it effective and useful in the attainment of their overall educational goals.

The Significance of The League of Cities

At this writing, the significance of the League's experience appears to be threefold:

First, six urban school systems of widely different size, geographical location, and educational structure have agreed that it is beneficial to meet regularly and work together in common cause with the understanding that differences are to be both respected and cherished.

Second, the plan that was originated in New York City in 1973 has become known as the League's model process for school change and development through the arts. Collective ownership and experience have refined, altered, extended, and in some cases given practical meaning to theoretical ideas, but the basic goal statement and general approach is still intact and in evidence in each district.

Third, the League's model process is not a single rigid formula with a set of unalterable strategies to be followed in lock-step fashion. Rather, since the process has already been orchestrated into six variations on a theme in which each program reflects local needs, conditions, and opportunities, it offers a variety of flexible options to school systems interested in following a similar course. Schemes for management and co-ordination, specific program content, approaches to leadership, staff and curriculum development, and the means for expanding the program from a small network of demonstration schools to a much larger number of schools are highly individual.

Members of the League continue to learn from one another and to provide mutual moral support and professional guidance. It is interesting to note that the fundamental principles of networking, collaboration, individualization, and choice so clearly enunciated in "Design for Change" back in 1972 have proved viable and profitable not only for individual schools but for school districts nationally.

The League's model process is comprehensive, complex, and time-consuming. It requires patience, persistence, and creative leadership since it operates horizontally and collaboratively and tends to fly in the face of standard bureaucratic procedures which operate vertically, from the top down. It is an approach that may not appeal to everyone. However, in the past few years, especially as the League and the Fund have begun to document and share their experience and to provide technical and consulting assistance to a number of school districts and state education departments across the country, it seems increasingly clear that school systems that opt for this approach are finding it effective and useful in the attainment of their overall educational goals.

Getting Down to Cases

The two case studies on the following pages provide insights into and information about the planning and development of two of the League's six programs. They were selected for inclusion in this source book for two reasons: First, New York City was the first and Winston-Salem the most recent school district to establish individual partnerships with the Fund. Second, New York and Winston are vastly different cities and the fact that both have flourishing arts in general education programs with different emphases and modes of operation makes the study in contrast interesting and potentially worthwhile.

In a source book of this kind that covers a period of twelve years and is intended to provide an overview of the arts in education from the Fund's perspective, space does not permit similar attention to the other League programs. However, plans are now under way for a separate book about the League of Cities which will document its origin, growth, and development, and go into detail about the components of an arts in general or basic education program. It is hoped that some of the practical questions which the following case studies may provoke will be answered at a later date.

CHAPTER FIVE
Case Study: New York City— School Development Through the Arts

Charles Fowler

Perceptions of New York City's Public School System[1] generally run the gamut from bad to hopeless. The City's educational system is probably the most maligned in the world. Some have made it analogous to the slums—a worn-out and depleted operation bogged down with teacher strikes, bureaucratic snares, and budget cuts.

Everyone likes to attack a monster, and as large as it is, this complex of a central board, 32 school districts, and more than 900 schools, by the law of averages, must collectively encompass every flaw known to education. But with all its vulnerability, by the same law, the system must also embody much of the best of what education is all about.

True, the odds against any new mode of operation taking hold in N.Y.C. schools are enormous. It has been said of education that it is easier to move a cemetery than to change a

---

[1]This case study has been formulated with the assistance of on-site research by Nancy Shuker.

The arts are the minority subjects of American education, and they suffer all the attendant problems associated with the disadvantaged—neglect, malnutrition, segregation, instability, isolation, powerlessness, poverty, and high unemployment.

school. Any plan to change the N.Y.C. School System has to deal with the separate governance of the senior high schools and the isolation and quasi-autonomy of the independent districts, a result of decentralization. It has to account for the sheer size of the city, covering five boroughs and 300 square miles. It has to take into consideration that there are more than 50,000 teachers who teach 1.1 million students, two-thirds of them black or Hispanic. And it has to make allowances for the financial plight of the system which seems to grow more severe by the year.

If that change is to embrace the arts, the plan must also take into account the low status generally accorded these subjects. It must be acknowledged that the arts are the minority subjects of American education and that they suffer all the attendant problems associated with the disadvantaged—neglect, malnutrition, segregation, instability, isolation, powerlessness, poverty, and high unemployment.

Considering all these problems, the apparent success of N.Y.C.'s Arts in General Education (AGE) Program is all the more startling. Walk into any one of the 16 demonstration schools in this project and you will sense, immediately, an educational environment that is positive and productive. Children are friendly and open and happily engaged. Teachers are enthusiastic and creative. Principals are animated, even excited. There seems to be a cooperative energy that pervades everything.

The arts are everywhere. An architect is doing city planning with a group of sixth graders as part of a social studies unit. A dancer is working with a fifth grade to study, through movement, the Near East as the cradle for the three great religions of the world. A kindergarten class is making a painting of animals as a prelude to going to the zoo to perceive the real thing. Children in a fourth grade are writing their own stories and acting them out with handmade puppets. Third graders are making their own storyboards with the help of their own cameras and photographs. A junior high school is putting together an anthology of their own poems written under the guidance of a visiting poet. A second grade creates its own musical backgrounds to set the moods for reciting a favorite story. So it goes. The arts are thoroughly enmeshed in the fabric of learning. The quality of education is tied, unbelievably, to an infusion of the arts into the total curriculum.

But that's not all. Look a little deeper and you will find an undergirding structure to the program that is both powerful and pervasive. There is, for example, a carefully designed network—really a number of interlocking networks—that deliberately link all of the people in the AGE Program. The quintessential entity in the network is the "hub" which coordinates and manages all the elements of the program. This hub consists of a somewhat unusual alliance of organizations that has stood behind the operation, the first two of them, from its inception. The N.Y.C. Board of Education (a public institution), The JDR 3rd Fund (a private foundation), and The New York Foundation for the Arts (a non-profit organization affiliated with the New York State Council on the Arts which is in charge of the Artists-in-Schools Program in the state) serve as a cooperative triumvirate. The particular personalities representing those organizations—Jane Remer for the Fund, Ted Berger for the New York Foundation, and at first Carol Fineberg then subsequently Leslie Goldman as Program Coordinator for the Board of Education—function as the gravitational center around which everything else in the project revolves.

And revolve it does. As the program moves at present into its sixth year of operation, it has captured system-wide attention. Numbers of schools that have not been involved are now looking at and studying the program with the serious intention of moving in the same direction. Several district superintendents are already supporting or considering bringing the program into all the schools in their districts. Numbers of principals, parents, and teachers have expressed an interest in learning more about how the arts can possibly be employed as the central agents for improving the quality of general education.

Unquestionably, the program has caught the imagination of the people involved in it. Like the newly converted, these principals, teachers, and in some cases even the students are eager to preach their gospel to the uninitiated. Principals and teachers have launched their own initiatives to spread the word, and their own convictions are perhaps the best proof of the amazing transformation that has taken place.

As the program moves into its sixth year of operation, it has captured system-wide attention. Numbers of schools that have not been involved are now looking at and studying the program with the serious intention of moving in the same direction.
Like the newly converted, these principals, teachers, and even the students are eager to preach their gospel to the uninitiated.

The Background and Planning Process

How was such a force unleashed, especially in light of all the severe problems that face education and the arts in N.Y.C. schools? In 1972, a group of educational reformers were working within N.Y.C.'s Learning Cooperative, an official arm of the Office of the Chancellor of the schools that was brought into being to foster change and improvement in education in light of school decentralization. That group published a document called, "Design for Change," a four-page bulletin that planted many of the seeds from which the plan for the AGE Program grew.

This document redefined education and suggested that it could be achieved "only through a network of interacting social systems and institutions of which the 'school' is one part." It viewed education as a process rather than the mere acquisition of knowledges, skills, and course credits. It maintained that students "must have maximum choice—choice as to learning objective, choice as to learning environment, choice as to learning style." And it spoke of linkages between the schools and educational, cultural, and scientific institutions and organizations.

Dr. Edythe Gaines, director of the Cooperative, believed that the cultural life of N.Y.C. offered an almost limitless potential resource for the schools, if ways could be found to tap it. In response, Jane Remer, who had been assistant director of Lincoln Center's Education Program and was then her assistant, agreed, and designed and developed an Urban Resources Program. During this period, she came in contact with the Fund and Kathryn Bloom, its director. It wasn't long before Bloom and Remer realized that there was enormous potential in combining a comprehensive approach to the arts in education with a school development program that incorporated the basic tenets of the Learning Cooperative's philosophy.

Bloom knew that the creative process of learning in the arts was self-motivating. It tended to envelop students and, provided the teacher gave sufficient challenge at the outset, cause them to explore their own inner resources. As media for communication, the arts afforded a means to convey—and therefore to study—any subject matter. By getting people to engage themselves, the arts could liberate human potential. She knew all this from earlier projects the Fund had initiated in schools and school districts across the country.

While the main thrust of the Fund was to advance the idea of all the arts for all the children, Bloom now saw the arts as a potential force for improving education in general. She chided arts educators: "We should stop asking educators what they are going to do for the arts and start showing them what the arts can do for education." Bloom and Remer became interested in formulating a project for N.Y.C. schools that would focus on school change through the arts. If it could be done in N.Y.C., it could be done anywhere.

Remer joined the staff of the JDR 3rd Fund in July 1973 and, on request from Gaines, now executive director of the newly organized Division of Educational Planning and Support, began work on a position paper and a detailed plan for organizing and implementing an Arts in General Education Program for the N.Y.C. schools. An ambitious undertaking, the plan took ten months to produce. While none of the ideas on which the program was based were new, this particular combination of goals and processes had not been tried anywhere. To test the arts as a vehicle for educational change in N.Y.C. was audacious, indeed, more audacious than anyone could have predicted.

In working out the basic structure and rationale for the AGE Program, several issues had to be resolved. Surprisingly, Gaines insisted that, if the JDR 3rd Fund joined with the Board of Education in this venture, the Fund could not put substantial grant money into it. She did not want to put the Board in the position of being dependent upon or intimidated by the power of outside money. But more important, she felt that the project could only succeed in the long run if it was school-system based. There had to be strong commitment from the inside.

Bloom agreed. As a veteran of the plush 1960's in the U.S. Office of Education, she knew that substantial outside money created dependency. When the funds dried up, so did the programs, and temporary programs do not change schools.

Accordingly, the only outright grant the Fund made was for $500 to each of the original 12 demonstration schools. These funds were specified for planning and development, not for artists or supplies. The Fund also covered expenses for travel to observe programs in other cities, certain meetings, seminars and workshops, fees for consultants, and the contribution of Remer's services. Most important, it was agreed that the participating schools, their districts, and the Learning Cooperative would reallocate existing funds and resources to support the program.

Gaines believed that school change depends upon establishing the new mode of operation in a number of strategically located, highly visible schools. This "critical mass" of schools would theoretically provide enough weight to "tip the balance" in any school system, so that other schools would be inspired to follow their example. Inherent in this belief is the notion of establishing demonstration schools—an array of sites that can convincingly demonstrate the new idea in action. Setting up a group of demonstration schools thus became a major component of the AGE plan. From the beginning, then, the plan centered upon the system-wide institutionalization of the idea. This was an elaborate design to change an entire educational system through the arts.

In retrospect, Remer says that they learned that other schools have become persuaded, not only because a number of schools were doing something new and different, but also because the network of people in those schools became dedicated to the new concept and articulate about its value. It is this "people network" that can tip the balance. This is a key element in the change process, for it is the network that provides the talent bank that can assist the uninitiated, that gives visible and tangible proof of the validity of the idea in operation, and that can testify with certitude on the viability of the new approach.

Networks do not run by themselves. They need to be facilitated, and this implies some kind of management. The AGE plan designated the Learning Cooperative as the administrative arm of the program and called for setting up a management team to supply leadership in the initial planning and implementation of the program in each selected school. This hub has served as the official liaison between the participating schools and the city's cultural and educational resources; it functions as a central repository of knowledge about the program and a source of ready assistance; and it coordinates the network of people involved in the program.

Since there were no textbooks that showed how to integrate the arts into regular classroom work, curriculum development necessarily constituted another basic component of the plan. Many classroom teachers have limited arts training making it difficult for them to create their own new approaches in order to incorporate the arts into their teaching. They need the support and encouragement of their principals, the management team, consultants, artists, specialists, and volunteers from the community. Workshops and inservice training were 99

Substantial outside money creates dependency. When the funds dry up, so do the programs. Temporary programs do not change schools.

School change that evolves from the cooperative efforts of the total educational constituency is a long-term process. Before any program can be implemented in the classroom, adequate planning time must be provided.

planned in order to assist both administrators and teachers in rethinking the entire teaching and learning process.

School change that evolves from the cooperative efforts of the total educational constituency is a long-term process. Before any program can be implemented in the classroom, adequate planning time must be provided. The plan called for a whole year to be devoted to meetings of principals and teachers, workshops, and site visitations by Gaines and members of her Division to some of the Fund's earlier projects prior to making the program operative in the classroom.

On May 7, 1974, ceremonies at the Board of Education offices in Brooklyn officially inaugurated the program. Chancellor Irving Anker told the assembled school and community representatives that he hoped the program would help combat "joyless classrooms" and put children in touch with the riches of their city, which he called "the arts and cultural capital of the world." John D. Rockefeller 3rd, who had expressed a deep interest in doing something to bring more arts to children in N.Y.C., stated that his personal objective was to give young people "a chance to find out if the arts will be a meaningful factor in their lives." Gaines made her commitment clear and firm: "In this concept of education," she stated, "the arts are not the frosting on the cake; they are not the frills; they are the rice and beans of the teaching and learning process."

Getting the Program Rolling

Why were Gaines, Bloom, and Remer willing to put their professional careers on the line to try to institute comprehensive change through the arts in the largest and most overwhelming city school system in the United States? All three knew that, in spite of its problems, the N.Y.C. Public School System had many strengths to build upon. No single part of the program that they were putting together had to be created from scratch.

There was a Beacon Light Network of principals that could serve as a reference point for a network of AGE principals. The Learning Cooperative's Urban Resources Program had established strategies for forming linkages with many institutions and organizations outside the schools. A number of cultural organizations were already at work in the schools using the arts in innovative ways. There was a long history of the use of artists in the schools.

Resources for an Arts in General Education Program could be found all over the city. They simply had to be organized within a cohesive framework that would insure their contribution to the larger goal of making the schools better and more effective learning environments for children.

In order to get the program underway, Gaines notified all the administrators, community superintendents, and principals about the program in June 1974. A second mailing in September brought about 100 school and community representatives to a meeting to discuss possible participation in the venture. This meeting was hosted by the management team.

Typically, the first reactions of many of those in attendance was, "What do I get out of this for my school?" There were misconceptions about large infusions of outside grant funds to be expended, so some thought, to implement a preconceived set of cultural enrichment plans. Remer says, "There had to be frank discussion about the nature of the project as a joint school development effort that would rely from the start primarily on existing resources—human, physical, and financial. Participation in the project, therefore, depended on the school's and district's commitment to the program's goals and objectives."

As a consequence of this meeting, 32 schools submitted written proposals to participate in the program. The selection process began in mid-October. The project management team worked together with a screening committee of educators and representatives from arts and cultural organizations. Selection was based upon evaluation of the written proposals, site visits to the schools, and advice from teachers and administrators who were familiar with both the project and the applying schools.

According to Remer, the selection process was an encouraging exercise, because it revealed a depth of leadership and commitment in the schools that had not been anticipated, and it showed that much of what the program was designed to achieve in the schools was already under way in many of them. Although the original plan called for only four demonstration schools and an undetermined number of cooperating schools in a less intensively served network, the management team, with Gaines' approval, decided to accept all 32 schools in the program with 12 demonstration schools as the core. (Later the number of demonstration schools was increased to 16.)

The 12 selected demonstration schools—eight elementary and four intermediate or junior high schools—represented a pairing of schools in each of six districts. The 17 cooperating schools—nine elementary, six intermediate or junior high, and two senior high schools—represented an additional seven school districts. Three specialized secondary schools—the High Schools of Art and Design, Fashion Industries, and Music and Art—made up a new consultative category with an advisory and support role. All five boroughs of the city were represented.

Each of the demonstration schools received the small planning grant from the Fund, modest incentive grants and limited teacher-released time from the Learning Cooperative, and intensive technical assistance to aid in program planning, leadership training, staff and curriculum development, and identification of resources.

In contrast, the cooperating schools received some limited technical assistance from the management team, but were invited to participate in many of the planning and training activities designed for the demonstration schools.

The consultative high schools, which were strong in specialized arts already, were considered resources. They sent staff

The school selection process was an encouraging exercise, because it revealed a depth of leadership and commitment that had not been anticipated, and it showed that much of what the program was designed to achieve was already on the way to happening.

101

The greatest schools in the country and across the world are those that have clearly definable philosophies.

and students to training and planning sessions and were also asked to offer technical assistance to other schools. (This category proved to be the least effective. In September 1977, it was dropped. Two of the high schools became demonstration schools and the other was absorbed into the cooperating network.)

Dr. John Goodlad, Dr. Robert Stake, and other consultants, whom the Fund had involved in the project in its formative phase, returned for a three-day seminar sponsored by the Learning Cooperative and the Fund to discuss with key administrators the processes of school change and program evaluation. The Fund organized a traveling seminar for the project management team, staff of the Division of Educational Planning and Support, and several community arts organization representatives. The group observed the arts in education program in the University City Public Schools. In St. Louis, they met with Dr. Stanley Madeja and the staff of the Aesthetic Education Program of CEMREL (the Central Midwestern Regional Educational Laboratory). They went on to Oklahoma City where they met with representatives of the schools and cultural institutions involved in the Opening Doors Program, a project that explored the use of cultural resources in the schools.

By January 1975, when the participating schools were announced and the first meeting of the AGE principals' network was held, the project management team had amassed a list of 58 arts organizations, 11 colleges and universities, and 10 foundations that were interested in working with the program.

From January to June, principals, district liaison personnel, and school staffs met monthly with the project management team to plan and to assess individual school needs. Each school organized a planning team of its own. School budgets were analyzed and redirected to support AGE activities. The management team continued its inventory of available community resources and wrote proposals for state, federal, and private grants to support different components of the program. Schools made inventories of arts expertise at hand among their teachers and staff. Monthly meetings of the principals were held so that by June their network was in place. They set September as the time to begin taking the program into the classroom.

The Concept of School Development

In the AGE Program, the concept of school development is crucial. This program was designed not only to make the arts—all of them—more central to the education of youth, but also to transform and humanize the whole notion of schooling itself.

When the arts become the pivot of the learning process, the whole school changes. "The greatest schools in the country and across the world," states "Tev" Sumner, principal of elementary demonstration school 152 in the Bronx, "are those that

102

have clearly definable philosophies." The reason, he says, is that "parents know why they are sending their children there; the children know why they are there. The expectations of the children are increased. They know that their talents are going to be explored and developed and that they can use their talents as a way to succeed in school. Up 'til now, people have had the philosophy that the child has to continually adjust to the school, without the school representing or standing for anything. The child never knew what he had to adjust to. That is not the case with an AGE school."

Luis Mercado, principal of elementary demonstration school 75 in Manhattan, says, "I think to be a better teacher, you have to be a better human being. The AGE concept gets teachers involved in their own value system, their own appreciations, and what they consider to be important. If, indeed, you can get that kind of response from a whole staff, then there is no doubt that the project has contributed a great deal to staff development."

A good part of the reason that the program has had an effect on staff is that it has not been imposed on schools from the top down. The idea of school development within the AGE framework is that planning is multilateral. Everyone who has a personal and professional stake in the total school program is invited to be a part of the decision-making process.

The idea may sound simple. In practice, it is complex. Getting a number of people to work together to make the concept operational is a long and involved process. To the observer who visits an AGE school, the process tends to be intangible and invisible. It is not something that you can see or photograph.

Remer has observed that within the AGE approach, school development occurs when the principal, acting as educational and administrative leader, involves the staff, parents, students, and community in discussions and decisions that affect the school's philosophy, its programs, and the way in which resources, existing or new, are allocated. It is sometimes an agonizing process, and it never works with all of the people all of the time. It is hindered by all sorts of constraints and obstacles: educational mandates, union regulations, political considerations, and lack of time. It presumes that chief administrative officials are willing to delegate power to individual school communities within the boundaries of reason and law.

Remer has also noted that a functioning program will result in some or all of the following:

- Principals, teachers, parents, and resource personnel behave in different ways both individually and as a group. Roles and responsibilities change. New talents, abilities, and interests are identified and tapped.
- Students take a more active part in the life of the school. Their motivation for learning is increased. They find new avenues of self-expression and success, and they relate more freely to their peers and "mentors."

To be a better teacher, you have to be a better human being. The AGE concept gets teachers involved in their own value system, their own appreciations, and what they consider to be important.

The developent of decision-making capacity on the part of other people in the school has been the most valuable part of the AGE Program for me.

• New and improved programs, services, and activities emerge. New instructional approaches and materials are developed.
• The climate of the school becomes livelier, more vital, more colorful. The environment itself changes from drab to vibrant, a result of adopting creative teaching and learning styles.
• Attendance improves among both students and teachers. Vandalism, alienation, and violence wane, and a sense of personal pride in the school develops.

Deliberately, this list omits the claim that basic achievement skills rise because of the arts, or that standardized test scores, minimum competency ratings, or the like, improve solely because of an AGE program. Variables influencing these evaluative devices have yet to be isolated, let alone controlled. However, experience and common sense decree that, if the school, its atmosphere, its inhabitants, and its program become vital and exciting, improved learning will be an outcome. Indeed, this is what the AGE Program is all about.

The AGE Program in Operation

Each AGE school has an AGE Steering Committee consisting of those faculty who are most interested in the arts in education. The Steering Committee at PS 98, an elementary demonstration school in Manhattan, is typical. Mark Shapiro, the principal says, "The committee functions as a cabinet. With a staff of 80, about 12 attend. An assistant principal, who happens to be a former art teacher, serves as administrator. Each grade level is represented on the committee, and those teachers report back to their colleagues. Parents and students are also represented."

Whenever possible, the committee decides such things as what kind of visiting artists they would like. (This year, for example, one of the choices the committee made was to have a printmaker.) They plan a yearly "think tank" session for all faculty on the AGE concept. (This year the meeting centered around social studies and how it can be approached through the AGE Program.) They plan an annual arts fair and residencies they would like in the future. (After considerable discussion, the committee at PS 98 opted for a ceramist.) They suggest new resources that can be used. They fashion proposals. (A group of fourth grade teachers created a puppet project to help teach Colonial Times, part of their Social Studies curriculum, and got it funded.) They evaluate various aspects of the program. (If an artist bombs out, they let it be known.) And they carry on a continual dialogue to clarify goals, asking essentially, "What does this program have to do with my work?" These committees generally meet monthly and on an emergency basis as the need arises.

At another demonstration school, PS 152 in Brooklyn, Dr. Herbert Shapiro, the principal, credits the Steering Committee with altering the whole operation of his school. He claims, "The development of decision-making capacity on the part of other people in the school has been the most valuable part of the AGE Program for me. The school's voluntary AGE Committee, which consists of seven teachers, two parents, and myself, meets a minimum of 12 to 15 times during the year. When we met last spring, the committee made the decision to apply for an architect-in-residence and to plan how to raise the matching funds. In the fall, when we were notified that we had won the grant, we met to interview three architects. The committee also decided how three teachers were to be chosen to work with the architect.

"The June meeting," Shapiro says, "was devoted to evaluation and to planning for next year. When the school became a Title I school last year, the committee met to discuss what kinds of specialists we could use to strengthen our arts program. Under Title I, the number of specialists or so-called 'cluster' teachers was increased from 4 to 12. The committee recommended to staff a number of arts specialists, which by and large they accepted. As a consequence, we added two instrumental teachers, a second vocal music teacher, and two creative dramatics teachers."

Shapiro explains that there is "no visual arts person on the staff, because, of all the arts, classroom teachers are most comfortable and competent in this area. We want to strengthen dance and movement, but we simply do not have space because we are so overcrowded. The auditorium is used full-time for instrumental music. We do have a voluntary dance program that accommodates 60 youngsters twice a week. There are two choral groups and a poetry group that meets twice a week. These are voluntary for fifth and sixth graders. The band is not a performing group. It is made up of every student in the fourth grade. This is a mandated, exploratory program for all fourth grade students that meets three times a week. Every student goes to gym," Shapiro reasons, "why not band?"

Shapiro's school is one of three AGE schools to have an architect-in-residence this school year. The architect worked with three classes—a fourth, fifth, and sixth grade—for a whole year. "This is a dramatic and exciting program," Shapiro says, "because of its scope. The students have designed, constructed, and installed a 30-foot-long wooden kiosk in front of the school for the purpose of displaying to the community what goes on in school. Through this project, these students have learned problem solving, cooperation, persistence, and creative thinking. They have learned to read plans, take measurements, make computations, and build scale models. They have taken photographs and learned to develop them and then use them to formulate plans and to make aesthetic judgments about the size, look, and placement of their structure. They have also won the pride that comes from making a contribution to the community."

At the junior high school level, compartmentalization of classes and subject matters makes the integration of disciplines

The band is made up of every fourth grade student. This is a mandated, exploratory program that meets three times a week. Every student goes to gym. Why not band?

more difficult. But according to Bernice Frankenthaler, principal of the junior high demonstration school 167 in Manhattan, "crossing lines is possible, if faculty see the value and set their minds to doing it." Project Synergy in this school is a good example. This project, which was started by Gerry Segal in the math department to study Buckminster Fuller's concepts of form and structure, encompasses science, visual arts, and dance. "In such cases," Frankenthaler says, "one subject builds upon the other, and one project stimulates others in the school."

In AGE schools, the arts are often the impetus for learning in other subject matters. Each one of the arts stimulates the students' creative urges and provides them with an activity that involves their mind, body, and spirit.

Weathering Crises

"The AGE Program began when 'Big Mac' was still the name of a hamburger," Carol Fineberg, the program's first coordinator, observes. But by September 1975, "Big Mac" referred to the Metropolitan Assistance Corporation, a body set up to cope with the city's impending bankruptcy. In order for the city to qualify for federal loan assistance, Big Mac's Emergency Financial Control Board had the powers to slash all city budgets.

And cut they did. In one stroke, the school budget was reduced by $262 million. Nearly 8,000 teachers were laid off. To protest the way cuts were made, the United Federation of Teachers struck.

The settlement with the teachers' union called for the school week in elementary and junior high schools to be cut by 90 minutes, which represented a loss of teacher preparation time. This time had been made available through the use of cluster teachers—usually specialists in the arts or other areas—who took over classrooms to free the regular teachers. With the shortened school week, the need for these cluster teachers was eliminated and so were the jobs. Since staff cuts were based upon a seniority system, some AGE schools with young staffs suffered as high as a 90 percent turnover in teachers.

But this was only the beginning. In less than two years, further layoffs and budget cuts brought the total teacher reduction to 22.9 percent. The average age of N.Y.C. public school teachers went from 28 to 41 during this period.

Clinton Howze, Superintendent of District Three, the home district of two AGE demonstration schools, described the devastating effect of these changes in *The New York Times:*

> Cutting teachers has meant less music, less remediation and less physical education. Our classes are up from 29 to 40 students. There are no teachers for anything but the classroom. Teachers trained in early childhood education are teaching fifth and sixth grade classes. I've lost most of my assistant principals.

We haven't aides. We have had many instances of people walking in off the streets and we've had assaults and other incidents. Fights occur in the school yards and we can't do anything about them until it is too late.

As if all this wasn't enough of a blow to the AGE Program, there was a central administrative reorganization and a corresponding change in administrative positions. Gaines, the key top administrator who supported the program, left the N.Y.C. School System. Her position as head of the Division of Educational Planning and Support was filled by Arnold Webb, who was formerly the director of the Office of Planning, Programming, and Budgeting.

Dr. Webb was in a difficult position. "I was appointed to this position at the time of the most grievous cuts in the history of the board of education and at a time when there was increasing agitation to 'cut the fat' at central headquarters and put every available dollar into the classroom." Right after he accepted the job, the Division's budget was cut by 40 percent—from $10 to $6 million. In order to make sense out of this reduction, Webb undertook a massive reassessment of the Division's work.

Of course, a fledgling project such as the AGE Program is extremely vulnerable in such dire circumstances. So much depends upon administrative support at the top. Webb had no track record in the arts. Would he or wouldn't he stand behind the AGE Program?

"What won me over to the AGE concept," Webb recalls, "was that it was a program I didn't have to just read about. I could see it. I visited schools and saw the program in various stages of development. The demonstration schools were very effective in this respect."

Webb asserted his support. "One thing that helped me to understand the potential worth of the program," he says, "was developing a relationship with the principals involved. I watched them grow in the process of taking a concept and translating it into a more meaningful education for kids in their schools. I found the principals in the program to be remarkable people. Tev Sumner lost 80 to 90 percent of his staff that fall, but he was willing to start over. Within a remarkably short time, he was able to instill a commitment to AGE in his new teachers."

Nola Whiteman, an avid supporter of the program from its inception, who became Webb's executive assistant, says that, "I didn't have to sell the program; it sold itself." Webb credits Whiteman for being wise enough not to push the program on him. "She answered all my questions, and she pointed out people I should see and talk to," he remembers, "but she left it to me to decide."

During this uncertain period, the Fund's organization of the League of Cities for the Arts in Education was of strategic significance. For the people in the N.Y.C. program, the League had an important reinforcing effect. Webb acknowledges that,

What won me over to the AGE concept was that it was a program I didn't have to just read about. I could see it. I visited schools and saw the program in various stages of development. The demonstration schools were very effective in this respect.

The impact of having other school districts interested in and impressed by what N.Y.C.'s public schools were doing was both exciting and reassuring. The Fund gave the program enormous credibility.

"The impact of having other school districts interested in and impressed by what N.Y.C.'s public schools were doing was both exciting and reassuring. The Fund gave the program enormous credibility."

Once Webb made the decision to keep the AGE Program, it was placed in the newly formed Center for School Development under its director, Hortense Jones.

Unquestionably, administrative support on every level has been a key to sustaining and developing the program. "But," Webb cautions, "it is not enough for a supportive administrator to simply understand and endorse a concept of education. To really be effective, an administrator must participate in the developmental process." Webb was explaining his own commitments of time to principal's meetings, to meetings of the League of Cities, and to arts in education conferences. He was also describing the deep involvement of the principals who are participants in the program. Without such personal commitment on the part of administrators, it is doubtful whether the program could have survived.

Herbert Shapiro thinks that the program helped the principals survive. "In a very practical way," he says, "the AGE Program minimized the impact of the budget cuts in terms of the depression that hit us in 1975. All of a sudden all of our dreams seemed to come crashing down on our heads. The AGE Program, because it did not require a lot of money, and because it gave us a focus again, sustained us through this period."

Webb indicates that another major factor in the survival of the program in a period of retrenchment was that "it provided so many tangible educational benefits for a relatively modest investment on the part of the school system. This is no small consideration at any time for cost-conscious school administrators, but was particularly applicable during this period of unprecedented cutbacks."

The Network in Action

If there is any one factor that makes the AGE Program unique, it is its network. Principals of all the schools involved meet once a month, chair their own meetings, and evolve their own strategies for curriculum and staff development. In the past year, especially, principals have asserted true ownership of the program. As Webb sees it, "There have been some interesting struggles for power and bloodless coups that have taken place in terms of moving from a management-team-directed project to a principal-directed program. This is all to the good."

The principals themselves praise the network meetings without reservation. Tev Sumner declares that, "N.Y.C. has one of the most parochial educational systems in the United States. Probably the single most important consequence of the AGE Program is the opportunity it has provided for educators from various parts of the city to get together to explore, to exchange, to listen, to grow, and to share."

In a system like New York's where districts are run by independent school boards, principals rarely have an opportunity to cross over district lines, let alone join in a consortium to coordinate a program collectively. When the principal's network was first started, the program coordinator, Carol Fineberg, literally managed it, and the management team—the hub—made most of the decisions regarding policies and programs. While this approach was dictated by the practical realities of this early developmental phase of the networking process, Fineberg operated on the belief that, "the hub cannot determine what is good for principals but must operate on a consultative basis with its clients, in this case the principals and their staffs. Moreover," she says, "the network cannot be perceived as a closed organization—a club, if you will—but rather as an open, accessible, and growing organism that reflects the status of school development options within a given district."

As it matures, a true network should evolve toward collective ownership, and this is the direction that has emerged in N.Y.C. in the past year. Leslie Goldman, the present program coordinator, says, "Principals have now reached a point where they understand the concept well enough to assert their own leadership in the development of the program." In keeping with this belief, Goldman does not manage the network; she facilitates it. "My role is catalytic," she says firmly.

The participating principals seem to agree with Herbert Shapiro, who says, "The network, for me, has been personally satisfying. I have enjoyed the interaction with colleagues who are professionally committed to the same ideas I am. It has provided me with the opportunity to think anew about my job and the way in which I perform as a principal. I've had the opportunity to hear people talk and to have that whole ferment of ideas. This is an essential part of the program for me—and a delight. Without question, it has helped solidify my ideas about the AGE concept."

Shapiro has taken those ideas back to his own teachers. "We found that we have had to do the same kind of talking to get our teachers to accept and understand what the AGE Program is all about."

Nola Whiteman says that one of the most significant outcomes of the program to date "is the change in the principals. When this project began, many of the principals involved seemed to view themselves mainly as creative administrators. They now seem to place a much heavier emphasis on their role as educational leaders."

Virginia Flanagan, principal of elementary demonstration school 312 in Brooklyn, says it this way: "If you're in a school like this with relatively few problems, your life as a principal could be very humdrum. You could come in, do the reports that you have to do, do the little disciplining that has to be done, and at the end of the day, go home and forget about it. I find myself looking forward to being here. There is something

It is not enough for a supportive administrator to simply understand and endorse a concept of education. To really be effective, an administrator must participate in the developmental process.

109

happening every day. The kids are happy. They're outgoing. They are thrilled to be here. An AGE school is exciting to the children, to the teachers, and to the principal."

Principals have also gained techniques and approaches that they have applied beyond the AGE program. "There has been a marked increase in comprehensive planning in general among the participating principals," Whiteman notes. "These administrators have an overall picture, if not in writing then in their heads, of what they want their schools to look like. As resources become available, they can place them in perspective and use them in a more effective way as part of their overall philosophical thrust."

What the principals' network boils down to, then, is leadership training and on-the-job professional development that involves a redefinition by the practitioners of their own roles and functions. The management team testifies to the tremendous broadening of people who have participated in the program. Remer says that such change does not come about without a certain amount of risk. "Schools generally work from the top down. In a comprehensive program of this kind, there has to be involvement of staff, parents, and outside groups. It is a lateral type of decision-making process where people are delegated power by those above. The AGE committee in each school makes certain programmatic decisions for that school and helps to carry them out. That is not the traditional bureaucratic process. This represents a personal risk on the part of principals, who must say to themselves, 'I'm in charge, but I'm willing to delegate authority.'"

The principals have also gotten a certain amount of ego reinforcement by being a part of the network. Sumner says, "It has given me the opportunity to travel, to serve on panels, and to articulate what I believe throughout the city and nationwide. You cannot overestimate the kind of personal replenishment that a principal needs. Every now and then we need the same kind of recognition that teachers need."

As if coping with N.Y.C. isn't enough, the network and its hub (the program's management team) have reached out to other cities. The superintendent of schools and key staff members from the Syracuse (New York) Public Schools visited the demonstration schools in N.Y.C. and met with Webb and the management team with the idea of setting up an AGE Program in Syracuse. As a follow-up to that meeting, Whiteman, Goldman, two teachers, and a principal went to Syracuse to talk with over 80 teachers and administrators on what the AGE Program is all about. This is only the beginning of what the New York State Education Department and management team hope will become a state-wide network.

This past year the program's management team (enlarged to include Jones and Whiteman) recognized the need to form a teachers' network parallel to the principals'. Webb acknowledges that this may be getting at one of the weaknesses of the program: "When you talk to teachers in AGE schools, you find many have difficulty articulating the AGE approach conceptually and philosophically. They need to be more aware of what is happening and be more involved in the total concept. There is a discrepancy between what the principals have come to understand and where the teachers are." He feels that if this network is effective—and it is too early to tell at this time—"then we would truly have an AGE Program that is built from the bottom up."

The Mini-networks

Any design for widespread educational change through a demonstration-type format must make provision for disseminating the program. There seems to be no easy mechanism for accomplishing this, particularly with the AGE approach which depends heavily upon a process of human interaction. Whiteman has observed that, "It is a difficult concept to translate to other people outside the network. People want a recipe. This is a process, and it can't easily be put down in writing."

She sees that process as "a way of looking at a school as a whole, of examining all the parts of the system, tying them together, and strengthening those that need it, all for the purpose of improving the quality of education for all students. I believe in a joint planning process of all those people who impact on children—the principal, the teachers, and the parents. It creates a common philosophy, in this case one focused around the arts."

The project management team has tried a number of different means to move the philosophy out to other sites. "There are many ways to skin a cat," Goldman says. "One means of reaching superintendents has been to invite them on site visits to other cities." In Sumner's school district, for example, Max Messer, the superintendent, was invited to go to Minneapolis on a League of Cities Site Visit. As a result of his participation there, his belief in the AGE concept was reinforced, and he was willing to devote one of his monthly district meetings with principals to a demonstration of the AGE concept.

These monthly meetings of principals in each district do provide a means to bring the program to the attention of all the administrators in the system. Many principals in the network have led a discussion about the AGE Program at one of these district meetings. Goldman says, "A meeting on the arts would be rare without the impetus of the AGE Program and the enthusiasm and know-how it has engendered among the participating principals and superintendents."

Members of the program's management team have also taken the initiative in spreading the word through what they call their traveling "Dog and Pony Show." In order to spotlight the AGE approach, Berger, Goldman, Remer, and others often hop in a car and go to one of the demonstration sites to meet with superintendents and principals from another district. The team introduces the administrators to the concept, distributes documentary reports, manuals, and descriptive materials, then

The AGE concept is difficult to translate to other people outside the network. People want a recipe. This is a process, and it can't easily be put down in writing.

invites them to observe the program in operation. Discussions follow that often lead to some kind of commitment and action in the other district.

In May 1979, for example, the superintendent, two deputy superintendents, and three principals from District 21 met with the management team at a demonstration school in District 22. There they had the opportunity to talk with the principal and some of the staff and to observe classes. The superintendent has already agreed to district-wide meetings in the fall devoted to the AGE Program, which he is interested in installing throughout his district.

Berger says that such visitations to a nearby district have a powerful effect upon administrators. "They don't see it in their own district, but they do see it elsewhere. And then they say, 'Oh, we could do that at home.'"

Remer points out that, whenever possible, "the program uses a peer structure to spread the concept. Teachers talk with teachers, principals with principals, superintendents with superintendents, as well as an intermixture of teams of various kinds." Such networking involves considerable time and effort.

Goldman estimates that, "There are now eight or nine school districts in N.Y.C. that have made the commitment to make a comprehensive plan for all the schools in their district to move in the direction of the AGE philosophy." In addition, she says, "There are another 16 or 17 districts that are interested in moving toward a comprehensive plan for the arts in general education. It is a question of the time and energy that can be put into the traveling road show. If we could devote every day to this, we could reach all these districts now."

But, without doubt, the most effective means of moving the program to other schools is through mini-networks set up within districts. While many of the participating principals have held their own district-wide meeting for other principals, Mark Shapiro, principal of PS 98 in Manhattan, has taken the initiative in establishing the first district-wide AGE network. At the start of the project, District 6 had two demonstration schools and three schools that were designated cooperating schools. (One of the latter was later designated a demonstration school.) Thus five out of the 14 schools in this district were involved, which means that more than one-third of the district's schools were already committed.

At the monthly principals' conferences in this district, there has been considerable sharing of ideas about the arts in education. Two years ago, Shapiro conducted a conference for principals on the AGE Program using his own school for class visitations and discussions between his faculty and the other 13 principals in his district. "Because of the enthusiastic response of the principals," he says, "I suggested to Dr. Paul Treatman, our community superintendent, that we form our own AGE network within the district. The purpose was to further support the schools already involved and to help give impetus to those schools not yet deeply involved. He agreed."

Shapiro then consulted with the other principals to determine the makeup of the committee and its function. Representatives from schools may be principals, assistant principals, arts specialists, and/or classroom teachers. At a principals' conference in April 1979, the District 6 AGE Steering Committee planned the presentation. Shapiro says, "More than half the schools in the district gave demonstrations, including especially schools not designated as AGE schools. We wanted to show that you don't have to be called an AGE school to have an AGE program. This conference was very successful. There was articulation between all the principals and the teachers involved."

At the time of this writing, four schools in the district had not yet sent representatives to the district AGE meetings. Shapiro isn't worried. "I've deliberately planned the meetings from two to four o'clock so that they are split between school time and personal time. This little gimmick forces the schools to make a commitment to release the committee members, and it also forces committee members to give a little of their own time. The probable reason the other schools aren't represented is that they haven't yet found that person on their staff who is willing to give his/her own time. That is fine. I don't want them on the committee until they're willing to devote one of their own hours to it."

The formation of this intra-district network, envisioned in the original program design, is a significant breakthrough in the dissemination process. "What we have here," Goldman states, "is our prototype for expansion. With more than 900 schools in N.Y.C., we have to start accommodating other schools that want to get into the program. The project management team had considered expanding by increasing the number of cooperating schools. We decided we couldn't expand that way. What we want to do is replicate the model network started in District 6 and use this as the way to expand in every school district that so desires."

Shapiro says that, "The problem of dissemination of programs is not a problem of the arts but of education in general. This gets at the heart of what demonstration schools are all about—what the word 'demonstration' means. Too often demonstration is interpreted as showing something in your own school. The essential question is, 'What are you demonstrating for?' I'm really happy if something is being demonstrated that benefits all 1,350 of my students; but, if a school is truly a demonstration site, then you must take the concept out and share it, and let other people decide if it can work for them."

"What we have to do," Goldman declares, "is to have Mark (Shapiro) share his experiences as specifically as possible with the other demonstration-school principals. Then, they too can move to set up district-wide networks in their own districts." This will be a test of the real leadership that must emerge from the principals' network. Like Shapiro, the other demonstration-school principals must continue to show concern not just for their own school but for the entire school district.

In Shapiro's way of thinking, assuming this kind of responsibility is self-serving. "Why do I come to the city-wide

The problem of dissemination of programs is not a problem of the arts but of education in general. This gets at the heart of what demonstration schools are all about— what the word "demonstration" means.

In AGE schools, artists function differently. They fulfill the needs of that situation according to how the staff defines the AGE concept, and residencies often result in new courses that are teacher-designed and taught.

meetings? Because I get smarter listening to my colleagues and stealing ideas from them. It is no different on the district level. We all need the input and stimulus from other people."

Efforts to share knowledge about the AGE Program with other interested schools and districts have also taken the form of written documents. Two of these are worthy of special mention. The first, "All the Arts for All the Children," is a report on the AGE Program in N.Y.C. during the years 1974-77. This so called "Doorknob" Report (labeled as such because of the antique board of education doorknob pictured on the cover) explains the concept; provides profiles on the demonstration schools; quotes principals, teachers, and other participants on the merits of the approach; and lists funding sources and participating artists and organizations. The second document is an administrator's manual designed as a guide to help principals and superintendents understand and implement an AGE Program in their own school or school district. These and other materials are part of the dissemination efforts supported by the board of education with assistance from the Fund.

Artists and Arts Organizations

Perhaps the most severe criticism leveled against N.Y.C.'s AGE Program has been that it appears to be nothing more than a glorified artists-in-schools program. Remer says, "The same criticism has often been leveled against the Seattle and Minneapolis programs. There are simple reasons for it. Minneapolis, Seattle, and N.Y.C. abound in artistic and cultural resources, and they have a long tradition of using them in the schools. Every school district, whether urban, suburban, or rural, has got to start from its points of strength. One of N.Y.C.'s strengths was its involvement with artists in schools. For example, Lincoln Center and Young Audiences have been operating in the public schools for many years. We built on this experience and strength. But we also went beyond it to incorporate the elements of interdisciplinary teaching and learning and to focus the program on staff, curriculum, and total school development. In order to do this, we enlisted the cooperation of the many smaller and culturally diverse arts groups throughout the city."

Of course, an artists-in-schools program cannot be equated with an arts in general education program. "The two are quite different," says Ted Berger, who runs N.Y. State's Artists-in-Schools Program through the N.Y. Foundation for the Arts. "In AGE schools, artists usually function differently. They fulfill the needs of that situation according to how the staff defines the AGE concept," Berger observes, "and residencies often result in new courses that are teacher-designed and taught."

One of the needs has been for workshops in the arts for classroom teachers. "Our major thrust has been the inservicing of our teachers," explains Herbert Shapiro. "We expect that every artist we hire will leave behind sufficiently trained teachers who can carry on at least some of the activities that artist has done. When we found artists who were only interested in performance or who could not achieve our goals in teacher training, we didn't re-hire them."

Bernice Frankenthaler testifies that, "The artists in residence have worked closely with the classroom teachers to come up with projects that meld the arts with particular units of study."

Shapiro believes that, "It is the principal who makes a difference between whether a program is an artists-in-schools program or a school development effort. Where one principal sees it as an artists-in-schools program and another a school development program, you are going to have two different results at the end of the year. The students in the former case will have had some fine experiences with artists. That will be the end of it. In the latter case, much will have been inculcated into the faculty. They will be co-planning in an effort to further the experience the artists bring in. A whole different experience will result."

Mark Shapiro says, "You can have an artist in residence who will have nothing to do with the main thrust of the school. When we have had actors in residence, they have worked with both students and teachers. The four classroom teachers involved in the theater arts residency met weekly with the actor to pre- and co-plan the activities. Visiting artists offer workshops to teachers and to the community at large. Every residency has these ingredients. Yet it should be understood that, without any artists in residence, we would still have an AGE Program."

Berger, whose organization supplies many of the artists for the AGE Program, notes that many collaborations of artists and schools are superficial. "This is not generally the case with AGE schools," he says. "In the AGE Program, we are dealing with attitudinal changes in adults—parents as well as teachers and administrators. Until these changes occur, we will not have done enough for children. If you bring a dancer to a school, but the adults do not encourage the children to participate fully in the dance experience, you may be doing the children a disservice and have nothing lasting to show for it."

Berger talks as well of "artist development." He feels that artists have gained special personal and professional rewards from working in AGE schools. "These schools know what they can ask of artists and they know how to use their fullest potential. In turn, the artists have learned how to work in partnership with the schools and how to serve as a valuable educational resource. In addition, the experience of working in an AGE school has opened new professional vistas and new creative possibilities."

While the demonstration schools have for the most part mastered the art of selecting and using artists, this was not always the case. "In the beginning one of our biggest obstacles was that some principals and teachers thought that having artists come to the school was in itself the AGE Program,"

It is the principal who makes a difference between whether a program is an artist-in-schools program or a school development effort.

115

Rather than simply serving as cultural enrichment or entertainment, the artist residencies now have a built-in and lasting effect on staff development and the whole teaching-learning process.

Remer recalls. "They thought it was 'nice' to have artists come to the school, but they didn't fully understand how to integrate the artist's special knowledge and talent into the school program so that teaching and learning would be strengthened long after the artist had left."

The AGE committees in the demonstration schools have helped to develop techniques for using artists effectively. The hours of preplanning time, talks with teachers and administrators, and the evaluation of each residency have paid off. Rather than simply serving as cultural enrichment or entertainment, the residencies now have a built-in and lasting effect on staff development and the whole teaching-learning process.

Faculty development is sometimes surprising. In Junior High School 104 in Manhattan, a modern dance company from Young Audiences inspired a young male math teacher with no previous dance experience to volunteer to coordinate a dance program for the school. Harold Grill, the principal, helped by rearranging the school schedule so that two 90-minute dance periods could be offered each week. Because parents had been involved, a dancer from the company was hired with PTA funds to teach the class. Consequently, adolescents in this school—boys as well as girls—are getting a serious introduction to modern dance. In Mark Shapiro's school, a photographer's residency, which included workshops for teachers, inspired one teacher to take further photography courses on her own and to design a photo-journalism course for the school.

With their considerable experience in dealing with artists and their commitment to making the arts contribute to all their educational goals, the AGE schools have played a role in helping arts organizations work out more effective programs. Young Audiences' National Theatre Lab has used AGE schools to test an intensive new theater program. The New York Foundation for the Arts has used its extensive pilot work with AGE schools to benefit other artists-in-schools programs. In April 1979, eleven arts organizations that have worked with the AGE Program formed their own network called the Arts Consortium for Education (ACE).

ACE was formed to consider the organizational, technical, educational, and artistic needs of arts in education programs from an artistic perspective. It has two major objectives: (1) To provide ACE members with a means of sharing information, program ideas, and concerns with each other, and to give members access to information from the larger arts and education communities; and (2) To establish an advocacy group that will make the concerns of ACE members known to city, state, and federal agencies, private funding sources, and school districts.

Community Response

Goldman tells a story about the woman who called her asking for information about the AGE Program. It seems that she was sitting in a hospital waiting room sharing her anguish with another mother about whether her child should have a private or public education. The woman she was talking to told her that, if she decided to send her child to a public school, she should send her to an AGE demonstration school similar to the one her son was attending. The more the woman heard, the more she became fascinated. As large as the bureaucracy is in the N.Y.C. schools, the woman located Goldman, the AGE Coordinator, by phone. She was determined to enlist her daughter in an AGE school.

Goldman suggested that the woman write a letter to the principal in her district telling what she knew of the AGE Program. In response to this letter, the principal contacted Goldman and inquired about how he could become involved. In the meantime, Goldman carefully let the superintendent in the district know about the case. (There is nothing so persuasive to a superintendent than a parent who demands that her child attend an AGE demonstration school on the basis that it provides a better general education.) Goldman then met with him. Somewhat later, this superintendent and his steering committee went to an adjoining district to view a demonstration school and meet with the AGE management team. Plans for an AGE program in this district are now under way.

The AGE schools, from all appearances, have managed to win wide public support in their communities, something that cannot be taken for granted in a city like New York. The program has, in most cases, kept enrollment in these schools up, while in most schools it is declining. Luis Mercado, principal of PS 75 in Manhattan, a demonstration school, says, "There is no doubt that, if we had a voucher system, I'd have 10,000 kids trying to get into this school. We are a quality school on all levels—in terms of reading scores, the way we treat children, and the way we work with parents. The arts have been the way through. If we didn't have the arts here, this would be a dying school."

When the principal of PS 312, the elementary demonstration school in Brooklyn's District 22, retired, Community Superintendent Ralph Brande and the parents insisted that the new principal be willing to provide basic support for the AGE concept. Frank Macchiarola, the current Chancellor of the school system, happened to be chairman of the school board in this district at that time. In a system where parental indifference or outrage is often the case, this kind of insistent caring does not go unnoticed by school board members. Certainly, it is one reason why Macchiarola is supportive of the AGE Program today.

"Without doubt," Berger says, "the AGE schools have become important educational and cultural resources for their communities. For example, there are dance and theater programs that weren't there before that have attracted great community interest and support. As a result, there is a growing sophistication about the arts and their value in human development. There is also an increasing recognition by the school

The AGE schools, from all appearances, have managed to win wide public support in their communities, something that cannot be taken for granted in a city like New York.

117

As an educator, it makes sense to me, that a child isn't going to do well if he doesn't like what he is doing and he doesn't like school. Those things have to come first.

and its community of the need for specialist teachers in all the arts. Witness the fact that AGE principals, with strong parental support, are choosing specialists in the arts or teachers with a strong arts background whenever the opportunity presents itself."

One of the outgrowths of the AGE Program in the community around demonstration school 152 in the Bronx is the organization of the Soundview Arts Council, a group that was formed to promote arts in this community. The Council supports lessons in dance, voice, and instrumental music for talented students. AGE schools have a way of making parents aware of the arts by making the arts a natural part of the life of the community. Arts festivals and fairs, in-school arts events, and workshops in the arts for parents have attracted considerable attention and won broad community support, not just for the AGE Program, but for the arts in general.

Outcomes

In the final analysis, the measure of the worth of any educational program is what it does for students. Principals of the demonstration schools speak in glowing terms of these results. Tev Sumner says, "It has given kids a feeling of belief in themselves—a way to succeed in schools other than by the written word. It has been instrumental in working out more effective relationships between teachers and students."

Sumner's elementary school is 99 percent minority. About 92 percent receive free lunches, and upwards of 60 percent are on welfare. Yet he says, "We are more than holding our own in reading with 38 percent of the students reading on or above grade level." He attributes this as much to the emphasis placed on the arts in the daily learning process as to any other factor. "As an educator, it makes sense to me, that a child isn't going to do well, if he doesn't like what he is doing and he doesn't like school. Those things have to come first. If teachers and students are happy about what they do, that has to be a major factor in getting students to succeed."

In other words, Sumner says, "You don't have successful schools where there is a lack of job satisfaction. Attendance, vandalism, graffiti, assaults, break-ins, and suspensions are almost non-existent in this school. Even though this is a very rough neighborhood, we never have a major incident, and we have very few minor ones. The community cares about the school."

Edith Del Valle, coordinator of the AGE Program at LaGuardia High School of Music and the Arts in Manhattan, speaks of "another kind of poverty—one that can't be seen. It is a poverty of inspiration, of providing young people with a chance to dream—a vision—the ability to say, 'I can be . . .' Without the arts, young people dry up."

Children in AGE schools draw and paint, sculpt and
118   model, listen and sing, dance, act, write stories and poems,

play instruments, take photographs, and even build structures. But that isn't the real point. Arnold Webb says, "AGE is a lot more than putting pretty pictures on the walls. It is making the arts part of the instructional fabric of the school. It can turn a school around and change the entire environment for learning. If you can infuse this kind of spirit and belief in what you're doing into a school as the AGE schools have been able to do, that is more than half the battle. The rest is downhill. That is why there is such a remarkable contrast between AGE schools and comparable schools that draw from the same neighborhood population."

Webb has been a consistent and articulate supporter of the AGE Program. "Step into an AGE school and it seems to say, 'This is a place where we feel good about what we are doing.' It is on the lips of the teachers and the faces of the kids. These schools are definitely not drab and colorless places," he says. "I have to say, in all candor, that I do not believe that the arts are the only way to achieve this. But they are one striking and dramatic way to enhance learning." N.Y.C.'s AGE Program makes this obvious, and it also provides a clear example of the way N.Y.C.'s schools can and do work for kids.

AGE is a lot more than putting pretty pictures on the walls. It is making the arts part of the instructional fabric of the school. Step into an AGE school and it seems to say, "This is a place where we feel good about what we are doing." It is on the lips of the teachers and the faces of the kids.

CHAPTER SIX
Case Study: Winston-Salem – The Management of Adaptation

Nancy Shuker

The greatest achievements sometimes start with the small-est gesture. This is the case with the initiation of an arts in education program in the Winston-Salem/Forsyth County (North Carolina) school system. In 1974-75 the Winston-Salem Arts Council commissioned Louis Harris Associates to conduct an arts attitude study in Winston-Salem. One of the results of that study was the revelation that the community felt that the schools should be doing considerably more with the arts.

The survey revealed that:

> The people of Winston-Salem are overwhelm-ingly in favor of arts courses being taught in the public schools, not just as a non-credit activity but as part of the core curriculum like English and mathematics. Furthermore, they believe the courses should be taught at all levels of the public school system and that the funds to pay for them should come from the regular school budget.
>
> When people were asked specifically whether they thought each of eleven arts and crafts subjects

Trying out ideas developed in other school systems requires constant evaluation. People in Winston-Salem had to analyze when these ideas worked and when they didn't and come up with their own solutions.

should be taught in the public schools for "credit just like math or science or English," whether they should be taught only after school or as a non-credit activity, or not given at all, substantial majorities felt each subject should be part of the regular curriculum as a credit course, and only very small proportions felt any of the subjects should not be given at all.

The arts courses that were listed, and the percentages believing they should be given as credit courses in the public schools, were: playing a musical instrument (87%), voice or singing (84%), sewing, weaving or other handiwork (84%), woodworking or other crafts (84%), drawing, painting or sculpture (83%), writing stories or poems (82%), music appreciation (73%), photography or filmmaking (72%), art appreciation (70%), acting (66%), and ballet or modern dancing (61%).

It was this study that set the stage for expansion of arts activities in the schools.

Initiating the Program

In the spring of 1975, Milton Rhodes, executive secretary of the Arts Council, concerned about what the survey said, wrote to Kathryn Bloom at the JDR 3rd Fund. He knew her and was aware of the Fund's work in the arts. The Arts Council and the community wanted her help in starting an arts in education program in Winston-Salem.

Bloom, who by then was already working with public school systems in New York City, Seattle, Little Rock, Hartford, and Minneapolis, replied that she was impressed with what the Council had done so far and suggested that the next step should be to work directly with the superintendent of schools and the board of education.

Although she could not then go to Winston, she sent Gene Wenner from her staff to meet with the education committee of the Arts Council and to speak to school officials. Wenner distributed materials developed by the Fund's and New York City's arts in education program. A second meeting was arranged for early summer to permit Wenner to meet with school superintendent Marvin Ward and other administrators. In the fall, Jane Remer, who worked collaboratively with school personnel to design the New York City program and now also of the Fund's staff, joined Wenner in Winston-Salem. As a result of these meetings, the school administrators expressed an interest in establishing a comprehensive arts in education program in the Winston-Salem school system. Up to this time, arts offerings in the district followed a traditional pattern. Junior and senior high schools maintained elective courses in visual arts, music, and drama, and elementary schools shared the services of vocal and instrumental music teachers and physical education teachers.

The Planning Process

Superintendent Ward gave the job of developing a plan for an arts in education program to his special assistant for instruction, Douglas Carter. Carter interested two elementary schools in exploring the idea of developing such a program. In a subsequent visit, Wenner and Remer met with the principals and total staffs of these schools for an orientation session.

After their initial presentation, Wenner and Remer were met with silence, if not resistance. The teachers were mystified; they did not fully understand why they had been called together or why representatives of the Fund had come to Winston-Salem. The remainder of the two-day meeting was spent in small group discussions. The interest of the Fund and the New York City approach were carefully explained, including how to identify pilot schools, set up a coordinating hub, and clarify responsibilities. Interest was aroused. Carter felt he could begin to move.

The ultimate enthusiasm and eagerness of the school representatives and the supportiveness of the Arts Council impressed the Fund. Bloom and Remer saw an opportunity to apply the New York City model/process in a different kind of school system in another geographical area of the country.

At the same time, the Fund was planning to organize a meeting of representatives from school systems they were already working with. The idea was to set up a League of Cities similar to the Fund's Coalition of States. If networking proved valuable on a local level, why not on a national scale?

Later in the Fall of 1975, Bloom and Remer again visited Winston-Salem to observe the planning success that Carter had begun to implement. Trying out ideas developed in other school systems requires constant evaluation. People in Winston-Salem had to analyze when these ideas worked and when they didn't and come up with their own solutions. For a new system just beginning the process, the results were unique.

Task Forces

During the planning process that first year, it became clear that Carter understood the difference between an arts enrichment program and a school development program focused on the arts. Believing that the incorporation of the arts into the basic school program ultimately lay in the hands of classroom teachers, he formed a task force of teachers to design the basic goals, objectives, and strategies for the program. Because the leadership role of teachers was considered to be of utmost importance, Carter placed an enormous amount of planning and design responsibility in the hands of a core group of classroom teachers. This approach was destined to have an important effect. Interdisciplinary teaching and learning in the arts tends to be more widespread in Winston-Salem precisely be-

Because the leadership role of teachers was considered to be of utmost importance, an enormous amount of planning and design responsibility was placed in the hands of a core group of classroom teachers.

123

cause their generation by each classroom teacher serves as the crux of the program's focus.

The teacher task force was made up of 12 teachers from the two schools—Brunson and Diggs—which Carter had first enlisted in the program. Between them, the schools encompassed kindergarten through sixth grade with special classes for the trainable mentally retarded, the educable mentally retarded, and the gifted and talented. A second task force of supervisors and administrators was formed to help carry out the plan. The name chosen for the program reflected its major thrust—Arts in the Basic Curriculum (ABC).

The ABC Plan

Drawing on materials provided by the Fund and their own reading and discussions over a period of six weeks, the teachers produced a position paper. In it they committed themselves to some principles described by Remer in a paper written for the Fund called, "Ten Characteristics of School Systems that Have Developed Effective Arts in General Education Programs":

1. A commitment to quality education for all children
2. A commitment to quality education through the arts
3. The creative use of existing human, financial, and physical resources
4. A coherent, collaborative approach to program planning and development
5. An organic program design
6. A continuing curriculum and staff development effort
7. On-going internal and external documentation and evaluation
8. An effective communications network
9. A broadening and humanistic concept of schooling
10. An increased commitment to and understanding of the change process in education

The teachers also expressed some of their own concepts about the value of the arts which they incorporated into the ABC program: "The ABC program concentrates on having all children experience the arts as an integral part of their education. Emphasis is placed on the entire curriculum and on incorporating new dimensions of awareness through the arts. . . . The interdisciplinary approach to the arts in education prepares the individual to utilize, throughout his life, the emotional, intellectual, and aesthetic fulfillment found in the arts. . . . The arts are seen as a catalyst for intellectual stimulation and for bringing all types of instruction to students in a way that they can accept, that interest them, and that may motivate them to learn. . . . Arts in the schools enriches the total community."

Carter, Associate Superintendent Raymond Sarbaugh, Director of Elementary Education Grace Efrid, and Diggs' Principal Mary Jo Issacs took the position paper to a Fund-sponsored meeting in Chicago in March of 1976. Winston-Salem became a charter member of the League of Cities for the Arts in Education. The sharing experience between the various cities represented had a strong effect upon the planning process in Winston-Salem. Upon their return, they reopened the school identification procedure. They formed a network. They paid particular attention to the role of the principal as leader. They studied management and field service possibilities in conjunction with the Central Board of Education. They established a rapport with the Arts Council so that, in effect, the Council asked, "What can we do?".

Of course, progress is not accomplished without overcoming snags. In the spring of 1976, it became known that Superintendent Ward was approaching retirement. His successor had not been named. Aware of the need for administrative commitment and support, the task force questioned whether such a program should be undertaken without the approval of the new superintendent. However, with the encouragement of Raymond Sarbaugh, Carter and his task forces proceeded.

Interested elementary schools were asked to volunteer for the program. Of those that asked to be considered, five were chosen as pilot or demonstration sites by the central office. The choice was based on their interest and promise as innovative schools as well as their geographic distribution in the city and county. By June the principals of the five pilot schools had met with Carter and a representative of the central board's curriculum department to discuss the program. Each principal was asked to recommend a teacher for a summer task force to develop a card file of ideas for relating the arts to basic teaching situations. The file was designed to help stimulate a teacher's own thinking about ways to incorporate the arts. These "stimulus" cards were printed and boxed for distribution to all teachers in the demonstration schools.

Interdisciplinary teaching and learning in the arts tends to be more widespread in Winston-Salem precisely because their generation by each classroom teacher serves as the crux of the program's focus.

Community Resources

There is considerable precedent for using community arts resources in conjunction with the schools in Winston-Salem. The Little Theater, a local non-profit group, provides volunteer creative dramatics teachers to elementary schools and training in creative dramatics for junior and senior high school teachers. The Winston-Salem Symphony and the North Carolina School of the Arts present enrichment programs in the schools. The P.T.A. Council—through a federal grant—sponsors an experimental, paid cultural program that brings arts groups into the schools. (They recommended that the school system budget get $75,000 to continue the program for the school year 1975-76.)

The City of Winston Salem considers itself a cultural center of the Southeast for good reason. There are five colleges and universities there, including the first state-supported high 125 school and college for the performing arts in the United States, the North Carolina School of the Arts. Winston-Salem boasts of having not only the nation's oldest continuously active brass band—formed in 1778 by Moravian settlers—but also, more recently, the first chartered arts council in the country. Founded in 1949, the Winston-Salem Arts Council has served as a model for local arts councils all over the United States and Canada and has continued to be a moving force in the community. (In 1977, it received the first annual award of the national Business Committee for the Arts.)

It is not surprising, then, that the Education Committee of the Winston-Salem Arts Council agreed to work with Carter to coordinate community arts groups' and artists' activities with the ABC schools and to match funds for these services with the district. Carter estimates that the Arts Council contributes some $75,000 a year to the schools, through artists' performances, workshops, and after-school classes.

In addition, the school board took up the recommendation of the P.T.A. to allocate funds—$35,000—for cultural enrichment programs in the schools. A portion of this budget was set aside exclusively for the ABC schools, and this policy has continued.

The North Carolina Department of Public Instruction was contacted about the program and responded with matching funds for a National Endowment of the Arts' Artists-in-Schools dance residency. The residency "package" included four weeks of work with a movement specialist before a two-week visit by the North Carolina Dance Theater. Three teachers from the host school were sent to the American Dance Festival in New London, Connecticut, in preparation for the dance residency.

In Winston-Salem, as in other League programs, the use of community resources has been interpreted broadly to mean more than the use of artists in residence. Arts groups work cooperatively with the schools; the schools make intelligent decisions and plan collaboratively with these groups. And just as important: the schools are not afraid to blow the whistle when things don't work out.

Beginning the Second Year: 1976-1977

In July, Dr. James A. Adams was appointed the new superintendent of schools. Briefed by Carter on the Arts Council survey and plans for the ABC program, Adams immediately endorsed the concept and took it to the board of education. The program was officially approved that same month.

"I was a supporter of the arts in schools anyway," Adams says of his commitment. "I saw that there was a real void in the system, and I told the board that we had to address that need. I thought ABC could help us get at the goal of arts education in the schools. I also saw it as a combination of staff motivation and changing of attitude toward the arts that would help us make more budget commitment to the arts later."

A "kick-off" meeting to launch the ABC program was held in August for the entire faculties of the five demonstration schools. The guest speaker was Carol Fineberg, coordinator of the New York City Arts in General Education Program. This was the first in a series of workshop activities planned by the ABC administrative task force as a year-long staff development project.

The administrative task force asked appropriate central board staff and consultants to hold workshops on visual arts, drama, music, and movement in each of the demonstration schools. The district's coordinator of volunteers oriented teachers to community talent interested in working with the schools. "Feedback" sessions were scheduled with each school after the five workshops were completed. To help get plans rolling, the central office allocated $500 for each school to use for whatever ABC purpose it chose.

In late August, one of the ABC principals unexpectedly died, precipitating a shifting of two other principals. This change in personnel also changed one of the demonstration schools and certainly presented problems for principals who had new faculties to work with. However, ABC planning continued in each of the schools. The arts workshops were scheduled for September and October and the first feedback sessions for early November.

For the most part, staff shifts are avoided in Winston-Salem schools. In the process of integration, children are moved, not faculties. Turnover among teachers is therefore not a particular threat to maintaining continuity, so long as there is stable, committed administrative leadership.

The use of community resources has been interpreted broadly to mean more than the use of artists in residence. Arts groups work cooperatively with the schools; the schools make intelligent decisions and plan collaboratively with these groups. And just as important: the schools are not afraid to blow the whistle when things don't work out.

The Reaction of Teachers

Transcripts of the early feedback sessions show some continuing reluctance and bewilderment on the part of teachers. "It is very difficult to break into the middle of reading with something that is fun and try to get your class back together," one teacher observed.

"I know the children have to be tested at a particular point, and they have to know a certain amount, and I feel I have to stick with reading," another commented.

"It doesn't come naturally to me to use the arts in my teaching," another teacher anguished. "How am I to learn to feel comfortable with the arts?"

Similar concerns were expressed at a faculty meeting at one of the demonstration schools that fall. The Task Force Reports of that meeting state that:

"Someone pointed out the need for a good background in the basic curriculum before broadening into an arts program and felt that our students do not have this background yet."

"Most of the participants felt that full-fledged participation in ABC would cause us to 'spread ourselves too thin.'"

My attitude toward using the arts in the basic curriculum has changed completely. I now feel guilty if I don't use some area of the arts in each class I teach.

"One teacher also was concerned about the time element involved in any large program. Is the amount of time required justified in relation to the other needs of the students?"

However, there were also teachers who welcomed the challenge and encouragement of the ABC program. The same reports also state:

"It was felt by this group that teachers through the years have involved drama, music, art, and movement in the daily curriculum, if, perhaps, in unspectacular ways. The ABC program has served to encourage teachers to be more aware of opportunities to include stimulating teaching techniques in their classrooms.

The dance residency package—including the sending of the principal and two teachers to the movement workshop the preceding summer—had a catalytic effect on its school. In preparation for the residency, three movement workshops were held for the faculty that stimulated, as the principal testifies happily, "a lot of rolling around on the floor." Films were also shown. The dance company was asked to send over dance clothes before the residency so that the children could get used to the idea of leotards and tights.

A reception was held for the movement teacher whose residency preceded the dance company's. Guests included dancers and administrators from the dance company, parents, arts council members, and the principals of the ABC schools. A special movement workshop for the P.T.A. was scheduled during the residency. In response, the P.T.A. hosted a dinner for the dance company. At the end of the company's residency, students—in this case fifth and sixth graders—offered to raise money to keep the company longer. The leader of this student petition, who was vice-president of the student body, explained her feeling about the residency to a reporter for the *Winston-Salem Journal*:

"At first I just hated ballet. But now that I have seen it up close—how their muscles work, how tough their bodies are, how they have to work to do everything they do—I just love it!"

However exciting an artist's residency might be for a school, it is not the core of the ABC program. The in-school coordinator for the dance residency, who also served on the task force that developed the stimulus cards, explains her own metamorphosis through the ABC experience:

"As the reading coordinator for our school, I teach in each classroom for a short period of time. I used to feel guilty when I incorporated the arts in one of my classes, because it took time away from the lesson. When I was asked to serve on the ABC task force, I looked forward to learning from more experienced people an 'approved method' for using the arts in a more efficient way. I discovered that there is no approved way and that we would have to work out our own ideas.

"I had had workshops or college classes in most of the arts, but movement and dance were difficult for me to use in any but traditional ways—learning a folk dance in social studies

128

or dancing to music in a music class. When I went to the movement workshop in preparation for the dance residency, I learned new ways to use the whole body for learning or demonstrating concepts. This was a tremendous stimulation to my imagination (as well as a test of my physical endurance).

"My attitude toward using the arts in the basic curriculum has changed completely. I now feel guilty if I don't use some area of the arts in each class I teach. Students' reactions have convinced me that, even though I am not an artist, I can stimulate their talents, enjoyment, and appreciation of the arts."

Teachers at another school talk about the process they went through without an artist's residency.

"We were told that we would be given time to develop our own program. We read about what other places were doing, but we were told we had to do ours our own way. We were given copies of the JRD 3rd Fund monographs and position papers from other sites, but that didn't tell us what was going on in other classrooms," one remembers.

Another teacher adds, "There was resentment at first, as there is to anything new. Teachers wondered what this new program would contribute to their work. Then the ideas began to come."

"We were given released time for our ABC planning meetings in the morning, when we were fresh. That made a big difference," a teacher says.

Another comments that she felt it was important that the principal didn't tell the teachers what to do, but trusted them to develop valid concepts themselves. "Teachers also felt good about creating a program that would pass from them to the administration rather than the other way around."

During the first year of implementing the ABC program— school year 1976-77—Carter took Emily Hyatt, Staff Consultant, Arts in Education, and different principals, teachers, and other administrators to League of Cities meetings, to site visits in both Seattle and New York, and to a JDR 3rd Fund conference in Chicago that brought together representatives of the League of Cities and the Coalition of States for the Arts in Education. The new superintendent attended both the New York City site visit and the latter meeting.

Bloom and Remer made a consultative trip to Winston-Salem and met with central board administrators, principals, teachers, and several arts specialists who had been hired by individual schools to work with teachers and children in the classroom to demonstrate ways that the arts could be used to teach other subjects.

Teachers also felt good about creating a program that would pass from them to the administration rather than the other way around.

Networking

Enthusiasm for the program was such that first year that Carter was under pressure from both the superintendent and other principals to expand the program. "Educators are great

Educators are great competitors. They hear about parental excitement for a program in another school, and they want it in their schools.

competitors," Carter explains. "They hear about parental excitement for a program in another school, and they want it in their schools."

Spreading this new arts concept throughout such a large and complex school system presented formidable problems. The Winston-Salem/Forsyth County School System serves nearly 45,000 students from kindergarten through high school in 65 schools. The consolidation of separate city and county districts took place in 1963. Racial integration was instituted in 1970-71. Youngsters in the system—70 percent white and 30 percent black—come from inner-city, suburban, and rural backgrounds. Maintaining racial balance in the schools has involved an elaborate pupil assignment program and busing. It has generally divided the schools into small units: buildings house kindergarten through fourth, fifth and sixth, seventh and eighth, ninth and tenth, and eleventh and twelfth grades—a 4, 2, 2, 2, 2 plan.

While the community has accepted the need for the pupil assignment plan and, in fact, as one administrator says, the schools have moved from desegregation to integration, the necessary system of two-grade schools and extensive busing throughout the county present problems of continuity. But this problem is minor compared to difficulties encountered in other cities in the League. Winston-Salem is the only one of the six cities that has not suffered a budget crisis, a teacher strike, or a tax levy failure. There is ample released time for teachers, for example, a necessary prerequisite for retraining them to incorporate the arts.

Toward the end of the first full year of operation, Carter considered expanding the program immediately to all the elementary schools in the system. Remer encouraged him to look at the problems other League of Cities sites were having in providing services to the original demonstration schools after two or three years and the even greater problems they were having, after several years of experience, in effectively expanding the concept to other schools.

Taking the advice to heart, Carter invited additional schools to volunteer to be cooperating schools the following year. Only six were chosen. In the meantime, a new elementary school building was completed, and an ABC principal and many members of his staff were assigned to it. The new principal of the original ABC school wanted to keep it in the program. Fortuitously, Carter gained a demonstration school. His idea was to pair the cooperating schools with the demonstration schools so that there would be a principal-to-principal and teacher-to-teacher sharing of experiences. He felt that the staffs of the demonstration schools could act as resources for the faculties of the cooperating schools.

Carter reasoned that many teachers in the demonstration schools were still struggling with their own understanding of the arts processes and how these might be applied to classroom studies. He observed that most of the demonstration schools spent their ABC budget to hire arts specialists representing various disciplines to work with teachers and students to demonstrate ways in which the arts can be used to teach the fundamental concepts of other subjects.

The Arts Resource Team

Carter saw the need for a staff development project that would serve both the demonstration schools and the cooperating schools on a regular basis, would help spread the ABC concept, and would have the demonstration component that teachers wanted. He decided to hire an arts resource team: experts in different arts disciplines who all understood the ABC concept of using the arts to strengthen general education.

"Normally staff development is conceptualized into a curriculum guide," he says. "But we don't have a curriculum in ABC; we can't hand teachers scope and sequence ready-made. We want them to learn to integrate the arts themselves. So, we had to come up with a new idea for staff development."

Carter found specialists in music, visual arts, theater, and movement, each of whom had worked in the ABC schools as arts consultants for brief periods during the first year. All young women, the arts resource team was excited by the ABC concept,and each was eager to explore ways of using her expertise to help teachers approach their jobs in new ways.

Jane Musten, the music teacher of the team, has degrees in music and theater and has worked as a music specialist in the Winston-Salem schools and as a professional actress.

The visual arts member of the team, Carol Miller, has worked in the Winston-Salem schools for eight years as a specialist at the junior high school level and has taught teacher workshops as well as courses for the Arts Council.

For theater, Carter hired Jane Pfefferkorn, a parent in the community, who studied creative dramatics for five years and taught classes in basic theater experiences at the Children's Theater.

Jody Sutlive, the movement specialist on the Arts Resource Team, earned a masters degree in dance and taught dance at the college level for seven years before she became interested in movement education and began studying for her doctorate in educational dance at the University of North Carolina.

Carter indoctrinated the Arts Resource Team himself, gave them JDR 3rd Fund materials to read, and sent them into the demonstration and cooperating schools to work with teachers in their classrooms on whatever part of the curriculum the teachers wanted help on. He told them that they should feel satisfied if they touched only half the teachers in a school.

One of the problems with resource teams in general has been a confusion of roles. There is a difference between being an administrator, a supervisor, or a coordinator and being a resource person. In Winston-Salem this difference is apparently understood. Team members are helpful as specialists. Where this team runs into difficulty, perhaps, is in inadvertently en-

One of the problems with resource teams in general has been a confusion of roles. There is a difference between being an administrator, a supervisor, or a coordinator and being a resource person.

I do not think that a teacher must use an art form in all its complexity to feel success. You cannot give teachers arts expertise. They are eventually going to have to get that for themselves.

couraging too much dependence on the part of classroom teachers. It is also felt that there is a need to define more clearly the role of the resource team as compared to the role of the resident school arts specialist.

Teaching Teachers

The members of the arts team give priority to their mission of staff development. Pfefferkorn notes that, "Teaching teachers to handle the art form is our major goal, as I see it. I want them to know that drama is a powerful teaching tool and that there is nothing that is inappropriate to drama. I want to do several things, when I go into a school: First, I want to make a good friend of that teacher, because the job is to pass on to her what I can. Second, I want her to be able to upgrade everything she normally does in the classroom. Third, I want to show her a new way to think about educating children that is as valid as any way that she has known before.

"I correlate as closely as I can what I do with the material that the teacher wants transmitted to the children. While the work with the children is, I think, secondary to the job, it is very hard for me not to make it primary. If the teacher, in the time I am in her classroom, has seen the children grow academically and socially and has seen that drama has the power to make them act as a unit, then, I think, she is ready for me to give her some expertise in the art form."

Like Pfefferkorn, Miller also teaches teachers by working with children. "I want to open up a child's view of his world and help him respond to visual happenings in his own individual way, which has no right or wrong," she says. "I plan with teachers and encourage them to try new things when they are reluctant. They are often amazed at what children can do in the visual arts. I try to let the teachers know that I respect them as specialists in teaching their grade level. I show them how they can rearrange their rooms for certain kinds of arts activities. I want to make them comfortable with art materials. Their own motivation will take them a long way. I reassure them that, if they can handle the verbal part of an art experience, the children will do the rest."

The Arts Resource Team took on an ambitious assignment their first year as the official staff development unit of the ABC program. Working out their schedules with the principals of the demonstration and cooperating schools on a rotating basis, they worked with an average of 25 different teachers and 900 different children a week. They had monthly meetings with Carter to discuss problems and weekly meetings with each other to compare notes. They also wrote up descriptions of their activities to document the program.

Team members felt some frustration in not having the opportunity to go back to schools after their residencies to get feedback on their effectiveness. Generally, no time was allotted for revisitation, but there were exceptions. Musten taught a

132

sixth-grade class to write their own songs to complement a story. The youngsters became so inspired that they wrote their own musical version of *Tom Sawyer*. Their teacher was determined to help them carry their play into production, but felt very insecure in the new role of producer. She, with her principal's encouragement, asked Musten for help. It was rewarding to see how far the class and the teacher had taken their arts experience, and Musten offered technical assistance and moral support through the run of the play's two performances. She believes that this teacher could do it alone now.

The arts team members view themselves as educators rather than arts specialists. Pfefferkorn explains: "I do not think necessarily that a teacher must use an art form in all its complexity to feel success. One fine teacher with a very structured classroom came to me at the end of the year and said, 'You have given me new ways to manage my students.' You cannot give teachers arts expertise. They are eventually going to have to get that for themselves, just as we did."

Miller says that she was shocked in a summer workshop to discover that a number of elementary teachers did not know the primary colors. "But," she said, "I don't want to work myself out of a future job, either. I want to create a need for more art specialists."

Sutlive adds that the one fear they all share is that teachers will structure arts experiences in a restrictive and limiting way. "We are trying to give children more freedom to explore ways of learning, and let them make more decisions; putting an arts curriculum into a tedious form would contradict what we are trying to do."

We are trying to give children more freedom to explore ways of learning and let them make more decisions; putting an arts curriculum into a tedious form would contradict what we are trying to do.

Consolidating Gains

The second year of ABC implementation was an eventful one. A sixth demonstration school and the six cooperating schools had been added to the program, as well as the new arts resource team.

The team finished its first year with a two-week evaluation session. The scheduling was reorganized. They planned six-week residencies for each pair of schools with three days per week in the demonstration school and two at the cooperating school. Two-week periods at the end of residencies were set aside for documentation, meetings with administrative staff, consultation with previous schools, and working with specialists, new teachers, and special projects.

The team felt they would be more effective working for more concentrated periods of time with fewer teachers. They also realized that 20 hours of contact work with children is more realistic than the nearly 30 hours that were sometimes scheduled during the first year. One afternoon a week was reserved for team meetings.

Carter's assistant left, and instead of replacing her, he decided to strengthen the administrative hub of the ABC net-

You have to ask a lot of questions of yourselves and of each other, and the principal has to have patience and confidence in the staff to let the program grow organically.

work by recruiting liaison people for each school from the elementary supervisors at the central office. Carter had always felt that the program was unique in uniting central office staff, and he saw this as a way of reinforcing that unity while offering the schools a direct channel to central office support and help.

The central office's Coordinator of Volunteers added an arts section to their "Community Resource Guide" and developed a handbook to help teachers make effective use of the volunteers listed.

In October, six teachers and two principals from Winston-Salem accompanied Carter on a site visit to the Minneapolis Public Schools to see its Arts in General Education Program. At the League of Cities meeting there, the Fund announced plans for an experimental "Administrative Fellowship Training Program" which would enable each League site to put such a person on staff for five months, beginning in January 1978.

The superintendent presented the proposal for participation in the JDR 3rd Administrative Fellowship Training Program to the Board of Education, and it was approved. Wanda Crouse, a recent graduate of the North Carolina School of the Arts and a media teacher in the Art Council's Urban Arts Program, was awarded the fellowship. Crouse began documenting the ABC program with video tape, and she assisted Carter in strengthening the networking of principals and teachers in the program. Eventually, she put together a weekly ABC show on the school system's television network. She worked with the Arts Council's Education Committee and community arts groups to develop appropriate services for the ABC schools and helped in the scheduling of these services. Under Carter's direction, she also took on major organizing responsibilities for the Winston-Salem site visit scheduled for the League of Cities in May. So important has Crouse's work been that the school system has decided to hire her on their own, full-time.

While the three-and-a-half day site visit for some 70 League of Cities guests seemed an enormous undertaking so early in the program's life, Carter and Crouse saw it as an opportunity to mobilize the community and the school system around ABC. If it caused pressure for the participating schools, it also aroused attention.

For the participants in the ABC program, the League of Cities' site visit to Winston-Salem was a great success. The impact of peer recognition and approval from many different parts of the country only encouraged administrators, principals, and teachers to make a greater professional commitment to the program. The attention of educators from other school systems deepened local pride and interest in the program.

The League of Cities' visitors were particularly impressed with the understanding and confidence shown by classroom teachers in using ABC concepts. Several League of Cities' administrators and teachers stayed extra days in order to go back to talk to teachers and principals they had observed earlier and to see more classroom work.

134   Confronted with the accolades of his League of Cities'

colleagues, Carter modestly brushed them aside: "We have simply tried to do exactly what you as a group told us to do." What took some by surprise was that he had adapted their ideas so thoroughly and rapidly and with seeming ease.

Having to explain to visitors what the ABC program involved and how it took form in each school made the teachers and principals in the demonstration schools analyze the process they had been through and recognize the changes that had taken place in their own work and in their schools. This was a useful exercise for the demonstration schools to undergo as they took on the responsibility of extending the program to their cooperating schools.

"We are now sharing our process with our cooperating school," one principal said in an interview. "We feel they must really do it for themselves. I have talked to the principal of that school about the traumas of beginning organization. I told him to organize a faculty committee that represents all grade levels and special interests in his school. Specialists must be included from the beginning. I also told him that he should not be chairman of that committee. Then, he, as principal, must be prepared to let the creative blood flow in everybody's veins. That committee must determine how the school approaches the program. We, for example, do our own inservice training at all-school faculty meetings. They may want to do it differently. You have to ask a lot of questions of yourselves and of each other, and the principal has to have patience and confidence in the staff to let the program grow organically."

Teachers seem to agree that, as painful as the process of change might be, there is no shortcut to learning the ABC concept. "We always used the arts before, but not as so integral a part of the curriculum," a teacher explains. "The growing pains of learning how to integrate the arts by ourselves were very important to us. I wonder if a new school coming into the program will feel the same exhilaration we have felt, if they don't go through the same difficult process."

"Our greatest obstacle is ourselves," another teacher says. "You can do what you want to do, but you have to work at developing a whole new way of teaching, and that is hard."

"I get concerned," another teacher amplifies, "when I hear of schools that want an ABC program through a curriculum approach. I don't think it can be done that way. I think you have to go through the brainstorming and sharing of ideas and working out of your own curriculum that we did. It is a slow process, but that slowness has a great deal of merit."

The key role of the principal in making an ABC program work seems to be recognized by administrators, teachers, and the arts team. "When I walk into a new school, I go straight to the principal's office," an arts team member says. "After a half hour with the principal, I don't need to walk around the school; I know what it will be like." Teachers frequently say that it was the confidence and leadership of the principal that allowed them to risk making mistakes in the process of understanding the ABC Program. The arts team believes that it is the principal

I think you have to go through the brainstorming and sharing of ideas and working out of your own curriculum that we did. It is a slow process, but that slowness has a great deal of merit.

135

alone who can turn a school around."

Involvement of parents has helped the schools and the ABC program. At one school where the P.T.A. was encouraged to create its own ABC committee, a parent helped a teacher design a unit on the Middle Ages using the parent's expertise in creative dramatics. Other P.T.A.'s have raised money for specific arts projects. P.T.A. involvement helps educate parents on ABC, as well.

Expanding the Network

With the growing success of the program, the Winston-Salem/Forsyth County School System—the latecomer into comprehensive arts in education—was no longer the initiate taking counsel from more experienced programs. It, like all of the members of the League of Cities, began grappling with a new problem. As the ABC program began to work in the six pilot schools and to take effect in the six cooperating schools, other schools wanted to join the program. Their staffs expressed interest. Parents made demands. The superintendent was committed to making the ABC Program a part of all 63 schools in the system, because he viewed it as good educational practice. (And, just as he predicted, he received support for reinstating an elementary instrumental music program, including a strings program. ABC had changed the climate for other arts programs, as well.)

How could the program be expanded without making an equal expansion of central office staff and budget, which is unrealistic in any school system? How could the integrity of the program be maintained in the original schools as well as in the new schools? Nine new schools, including a junior high school, approached Carter about being included in the program. In response, he added two part-time drama specialists to the Arts Resource Team to work exclusively with these eight schools.

Carter admits that there is a necessary progression of activities as a new school enters the program. Each must make a commitment and then put itself through the process. "At first I thought there were too many fingers in the pie," he says, "but then I realized that the process had to include everybody, and that it had to continue as long as the program is in effect." He also admits that networks can collapse, if they are not deliberately kept alive.

The demonstration schools and cooperating schools became more sophisticated as they entered the third year of implementing the program. "Many of them are now concentrating on one arts area at a time and trying to get better at using it," Carter says.

The major part of the Arts Resource Team's time is still committed to the original six schools. The cooperating schools fill the rest of their schedule. The problem of effective expansion has not been totally solved in Winston-Salem anymore than it has been in other League of Cities sites, although Winston-

Salem has the luxury of working out its own strategies and timetable unlike Seattle, for example, which must use its arts in education program to help implement a desegregation plan.

Carter envisions the original six pilot schools and their six cooperating schools as being the core of his expansion. New schools will be paired with these 12 and go through the process of setting up ABC teams, assessing faculty arts strengths and weaknesses, brainstorming among the staff, all with the partner school as consultant and demonstration site. He foresees a time when the original schools can give up the team's services and free it to work with new schools exclusively. In the meantime, he accepts the fact that new schools really need a year of observation and exploration, before they can start developing their own programs. "When a school faculty begins planning together and trying out ideas in the classroom, it is ready to take advantage of what the arts team can provide," he says.

During the 1978-79 school year, the ABC program was being implemented in 21 out of 63 schools in the district. The number of arts resource specialists was expanded for 1978-79 from four full-time teachers to five full-time and two half-time teachers. In addition, five creative dramatists began introducing the ABC concept into kindergarten through sixth-grade schools in January 1979. It is expected that some of these employees will become full-time arts resource specialists during the 1979-80 school year, depending on budget appropriations.

Ironically, while Winston-Salem struggles with expansion within the district, it has no trouble in attracting attention and interest from other school districts. Superintendent Adams and Carter—both through the Fund and through regional education and arts organizations—have been asked to talk about the ABC program in a number of forums across the country. For example, in 1977-78, Carter was invited to speak in Kentucky three times. The executive director of the Lexington, Kentucky, Arts Council, a native of Winston-Salem, was instrumental in getting the Lexington school district interested in the League of Cities and the ABC program. A county-wide system similar to Winston-Salem in size and demographics, the Fayette County School District sent representatives to the Winston site visit. With encouragement and support from the Arts Council, the Lexington schools developed a plan based on the ABC model and put it into operation in the fall of 1978. Louisville also expressed interest in the ABC program as have several other districts and the state education department. The Fund has agreed to offer limited consultation to these school systems. In effect, then, Winston-Salem has established its own mini-network on an ad hoc basis. It serves as the hub of a communication system in the southeastern regional area.

At first I thought there were too many fingers in the pie, but then I realized that the process had to include everybody, and that it had to continue as long as the program is in effect.

Overview

There has been no formal evaluation of the ABC program, but there has been an eloquent exchange of reflections about 137

Discipline has been a problem in schools all over the world, but I am beginning to see children understand that it takes self-discipline to create something that is really your own.

it in many of the schools and in national meetings. Documentation of the program by the arts team, by the JDR 3rd Fund fellow, and by transcripts and minutes of meetings indicate a general sense of excitement about its possibilities on the part of those principals and teachers who have become truly involved.

Certainly not every teacher in every pilot school has been equally involved or stimulated by ABC. The arts team, after their first year, felt that only one school succeeded in involving the total staff, and they credited the principal with that accomplishment. Some arts specialists remain convinced that the program will eventually threaten their jobs. There are still some teachers who are bewildered by the program, disturbed by mixups in scheduling with the arts team, or who harbor unrealistic expectations. Others resent what they perceive as additional demands on their time.

But for those principals and teachers who have been actively involved in the planning and working out of the program, no formal measures seem to be needed for their endorsement of ABC. A principal, for example, says without hesitation, "The ABC program has given our school a humane atmosphere."

Teachers seem to agree. "There is a certain atmosphere here that is really difficult to explain," says one, "but people who come into the school feel it and comment on it. Children feel freer, and we are not afraid of noise anymore as a threat to our control."

A number of teachers have commented on the inner discipline that children have gained through the program. One says, for example, "We find that there is a certain discipline you have when you are involved in the arts. Discipline has been a problem in schools all over the world, but I am beginning to see children understand that it takes self-discipline to create something that is really your own. This carries over into a broader inner discipline that affects children in more than just the arts."

A principal acknowledges that, "There has been a carryover in the area of discipline, particularly from drama and movement. Children understand about finding their own space and having freedom with it."

The program has helped to bring faculties together. "There is a good supportive feeling on the faculty now. There is more sharing going on than ever before, and no one is afraid to admit that he needs help," a teacher comments. Another adds, "We're not embarrassed anymore about using somebody else's idea. At one time, if you didn't think up something original in your own head, you weren't doing your job."

Teachers say that, although they are working harder, they are more relaxed at school. "I used to feel very guilty, if something I tried didn't work," a teacher says. "Now, I just accept it and think I will have to do it differently next time. I think the children are reassured to see that even teachers aren't perfect."

And they find that their attitudes toward the children are changing. "I don't think we ever meant to before, but we did make children feel that there was a right and a wrong to everything. Through the ABC program, we have begun to make some 'wrong' children turn into 'right' children. Their parents see it and are grateful," a teacher says.

Attendance, too, has improved, and student participation in class has increased in the ABC schools. A principal observes that, "Students look forward to coming to school, because they know that every day there is going to be something to enjoy."

Many teachers are convinced that students are retaining what they learn through the arts. "It may take longer with the arts, but when it is finished, the children have something that lasts," a teacher says. Other teachers agree and say that the planning of lessons with the arts is getting easier, as they become more accustomed to doing it. Many comment that it has put the fun back into teaching. "It takes a lot of work to make a lesson plan that includes the arts and will really involve the children. There have been lots of problems that we have had to work out. But there are days when I wake up knowing that something really exciting is going to happen in my class, and I can hardly wait to get to work. Children pick up on that. They are saying, 'This has been a good year,'" a teacher says.

"We have found that the arts are a great motivator," another teacher adds. "Once the children realize that they are going to do something that doesn't mean opening a book and reading and writing, but that it will require a creative response, they are much more eager."

A teacher points out other benefits: "We are giving children things we thought couldn't be taught, like self-confidence, poise, and an ability to speak before a group. These are not things that can be measured, but we can see them."

While the one specific academic achievement of the program commented on by many ABC teachers and principals is marked improvement in very slow readers, the most dramatic social effect of the program has been with the mentally retarded, both "trainable" and "educable." Classes for such handicapped children have been held in regular school buildings for some 15 years in Winston-Salem. However, the retarded students have not necessarily been an integrated part of the school's total program. From the beginning of the ABC program planning, special education teachers have participated in the ABC dialogue.

The inclusion of the special education classes in the ABC program has been rewarding, according to one special education teacher. "Through the arts, there is real interaction between the handicapped children and the normal children. They can share movement class and the normal children can begin to appreciate and accept the handicapped. It is not just throwing children together and telling them to get along. A real understanding has begun to take place based on shared experiences in the arts. And we see it carrying over into other areas. In one school there are retarded youngsters in the chorus now, and the normal kids are becoming very supportive of them. After a performance in which one of the retarded young people had sung a brief solo, the other students vied to have that child sit

Many teachers are convinced that students are retaining what they learn through the arts. It may take longer with the arts, but when it is finished, the children have something that lasts.

139

If the program were to die tomorrow, if the arts team were never to come to our school again, I wouldn't stop using the arts in my classroom.

next to them afterwards. And we are seeing the retarded kids being asked to play ball on the playground now."

It has worked both ways. The retarded students have, according to teachers, gained a sense of confidence about their own abilities to do some of the things that the normal children do. "It has made them feel a part of the school at last," a teacher says.

If the program has proved of benefit to students, it has also changed the teachers. One teacher acknowledges that, "If the program were to die tomorrow, if the arts team were never to come to our school again, I wouldn't stop using the arts in my classroom." This remark summarizes the extent of impact the program has had on many teachers.

Perhaps the oddest phenomenon about the extraordinary developments in Winston-Salem is that an idea that originated in New York City had enough appeal to initiate this kind of momentum in such a different environment. The reason the program is working in Winston-Salem is that it is teacher-centered and the management is sound. This is critical. Whereas, in the beginning, it was essentially a one-man effort, Carter has since established a team effort. Administrators demonstrate strong commitment to the concept, because they see it as a way to improve general education. With this kind of basic support, money is not permitted to be a problem. If there is a lesson to be learned from this, it is that a good plan plus good leadership equals a good educational program. That seems to be the case in Winston-Salem.

PART III

The Second
Six Years: State
Education Departments

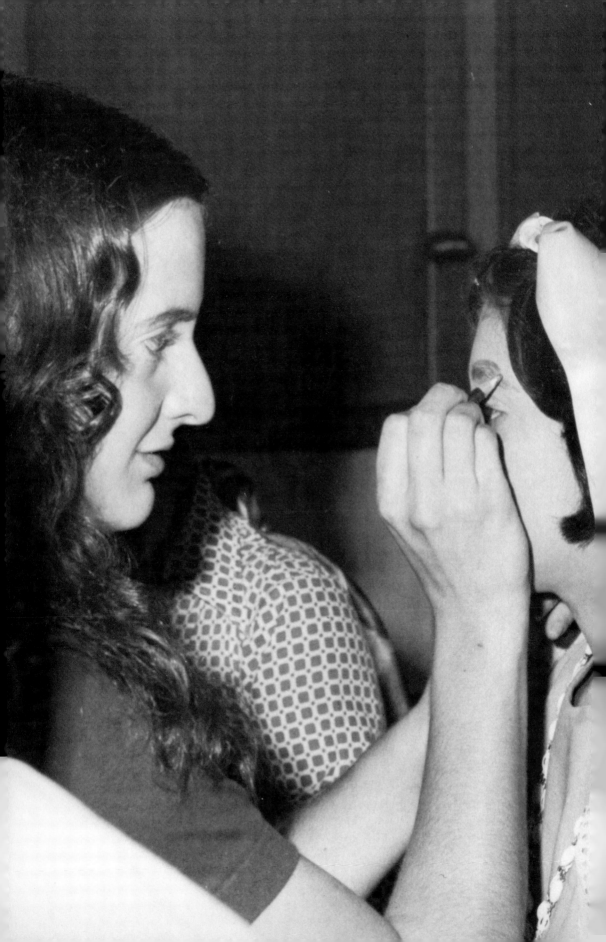

INTRODUCTION
The Ad Hoc Coaliton of States for the Arts in Education

Kathryn Bloom

The work done initially with the nine state education departments that are members of the Coalition paralleled almost exactly the Fund's earlier efforts to encourage the establishment of comprehensive arts in education programs in schools and school districts.[1]

The interests of persons in these state education agencies and the staff of the JDR 3rd Fund came together in a variety of ways. The relationship with New York State developed as an outgrowth of Project SEARCH, a major Title III humanities and arts program. It has been strengthened by the existence of the Mineola, Long Island, pilot project and New York City's Arts in General Education Program.

With Pennsylvania, long-standing professional relationships existed between Department of Education representatives and Fund staff members that encouraged collaborative efforts

---

[1]This introduction draws substantially upon a paper, "Comprehensive Arts Planning," written by Gene Wenner, former Assistant Director of the Fund. 145

in the establishment of a state-wide priority for the arts in basic education.

During 1973 and 1974, the Fund's staff provided consulting services to the Alliance for Arts Education when it was established jointly by the John F. Kennedy Center for the Performing Arts and the U.S. Office of Education. A series of working sessions with Forbes Rogers, then director of AAE, resulted in, among other items, a set of draft materials, guidelines, and criteria for use by state AAE committees in establishing arts in education efforts. The California AAE meeting was the test site for these materials, and that meeting initiated our relationship with the California Department of Education.

In Oklahoma, Massachusetts, and Washington, collaborative efforts were an outgrowth of our earlier involvement with arts in education programs in Oklahoma City, Boston, and Seattle.

Beginning in 1972, Gene Wenner provided extensive consultant and technical services to these six state departments, as well as to state departments in Arizona, Indiana, and Michigan, which are also members of the Coalition. As was the case with earlier projects and programs in schools and school systems, this one-by-one relationship resulted in the accumulation of a body of knowledge about successful approaches. Further, it placed Wenner in the role of agent for transmitting information among sites.

By 1975, it seemed desirable to form a network of these states to expedite the exploration of problems and solutions, the identification of major issues for collective action, and the exchange of information among the states. In May representatives of these state education departments were brought together for a planning meeting, and several decisions were made:

1. The Ad Hoc Coalition of States for the Arts in Education was established.

2. The work of the Coalition would be carried on by a Steering Committee comprised of two representatives from each state education department appointed by the chief state school officer. One representative would have responsibilities in his or her state department for curriculum and instruction; the second representative would have equivalent responsibilities for the arts in education.

3. The JDR 3rd Fund would coordinate and provide financial support for the Coalition and its Steering Committee. (Meetings have been held periodically, usually three times each year.)

4. The Following Mission Statement was adopted:
The purpose of the Ad Hoc Coalition of States for the Arts in Education is:
To promote the arts as a means for improving the quality of education for all students by establishing a network of state education agencies working cooperatively to provide mutual assistance and support to local, state, and national agencies in the planning and

development of comprehensive arts in education programs.

State education departments have much in common as far as basic roles and functions are concerned. There is wide variance, however, in ways in which they operate administratively and organizationally. As one example, the process for establishing a comprehensive state plan for the arts in education in a state department that has an organizational unit and a staff of six or seven professional employees in the arts can be addressed in a quite different fashion than is the case in a state department that has only one person who is responsible for the arts in education.

As a second example, there are differences from state to state in relationships between the state agencies and their school systems. The federal contribution, nationally, is about eight percent of the total budget of school districts. State departments are the conduit, administering these funds according to federal guidelines, which may be further modified by the interpretation of these guidelines at the state level. There is, however, no formula from state to state for the percentage of funds that come from state and local sources. The result is that in states where substantial funding comes from the state education agency, there tends to be a close relationship between this agency and local school systems. In instances where a larger proportion of funding originates at the local level, there may be a greater sense of autonomy and independence by school districts. Despite these differences, certain generalizations have emerged, and one of the most important considerations is the establishment of priorities.

Priorities are most often set by the chief state school officer with the endorsement and approval of the state board of education. Initiatives may come from the state board, but this is not ordinarily the case. Any priority that is established may be the result of personal and professional interests of the chief state school officer, but more frequently the identification of these goals is influenced by external forces.

Such forces include the United States Congress, the U.S. Office of Education, State Legislatures, professional educational organizations, lobbies, unions, corporations and foundations, local school boards and administrators, parent groups and voters (since many chief state school officers are elected). Contrary to popular belief, priorities are initiated less frequently by staff members within state education departments than by the agencies and organizations mentioned above.

One of the most powerful forces in setting priorities is the legislative process and funds appropriated at federal and state levels. Well known examples include compensatory programs to improve achievement levels in basic skills including reading, writing, and mathematics; vocational and, more recently, career education; and the education of the handicapped. Additional priorities may be—and are—established, but clearly, all priorities are not equal in the attention and support given to their implementation.

It seemed desirable to form a network of states to expedite the exploration of problems and solutions, the identification of major issues for collective action, and the exchange of information among the states.

147

Once a state department of education and/or state board of education commits itself to the arts in education as a priority and allocates resources to support comprehensive arts in education programs, a major multiplier effort is under way which can affect large numbers of children.

Educational goals grow out of broad educational and social concerns rather than bear directly on the need to improve traditional subjects of instruction. In order for the arts in education to be established as a priority by a state department of education and, in turn, by school districts in the state, plans and programs must relate to these larger concerns and trends. The same forces and processes can be used to establish the arts as a priority that are effective in identifying and implementing other priorities. However, this action c..linarily will take place only if the arts are perceived as contributing to the quality of education for all students, rather than viewed in the narrower context of the arts for their own sake. Once a state department of education and/or state board of education commits itself to the arts in education as a priority and allocates resources to support comprehensive arts in education programs within the department and in school districts, a major multiplier effort is under way which can affect large numbers of children.

The following are key concepts relating to comprehensive arts in education plans that have emerged from the experience of the nine state education departments in the Coalition:

1. A comprehensive plan for the arts in education must have the endorsement of key decision-makers.

Any educational priority must have the endorsement of the chief state school officer, as well as his assistants and/or associates responsible for the content of instruction. Active involvement and support by administrators who make policy-level decisions on both federal and state programs within the department of education is essential.

2. A comprehensive plan must reflect and relate clearly to existing goals and operations of the state education department.

Conceiving of the arts in education as a special project or set of projects is not enough. The comprehensive plan must take into account the wide variety of programs that already exist, and interrelationships with them must be developed.

3. Program planning requires the involvement of arts personnel within the department who view the arts broadly as an integral part of every child's education. Further, specialists in the arts must relate effectively to staff members responsible for other programs within the state department.

4. A comprehensive plan should involve resources outside the educational system at both the state and local level. The arts community can be an invaluable resource. Effective relationships should be maintained with professional educational associations and organizations such as the Alliance for Arts Education. Comprehensive programs require a support system that is a mosaic of related programs and services rather than isolated efforts to improve the role of the arts in education.

The experience of state education departments that are members of the Coalition demonstrates that planning, setting a priority, and implementing successful state-wide comprehensive arts in education programs involve the following elements:

148

1. Awareness/Commitment

A. Develop a working or operational definition of the arts in education that will describe it effectively to a very broad audience.

B. If data is not available, conduct a state-wide needs assessment to collect accurate information on the status of the arts in the curriculum, budgetary support, and staffing in the schools. This serves as the basis for determining what must be done to reach a more comprehensive goal.

C. Develop a state-wide plan which is organically related to broad educational goals, and which takes into account how various organizational units in the department, the state arts agency and the state legislature can support the work to be done, both financially and with human resources.

D. Draw upon the capabilities of state educational and arts associations (school boards, chief school officers, parent-teacher organizations, state arts agencies, art and music associations) to provide organized support for the program.

E. Establish the arts in education as a priority of the department of education and/or the state board of education. The establishment of a priority means more than just a statement that the arts in education are important. It means that support is provided from federal and state categorical funds, in accordance with established criteria, to enable local school systems to plan, implement, and evaluate comprehensive arts in education programs, and to disseminate the outcomes of these programs.

Initially such a priority will effect changes within the state department. If the priority is meaningful, a support system can evolve that will provide encouragement and assistance to local school systems in developing their own arts in education programs.

2. Demonstration/Technical Assistance

A. Establish criteria and procedures for identifying demonstration sites for comprehensive arts programs. The implementation of programs in these sites can be of great value to other school systems in developing similar programs.

b. Involve existing regional mechanisms such as Intermediate Units or BOCES (Boards of Cooperative Educational Services) to act as linkages between state departments and schools.

C. Identify professionals with leadership capabilities who can be trained to provide consulting assistance as needed by school systems.

D. Identify curriculum tools and resource personnel, both within the state department and outside, and make them available to school districts as needed.

Comprehensive programs require a support system that is a mosaic of related programs and services rather than isolated efforts to improve the role of the arts in education.

149

3. Assessment/Dissemination

    A. Assist school districts in the evaluation of their comprehensive arts in education programs.

    B. Develop an evaluation of the effectiveness of the state department plan, priority, and comprehensive program and provide generalizable information on results to a large national audience.

The two case studies that follow contain information regarding ways in which state education departments plan, develop, and implement comprehensive arts in education programs. They also reveal the wealth of opportunities for restructuring working patterns within the departments and with local schools and school systems, as well as with other agencies, organizations, and institutions of higher education.

These two particular state education agencies were chosen as subjects of case studies for two reasons. First, the Pennsylvania Department of Education was first, and the Oklahoma State Department of Education the most recent of the state education departments to form cooperative relationships with the JDR 3rd Fund. Second, Pennsylvania is large, both geographically and in the size of its school population. Oklahoma is much more sparsely populated and, aside from two large cities, is mainly rural. Since both state education departments have developed sophisticated and effective comprehensive arts in education programs, it was felt that a comparative study of their approaches would have value for a broad audience.

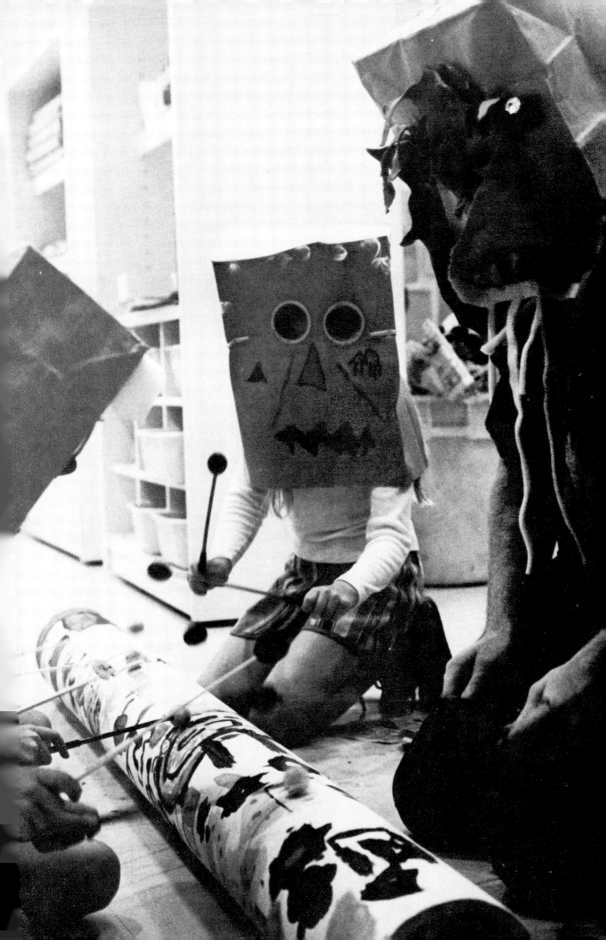

CHAPTER SEVEN
Case Study:
The Influence of Pennsylvania's Department of Education and the Fund's Role

Charles Fowler

There are ways that you can intrigue children into learning what many people call the "basics" of education through the arts. Can you think of a better move into chemistry than through the color combinations? When you put blue and yellow together and you get green, children begin to wonder . . .

> *Dr. Caryl M. Kline*
> Secretary of Education (1977-79)
> The Pennsylvania Department of Education

For years the School of Education has neglected the area of arts education. In my role, I am attempting to get classroom teachers and arts specialists together to think about how you train people today to handle the arts. Administratively, we are trying to provide encouragement and support for faculty to move the arts and humanities from the back to the front burner.

> *Dr. Horton Southworth*
> Chairperson, Teacher Development
> University of Pittsburgh

We consider that the arts are basic, and this is reflected in the budget as well as the classroom.
Dr. Rodney Tolbert
Superintendent (1978)
Lewisburg Area School District

These statements by educational administrators in Pennsylvania demonstrate that they are strong advocates of comprehensive arts education programs. In a state that is the third largest in population and has 505 public school districts that enroll 2.2 million students (1967), do these administrators represent exceptions, what might be called "happy accidents"? Given the possibility that their attitude toward the arts is atypical, did they come to give priority to the arts in education completely on their own, or are their attitudes the result of some kind of persuasive master plan for the arts in education in the Commonwealth?

As is the case with many people, these three administrators came to value the arts through their own personal experiences in their early home life and schooling. But it is equally true that in each case their commitment has been reinforced and expanded by influences, both subtle and dynamic, that can be traced back to the Fine Arts Program of the Pennsylvania Department of Education (PDE). In this sense, these administrators are like key pictorial details in a vast and carefully planned, but as yet incomplete, mosaic.

The Fund's Initial Role in Pennsylvania

A state education agency can be a pivotal force for improving arts education programs in the schools. That basic article of faith, along with a number of bona fide affidavits of proof, drew the JDR 3rd Fund together with the PDE in late 1971. Pennsylvania submitted its first proposal to the Fund in June 1972. The proposal was in response to John C. Pittenger's (then the Secretary of Education) mandate that PDE personnel *anticipate* rather than merely react to educational change.

Donald M. Carroll, Jr., then Commissioner of Basic Education, made the initial request. Thus, in 1972, the Fund issued a grant of $25,000 to assist the PDE with a project entitled, "Plan for a Statewide Aesthetic Education Program, Kindergarten through High School."

The grant was given to the Pennsylvania Center for the Arts, a non-profit body set up to receive and administer the funds in order to keep them free of state restriction and to provide maximum flexibility in their use. The purpose of the grant was, "to assist the Department of Education to establish its position regarding the arts in general education and to work in the direction of a state plan."[1] The main objective of the Fund's own Arts in Education Program is to make all the arts

154 [1]Letter from Kathryn Bloom to Dr. Donald M. Carroll, Jr., August 4, 1972.

integral to the general education of all children in the schools.

According to Carroll, the Fund's own role in Pennsylvania accomplished three things: (1) *Recognition from outside*. The Fund "legitimized our effort," Carroll says. "If the Fund would simply bless what we were doing and give us a letter to that effect and show up periodically and say, 'You're doing good things,' then that was an immense help." (2) *Technical assistance*. "The Fund was in University City and other places. The technical assistance they provided enabled us to hear about what was going on and, in some cases, go visit." (3) *Small grants*. "Those relatively small grants permitted us to do just those little extra things that made a difference—to visit a site without worrying whether the state treasury can pay for it, or hiring an administrative assistant to collect some data—and that's a good thing. They weren't big grants. That, to me, is the success of the Fund. They have an uncanny way of figuring out what little bit of money is needed to tip you over."

Clyde McGeary, presently Chief of the Division of General Education within the Bureau of Curriculum Services and formerly Senior Arts Advisor of the Fine Arts Program, also acknowledges the importance of the Fund's role. "They provided funds to break through the restraints of the bureaucracy," McGeary says. "We could have meetings on our own." In addition, "It built in a level of accountability. There was a moral responsibility to produce. That was a different kind of personal pressure than one finds in government. It also allowed us to bring in and work with quality people from the rest of the country. The funds took us outside our normal resources. We could lean on the expertise of the Fund's own staff."

A state education agency can be a pivotal force for improving arts education programs in the schools, particularly if personnel anticipate rather than merely react to educational change.

Factors Favorable to Pennsylvania

It seems clear that the Fund's interest in working with state departments of education, which started with Pennsylvania and has since spread to a consortium of nine states, was set in motion because certain key elements were already in place. For one thing, the unification of the various arts within the PDE's Bureau of General and Academic Education in the form of a Fine Arts Division (FAD) had already set an example for public school districts within the Commonwealth. Then, too, there was a strong staff of five persons in the arts, who collectively gave representation to theater, dance, and film as well as visual arts and music.

There was a history in the FAD of imaginative and visionary leadership. When the Division was formed in 1964, Russell Getz, who was appointed program coordinator, and Clyde McGeary were new to the PDE. Both were highly respected in their professional associations in the state, Getz in music, McGeary in visual arts. McGeary says, "We agreed to teach one another." Together they made a dynamic team. With the passage of the federal Elementary and Secondary Education

155

Beginning in 1965, Pennsylvania took the lead in establishing related arts courses, publishing materials, holding workshops and conferences, and otherwise supplying technical assistance to train teachers in this approach.

Act (ESEA) in 1965, for example, they quickly perceived an opportunity to obtain funds to remedy some of the inadequacies they saw in arts education. One evening, they got together and wrote a proposal that brought them $500,000.

To prevent their efforts from being haphazard and to rally support across the state, they developed the first "State Plan" for the arts in Pennsylvania, which analyzed the needs and set up goals and objectives. In working with more than 60 arts supervisors in various local school districts at that time, they encouraged the development of proposals that resulted in the first requests for funds provided to Pennsylvania through Title I of ESEA. With the State Plan in hand to keep them focused on and responsive to state-wide needs, by 1968 FAD had commanded over $6 million of ESEA funds under Titles I, III, and V. They used these funds to expand their staff as well, bringing in people like Gene Wenner, Joseph McCarthy, Bernice Gottschalk-Roehner, and Robert Revicki.

Beginning in 1965, Pennsylvania took the lead in establishing related arts courses, publishing materials, holding workshops and conferences, and otherwise supplying technical assistance to train teachers in this approach. In addition, by 1970 FAD had aesthetic education programs established in more than 40 schools in the state supported in part by Title III funds. One of the five arts IMPACT[2] Projects was located in Philadelphia's Conwell Middle Magnet School.

Early in 1972, a "Celebration of Youth Arts," sponsored by the Governor, further convinced state education leaders of the need for all the arts in the educational curriculum. This event marked the beginning of state-funded arts education projects. Through the governor's interest in the arts and the strong support of Secretary of Education Pittenger, $121,000 of state money was provided to the FAD to facilitate program development. This was the first time that fine arts had commanded its own budget.

Another positive factor about Pennsylvania was the strong support for the arts shown by Donald M. Carroll, Jr., the Commissioner of Basic Education, as well as by John Pittenger, the Secretary of Education. Carroll was aware of the arts from having worked in the ESEA Title III Program. His wife just happened to be a music teacher. McGeary says of Carroll, "You could stand up to him and talk things out." As the fine arts staff recalls, it was Carroll who brought Pittenger to the arts through a cocktail party with the staff. ("We drank out of jelly glasses, remember?") Pittenger became convinced that the arts did have value in the schools, and he subsequently made monies available for the arts to back up that conviction.

With all the expanding projects, programs, and services sponsored by the FAD, what precipitated yet another project

[2]IMPACT, an acronym for "Interdisciplinary Model Programs in the Arts for Children and Teachers," was a U.S. Office of Education sponsored Project with assistance of the National Endowment for the Arts and the JDR 3rd Fund that established arts-centered school programs in selected schools in five different school systems in the United States.

and overtures to the Fund? Staff visitations throughout the state revealed that the majority of school districts treated the arts as compartmentalized entities apart from the total educational program. This specialization was directly counter to what the staff perceived to be a national educational trend toward seeking common humanistic values and processes.

The staff, then, faced a number of questions: How could this specialization be reversed and a trend toward generalization be translated into state policies and programs? How could such programs be carried to local school districts and be implemented by them? How could the arts effect an ordered change in basic education throughout Pennsylvania?

Such were the events that led to talks with the staff of the Arts in Education Program of the JDR 3rd Fund. Kathryn Bloom, Director of that Program, met with Pittenger, Carroll, and the FAD staff. Shortly after, a proposal was made by the PDE to the Fund for monies to carry out a program effort aimed at answering these questions. As a result, Pennsylvania's "Arts in Basic Education" project was launched in the summer of 1972. The PDE was intent upon transforming its many diverse programs into a coherent arts in basic education program designed to affect all of the schools in the Commonwealth.

A number of PDE staff other than those in fine arts participated in the project which brought together outside consultants along with teachers and administrators from around the state in a series of symposia to formulate a position paper on the arts in basic education. The project drew the FAD staff together innumerable times to share ideas, evaluate, and otherwise project plans for succeeding stages. The nature of the project and its demands caused the staff to develop an even greater cohesiveness. Another result of the project was the publication of a booklet entitled, "The Arts Process in Basic Education" (now in its eleventh printing), which represents the first full-blown attempt at exposition and articulation of the concept of the arts in basic education, now more often referred to as "the arts in general education" (AGE). This approach infuses the arts process into general subject-matter teaching. The booklet contained, in essence, a coherent posture for the arts in education in the Commonwealth—the utilization of the arts process as an integral part of basic education.

The position became firmly seated within the PDE, and the FAD decided to evaluate all proposed future projects and to reorder priorities in light of how they might serve this concept. The grant had enabled the fine arts staff to bring into focus an idea that had been around a long time but had not been clearly expressed or understood. The arts in education concept provided the necessary foundation and theoretical support for an organized presentation of arts projects and interdisciplinary studies within the basic education curriculum. The position also solidified priorities and pointed up the need for long-range plans in the form of a comprehensive new state plan for the arts. In important ways, the project altered the primary function of the FAD taking it beyond the role of a

The project altered the primary function of the state arts staff taking it beyond the role of a consulting body of specialists into the posture of exerting strong leadership for establishing arts-oriented basic curricula in school districts throughout the state.

157

consulting body of specialists into the posture of exerting strong leadership for establishing arts-oriented basic curricula in school districts throughout the state.

During the 1972-73 academic year, in the midst of the JDR 3rd Project, the PDE moved toward a tighter organization. The Bureau of General and Academic Education became the Bureau of Curriculum Services. Within this Bureau, the FAD was renamed the "Fine Arts Program" and was joined with the Language Arts and Social Studies Programs to form the Arts and Humanities Division. Russell Getz was appointed Chief of this new division and Clyde McGeary became Senior Arts Adviser. The reorganization facilitated interdisciplinary thinking and planning, and in this way lent additional support to the project. Of course, the fact that Secretary of Education Pittenger designated the Fine Arts Program as one of his priorities was also a distinct advantage.

Gaining Support

How did the Fine Arts Program establish its credibility within the PDE and command the support of people like Pittenger, Carroll, and others? For one thing, a base of support for the arts within the Department of Education had already been built before most of these people arrived on the scene. As Carroll recalls, Pittenger's support for the arts was strengthened by having a lot of the people he trusted walk in and say, "This is a good program." Then, too, Carroll says, "Everytime he tried out a project it worked. Bureaucrats like that. They put a CEMREL project in Mars, Pennsylvania, and it didn't blow up. And so, therefore, people could cite it. That's the name of the game."

The Fine Arts staff didn't just try to sell people on an idea. They offered specific programs. Carroll says, "When our arts staff came in to talk to me about something, it wasn't, 'We want your support for the arts.' It was, 'We are going to initiate nine pilot projects someplace, here's what those projects are going to do, and here's how we hope we can get them to spin off to other places.' We had a staff that could translate what they were thinking into specific programs that affected school districts."

The strategy for getting a new idea about the arts through a state department of education also involves the ability to adapt the arts to solve general curriculum problems. Carroll says, "The arts people were there to say, 'Hey, you guys, why not try the arts to do that?'" The arts staff, he said, created "a sort of sensitivity to what the arts were and how they'd fit in." They also had sites strategically placed to which they could refer people to demonstrate that the ideas were not, as Carroll says, "pie in the sky."

The point is, Carroll makes clear, that "in general, arts people speak vaguely and lack precision in what they're doing. They talk about funny things like 'aesthetics' and 'beauty' and 'truth' and all that, where people smile and say, 'Show me a beauty' or 'Show me a truth.' 'Okay, well, why don't you go to Reading. We'll show you a beauty or a truth out there.'" And, Carroll says, "once they demonstrated how useful this thing was, it was not very hard to say, 'Let's set aside ten percent of Title III, because that money isn't going to go down the drain. We know it will work.'"

Carroll is also convinced that the arts must have organized visibility. "There ought to be a place—just like you have a place for school subsidies, busing, certification, and all those other very important things—where the arts stand out organizationally. This ought to be true of school districts, too. We had a Bureau of Curriculum Services, but what we needed to have within there was some sub-group where you could recognize the arts as a very important part of the curriculum." This is exactly how the Fine Arts Program functions.

Carroll noticed another quality in the fine arts staff: "They made people look good. Even though they were doing the work, they didn't hesitate to make sure that everyone else that might be somewhere in that system got the credit. They didn't get possessive with their program. They shared it with everybody and made everyone eventually feel involved." In part, this strategy involved asking people like Carroll to speak on behalf of the arts. Carroll admits, "You stand up before a group and you say about the arts, 'This is what we believe in,' and if you say that long enough, even though you're not an arts person, you'll end up believing it."

In spite of the extent of successful arts-advocacy efforts, there are those at the PDE who have not been reached. One staff member from a non-arts discipline, who was around during the early phases, says that, "Pittenger did not make the arts alone a priority. Legal, political, and consumer education were also made priorities." Nor does this witness feel that raising funds from many sources was unique to fine arts. "If we had to rely on what the state gives us for our programs, we wouldn't do much. We all raise funds from government and other sources." He says, however, that "the JDR 3rd monies conveyed the feeling that the fine arts group operated in isolation with their Daddy Warbucks. It caused jealousy. As it was, the arts were a separate division. The structure inhibited an integrated approach. Now the arts have been made part of a larger bureau with many other subject matters, so this has been rectified."

One area where the Fine Arts Program has been successful in gaining and sustaining support is in the Title I and IV-C offices. William Dallam, Chief of the Division of Compensatory Programs (Title I), speaks in glowing terms of the results that have been achieved through the arts used to teach basics to students who have shown that they do not respond to conventional remedial techniques. Two recent projects brought four or five arts consultants in to work with low achieving delinquent and disadvantaged students. Dallam says, "The arts hold great promise for these students. I had deliberately chosen

You stand up before a group and you say about the arts, "This is what we believe in," and if you say that long enough, even though you're not an arts person, you'll end up believing it.

159

The arts hold great promise for delinquent and disadvantaged students. The pre- and post-achievement tests showed that a substantial number of students made unexpected gains, some as much as two years.

kids that everyone had given up on. The pre- and post-achievement tests showed that a substantial number of students made unexpected gains, some as much as two years. I consider it a very good investment."

Pennsylvania spends about $9 million in IV-C funds every year for innovative education programs at the district level. Of this amount, about $190,000 is going to the arts, which represents support for six programs, five of which are interdisciplinary. Proposals submitted are competitive, so that the arts are weighed against everything else. Considering the amount of competition for these funds from every possible source, the arts appear to be holding their own.

While efforts to gain support within the PDE have been generally successful, there is evidence that efforts to gain support from the state legislature and others on the outside have been less so. Marilyn Otto, Educational Consultant to Senator R. Budd Dwyer, Minority Chairman of the State's Education Committee, says that the arts are not a priority in the state budget at present. Neither, for that matter, is education. But Otto says, "We have pilot arts programs that show what can be done for all the students. Congressmen do not know about them. Arts people do not even send press clippings to gather support." She believes that support has to be built on the community level where parental enthusiasm is expressed to the superintendent.

A recent survey of the state's Intermediate Units (IU's)[3], conducted by Otto's office, reveals that three or four of the IU's (out of the 29) are very strong in the arts. But she says "about one-third of the IU responses are characterized by placing the arts on the lowest level of priority." Otto believes that the arts are hindered by a communications' breakdown due to the bureaucratic process in the PDE.

Karen Melton, Research Consultant for State Representative K. Leroy Irvis, echoes Otto's observations: "To the legislature, the arts are about as low a priority as you can get." She says that, "Representatives got very little support from their constituencies this year, so they followed suit. The arts council budget was cut by $175,000. No one has been successful in making senators and representatives aware of the importance of the arts in education."

Part of the reason, undoubtedly, is the general economic climate. But the lack of support, Melton believes, is also due to the fact that "arts educators are not aware of legislative processes." Like Otto, Melton states, "The parents must be the supporters of the arts. They bear the burden of taxes, and the arts are for their children." It should be mentioned that both Senator Dwyer and Representative Irvis are strong supporters of the arts.

---

[3]In 1970 Pennsylvania was divided geographically into 29 Intermediate Units (IU's) for the purpose of offering regional assistance to groups of local school districts. The IU's are sponsors for inservice education, and they provide shared services to the schools at minimal cost.

McGeary, who has a good working relationship with both Otto and Melton, is aware that advocacy efforts must be increased in the political arena. "We're so new at politics in the arts," he says, "that we are still not able to establish levels of trust." But it also a matter of how much a small arts staff can be expected to do. Unlike other subject areas, the arts must sell themselves on multiple fronts on a continual and often exhausting basis. Limitations of time and energy are factors that must be given consideration.

Implementing the Approach

How does a state department of education move a new idea out into the schools? As part of the initial project, a "Secretary's Conference on the Arts in Basic Education" was held in May of 1973. Invitations were sent to all school districts and Intermediate Units, and some 145 administrators and faculty representing most districts attended. The intent of this conference was to sell the administrators on the idea by showing them specific examples of the arts process at work. One of the important outcomes of the meeting was the announcement of the arts as a priority by the Secretary of Education. Fine arts staff prepared a multi-media presentation that highlighted the newly published booklet, "The Arts Process in Basic Education."

The conference was designed to determine not only if the administrators had grasped the concept of the "arts process," but also to ascertain their general reaction to it. In the small discussion groups, administrators showed both their understanding of and enthusiasm for the approach. They were eager to learn how to translate the concept into their curricula.

Directly out of this conference and the concern for implementation came a second project proposal to the Fund. PDE staff, meeting with Kathryn Bloom, developed the idea of an "Arts in Education Academy" that would be held at Penn State University in the summer of 1973 for the purpose of bringing together leaders from around the state to inform them about the concept of the arts in general education. The Fund agreed to support this activity with a $15,000 grant. The intent of the Academy was to launch regional and local efforts to establish such programs.

Participants of the Academy consisted of a five-member team from each of the 29 IU's, including one staff member of the IU, one faculty member from a college or university in the IU, and one administrator and two teachers from schools in the unit. The intensive five-day program provided "hands-on" experiences in all the arts, developed techniques for translating arts processes into the whole curriculum, and assisted the teams in designing an inservice workshop that they could operate in their own districts. It was anticipated that these school-based workshops would affect almost 12,000 teachers and administrators during the following year.

Unlike other subject areas, the arts must sell themselves on multiple fronts on a continual and often exhausting basis. Limitations of time and energy are factors that must be given consideration.

161

In spite of what appear to be considerable efforts on the part of the arts staff to bring administrators around the state to understand and give support to the arts in general education concept, Carroll says that, "The weakness, if any, was that there was a tendency—I think there still is—to talk to the committed. We had a hard time getting people to really want to go out to the principal's and the school director's meetings. But they really enjoyed—I think mostly—talking to the arts people. And that's still the case. I find all art educators are happier talking to each other, because they get a response."

As the demand from schools for information and technical assistance grew, the Department, with additional assistance from the Fund, began to develop a distribution system to report on and disseminate materials to arts in education programs within the state. A year's continuation grant of $8,000 was made in October of 1974 and another of $14,000 for the following school year. These grants provided for editorial and administrative assistance as well as the development of materials and the capacity for dissemination.

These monies also enabled the department to study and exchange ideas and information with other states. By the spring of 1975, working relationships had been established between nine state education departments and the Fund. The PDE had taken an early lead among states in establishing the arts in basic education as a state-wide educational priority, and they were instrumental in encouraging other states to move in the same direction. An Ad Hoc Coalition of States for the Arts in Education was established at a meeting of chief state school officers in Chicago in May 1974 at the invitation of Carroll, Pennsylvania's Commissioner of Basic Education. The Pennsylvania Arts in Education Program demonstrated to other states what may be accomplished to improve the quality of education for all children through the arts.

During 1975-76, many changes affected the Fine Arts Program. Dr. Frank Manchester replaced Carroll as Commissioner of Basic Education in 1975. Getz left his position as Chief, Division of General Education, in 1976 to be succeeded by McGeary. A new Bureau Director, David Campbell, was also appointed, and Secretary Pittenger was succeeded by Caryl M. Kline. Serious cutbacks in budgets within the PDE have not permitted the replacement of McGeary's position within the Fine Arts Program, although Joseph McCarthy of that staff was assigned McGeary's prior responsibilities as Senior Arts Adviser.

Manchester has been generally supportive of the arts, but, he says, "We have moved toward broader priorities—student achievement, discipline, and the right to education rather than stressing specific subject matters. These kind of priorities, he says "prevent jealousies between the disciplines. Within student achievement, there is Project 81.[4] That project is taking a

---

[4]Project 81, which refers to 1981, is the PDE's top priority for the next five years.

162

comprehensive look at a total curriculum that gives as much importance to the arts as basic skills." Manchester foresees that Project 81 will result in the arts being made part of graduation requirements.

From Manchester's perspective, "The Fund has given prestigious national support to the notion of the arts in general education, so that it is not just something thought up by our staff." He believes, however, that "the arts in education concept is still not in place in most schools. Project 81 is the way through." He says, "With its graduation requirements, new state goals, and 12 model districts, Project 81 will begin curriculum revision that will include the revision of the arts. The hurdle must include reaching the principals in massive numbers." He also believes that art and music teachers are presently protecting traditional ways.

Of course, every change in administration in the bureaucratic chain in the PDE means that the Fine Arts Program, renamed "Arts in Education Program," must re-establish its credibility. Such demands require shifts in concentration from external to internal. However, the transition of administrations appears to have been accomplished with the arts retaining some priority and continuity, even though the game plan is entirely different.

In spite of the changing circumstances in which the Arts in Education (AIE) Program finds itself, the staff continue to assault the field from every possible angle. For four years, the AIE Program has run four-day conferences for people who make decisions in the arts. Conferences are run under the auspices of the "Executive Academy," a PDE effort that the fine arts staff has plugged into. A typical conference calls together about 40 people from nine or ten school districts to work on their arts-management problems. Plans to increase this activity through the development of a Project on Leadership Development have been hampered by lack of sufficient funds. The Leadership Project, to be funded with $26,000 from the Rockefeller Foundation, was funded instead for $19,000. In January 1977, the Fund provided $3,000 for consultant assistance and travel and an additional $1,500 for travel and communication within the state and with the other Coalition state departments of education in connection with this project, which attempts to get state leaders in the arts moving.

Another effort involves the Pennsylvania Governor's School for the Arts, a summer program administered by the Central Susquehanna Intermediate Unit in cooperation with the department and funded by all 29 IU's. The project, which was piloted as a fine arts program in 1968, now provides five and one-half weeks of study each summer to 320 talented students, ten percent of whom are handicapped. Selection of students is made through a statewide screening process. While in residence, each student is required to elect an art form in addition to that in which he or she has primary competence and to develop understandings and appreciations for all modes of art.

Every administrative change in the bureaucratic chain in the department of education means that the AIE Program has to re-establish its credibility.

163

Students are required to participate in an "arts leadership" program that prepares them to assume responsibility in their school or community for new or expanded projects in the arts. This requirement has generated extensive peer-teaching and school/community programs throughout the state and has been adopted as a model for similar programs in the sciences and communications. In addition, the project has served as a model for developing regional summer programs for artistically talented youth. Graduates of the school are now being employed as student assistants in each of these regional programs, and a 1969 graduate of the pilot program has been engaged in a staff capacity for the 1979 session.

The AIE Program also works cooperatively with the Pennsylvania Alliance for Arts Education. The governing body of the Alliance is an eight-person steering committee representing the dominant state arts education associations, the Pennsylvania Council on the Arts, and the PDE. Funds awarded from the U.S. Office of Education are granted each year to several projects designed to infuse the arts into general education, to develop models for staff development, or to disseminate information on special problem areas in arts instruction. Other small grants support arts components of workshops and conferences sponsored by professional education associations. The overall strategy is to inject a concern for the arts into existing educational channels.

The Alliance is now supporting a network for delivery of technical services. Each of the three network "hubs" includes persons engaged in basic education, teacher preparation, and continuing education, as well as representatives of museums, theaters, and community arts and cultural organizations. By selecting only those projects that promise a high return on its investment, the Alliance has effectively directed its limited resources in support of the AIE Program.

To maximize the impact of artists' residencies in school and community settings, the arts staff works cooperatively with the Pennsylvania Council on the Arts to establish policies and procedures for the statewide Artists-in-Schools Program. Criteria for the selection of artists and schools (or communities) are mutually developed. The PDE and the Council work together to assure the program's educational effectiveness, which they know depends upon the productive interaction of the artist with students, teachers, administrators, and the general public.

This cooperation of the two agencies extends to projects funded under the Emergency School Aid Act (ESAA) and the Comprehensive Employment and Training Act (CETA), projects that are often carried out in districts with an AIE Program. The close working relationship with the Council has resulted in a unique curriculum development program for music teachers that provides them with grants to plan and implement innovative music education projects.

There is no question that all these initiatives by the AIE Program have been successful in increasing awareness and knowledge of the arts in general education approach among arts specialists, college arts faculty, administrators, and classroom teachers throughout the state. This has been achieved through workshops sponsored by the PDE or the IU's, publications of the AIE Program, technical assistance provided directly to local school systems, conference sessions at professional arts education meetings, and the publications of professional arts and education associations. Revicki, a member of the AIE staff, says, "We are developing a cadre of people who support the concept—college teachers, administrators, classroom teachers, and arts specialists." The implementation process is many-faceted and long-term.

Initiatives by the AIE Program have been successful in increasing awareness and knowledge of the arts in general education approach among arts specialists, college arts faculty, administrators, and classroom teachers.

Curriculum Regulations

In September 1976, the Pennsylvania State Board of Education unanimously adopted a policy statement in support of the essential role of the arts in education:

> The State Board of Education affirms its position that experience in the Arts is essential to the development of the human potential of every student in the Commonwealth of Pennsylvania. The Arts, including but not limited to music, art, drama, dance, film and creative writing, serve and express the needs, aspirations and acts of humanity. Therefore, the Arts, in both separate and interdisciplinary modes, should occupy a central place in the educational programs of all public schools.

Recently, the State Board of Education amended the fine arts sections of the curriculum requirements (a) to provide expanded opportunities in the arts for *all* students, kindergarten through twelfth grade, (b) to include drama, dance, film, and creative writing as components of arts education, and (c) to describe the objectives and content of planned courses in the arts. Effective July 1, 1979, the amended curriculum requirements mandate that, at a minimum, planned courses in music and art must be taught to *all* students in each year of the elementary school. The junior high school curriculum must include, at a minimum, one planned course in general music and one planned course in general art which must be taught to *every* student. Each senior high school must include course offerings in instrumental music, vocal music, music appreciation, studio art, art appreciation, drama, and related arts.

At the elementary and junior high school levels, instruction on band and orchestra instruments and both choral and instrumental ensemble experiences may be provided on an elective basis. Related arts, drama, film, and dance experiences may be incorporated in the music and art courses or offered as separate planned courses. At the high school level, experiences in creative writing, dance, and film may be incorporated in the music, art, drama, and related arts courses or offered as separate planned courses.

The planned courses in music and art at the elementary and junior high school levels must be designed to help *each* 165

State curriculum requirements are often and easily overlooked by local school districts. Nevertheless, they do establish an official and legal position toward which the schools should move.

student develop abilities to appreciate, create, and organize sounds and visual materials and to perceive and to respond to a broad range of symbols in sensitive and imaginative ways. Planned courses in the arts at the senior high school level must include historical, theoretical, philosophical, and ethnic considerations, in addition to technical and performance requirements.

These new, official regulations are the direct result of efforts on the part of the PDE's arts staff. Unquestionably, they set directions for school districts that are clearly in line with the concept of the arts in education. But "saying" doesn't make it so. Such "paper" regulations—and there are many of them governing the state's educational programs—are often and easily overlooked by local school districts. Nevertheless, they do establish an official and legal position toward which the schools should move. In this sense, they represent goals that tend to pull school systems onward from in front.

The Response in the Districts

Even though the AIE staff does not feel that the arts in general education concept has truly taken hold in the state, they can point with pride to strong signs that a movement is underway. Shortly before she left the staff, Gottschalk-Roehner acknowledged that, "There are no full-blown programs yet in the state, but there may be 100 school districts out of 505 that are making a concerted effort to develop an arts in education program; that is, integrating the arts at all levels, using artists in residence, incorporating related arts at the junior high school level, and hiring replacements for classroom teachers who have an arts background. There are probably another 100 where an individual teacher has developed his or her own program incorporating some of these elements."

McGeary says, "I am most pleased that we have won over a number of curriculum developers, building principals, and school superintendents. The commitment to the arts in general education concept has grown in the state."

Quite naturally, any state department of education elicits a varied response when it comes to the local school districts. In Intermediate Unit No. 16, for example, there has been very strong support. This IU, which has offices in Lewisburg, home of Bucknell University, has Susquehanna College 20 miles to the south and Bloomsburg State College 30 miles to the east. Immediately there are built in resources for the arts and for the support of the arts. Schools in this IU tend to be academically secure.

Patrick Toole, Director of IU 16, says, "There was not a lot of reason to get involved with things that are already going well, as in the general academic/cognitive kinds of areas. So here was the whole affective area of the arts that was ripe for people to work on."

166

Toole himself believes that more emphasis should be placed upon the residual value of education. He says that the things students do in the non-academic areas may "have more lasting value than those that they work on in the academic area." That developing artistic talents could "have utility beyond graduation, is a rather powerful notion," he says. "And when you talk to people who are influential, like board members, especially from rural central Pennsylvania where the practical is still very much appreciated, this makes sense for them."

IU 16 is one of two IU's in the state that have an arts coordinator connected directly with it. Jane Magnus, an energetic and imaginative creative drama teacher, runs a project in the arts in basic education in area schools that is supported by Title IV-C Funds that were assigned to the IU. They also tap CETA funds for their summer arts programs. They do not ask the recipients of the services—the school districts—to make a substantial contribution toward the underwriting of the activity. "If we had to make that kind of request, or if our activities depended upon school district funding, the level of activity would not be as high, because discretionary money that is available to a local school board or a superintendent is minimal," Toole explains.

Toole labels their arts operation "a spark plug." He says it's "the notion of getting more mileage out of available resources than somebody else might get." He is not ashamed that it is a shoestring operation. "It's the kind of nickle-and-dime approach that fits very much into the culture of the region—the way these small-town rural people see the world." They sought to capitalize upon the unique talents of the people involved.

Needless to say, with this kind of leadership exerting itself from the IU, schools in this region are beginning to move to incorporate arts in general education. David Heberlig, an elementary school principal in Lewisburg, became involved in curriculum development in the arts in the early 70's. He started with a related arts committee and spent several years in a planning phase that incorporated input from many sources. "We did a survey of the community trying to ascertain what it was that they felt we should be doing in the arts. We had meetings with the college and university professors in the area. Revicki came up from the state department. We invited students that were in the Governor's School for the Arts at Bucknell to talk about their experiences."

Heberlig succeeded in getting some IV-C funds that provided them with artists in the fields of movement, drama, and photography to supplement their staff in visual arts and music. During the 1976-77 school year, they assigned the artists to work with all the teachers in the elementary schools. Heberlig arranged schedules so that every teacher was forced to work with the consultants. He admits this caused problems.

"Some teachers felt that it was an encroachment upon their own personal planning time. Others felt that the use of the artists in the classroom was really a waste of time. They

There are no full-blown programs yet in the state, but there may be 100 school districts out of 505 that are making a concerted effort to develop an arts in education program.

167

couldn't see any benefits deriving from it, not either for themselves or their students. And they felt that they didn't have
enough time to really teach the basics anyway. We were putting
another thing on them that would usurp that amount of time."

Time seemed to help. Heberlig says, "As we worked
through the program and teachers became involved with the
consultant-artists, they became much more receptive to it. By
the time the third artist arrived in a school, in most cases the
teachers were cooperating and participating in the program."

The teacher's responses to the final questionnaire were
very positive, except they indicated that they would not have
forced the program. "But now I would suggest," Heberlig
reasons, "that if we wouldn't have forced, a lot of them
wouldn't have been involved in the program and would not
have reaped the benefits that they did from it."

Heberlig gives considerable credit to the AIE staff at the
PDE. "I've had close contact with Joe McCarthy, who in many
ways has influenced my thinking in terms of the arts and arts
education," he says. "Then, too, they approved our Title IV-C
project."

Initially, Heberlig concedes, "our expectations and goals
were too grandiose. It got watered down, because we were
trying to operate the program in kindergarden through the
twelfth grades. If I were to do it over again, I would try to keep
it more limited in scope." This year they are beginning a pilot
program at the North Ward School, and they hope there will
be spin-offs from that.

A number of other IU's in the state and a number of school
districts are moving toward adopting or promoting the arts in
basic education approach. While statistical data from across the
state is not available on programmatic changes in the arts, it is
apparent that the movement is gaining favor and following.
The Pittsburgh City School District, for example, has set a clear
course toward infusing the arts in basic education in the elementary schools.

Louise Brennan, Assistant Superintendent for Elementary
Schools in Pittsburgh, is a strong supporter. "A combination of
forces," she says, "moved me toward the arts in education
conception. It starts on the national level and filters down
through the state departments, then through the influence of
the local arts institutions." She attended a conference on the
subject with representatives of the Fund and has read materials
produced by the Fund. Two of the arts specialists on her staff
have attended meetings sponsored by the AIE Program of the
PDE.

Brennan is a member of the steering committee of a new
organization, The Collaborative for the Arts in Pittsburgh Education (CAPE), which sponsors workshops for principals designed to stimulate and motivate them to lead these programs.
She has set up a task force of teachers to draw up guidelines
for these programs. "We have a pilot program, and we hope
to implement others in the fall. Their goals, she says "is to
168 improve academic achievement through the infusion of the arts

into general subject matter teaching." She sees a problem with the arts specialists in moving in this direction. "They fear fusion, because they fear the loss of their autonomy," she states. But she hastens to add, "I see their roles expanding in this process and approach."

The Pittsburgh schools have a long tradition of strong programs in art and music, but, like many large city systems, declining enrollments and inflation have brought severe cuts in staff. A school population of 75,000 in 1965 is down to 55,000 in 1977. Gretchen Jacob, Coordinating Supervisory Instructional Specialist in Art, kindergarden through the twelfth grades, says, "We can never hope to regain the number of specialists, but we hope through workshops for teachers, better use of specialists we have, through the use of community resources, using select-teachers as coordinators of arts, placing artists in residence, and developing a new curriculum infusing the arts into basic education that we can provide all students with exposure to the arts."

IU 10, centered in State College, runs an arts program called, "The Arts in Elementary Education Project." Shirley Sturtz, Arts in Education Coordinator, and her assistant, Jonny Ramsey work with 11 school districts in this IU in implementing this program. They have employed community arts resources such as the Contemporary Dance Company, Orchesis, and the Children's Theatre Ensemble from Penn State to work directly with children and teachers. Creative Writing is handled with a consultant who works with teachers through inservice workshops.

Adrian Sorenson, Elementary Principal in the Penns Valley Area School District which is serviced by the program, was enthusiastic. "Many children in this rural community would not have the arts any other way. They need this exposure." All the elementary teachers in this district—between 45 and 50— have participated in an inservice program run by outstanding elementary school teachers from one of the other school districts who know how to use the arts in their classrooms. Sturtz and Ramsey assist with these workshops.

This project reaches over 24,000 elementary children in the IU. Parental support in the region is built through an active program of community awareness—newspaper accounts, participation in some workshops, the distribution of flyers, a "Week-end of the Arts" for 1,000 children and their parents, and television programs that show what the project is trying to accomplish. The Parent Teachers Association pays for many of the resources for the project which is financed primarily with IV-C funds.

Sturtz is complimentary about the efforts of the state's AIE Program. "I have always felt directly responsible to the PDE," she says. "I have met with the arts staff as often as possible. These contacts give me confidence. Through technical assistance, they helped me know how to begin, and they put me in touch with various resources. The state department is needed to back us up. We rely upon them for philosophy. They give   169

Through technical assistance, the state arts staff helped me know how to begin, and they put me in touch with various resources. The state department is needed to back us up. We rely upon them for philosophy.

Our teachers should not see the arts in isolation. People will be more favorably disposed toward the arts, and the students will appreciate them more when they are infused with the entire curriculum.

moral support in terms of assuring us that we are moving in the right direction."

The North Hills School District is a suburban community north of Pittsburgh that has ample resources and a strong traditional program of music and visual arts. The district has just appointed Dr. Karen Cercone as Facilitator for Fine Arts and Arts in the Basics. Her duties are to help write and administrate grants that have an arts component in order to move the arts into the basics, kindergarden through the twelfth grades, and to help implement the arts as an aesthetic experience.

Dr. Joshua S. Geller, Superintendent of Schools, is highly supportive of this approach having seen the arts used to teach other subjects successfully in his previous position as Superintendent of Schools in Hastings-on-the-Hudson in New York State. He says, "Our teachers should not see the arts in isolation. People will be more favorably disposed toward the arts and the students will appreciate them more, when they are infused with the entire curriculum."

The district already has a number of projects in operation that are demonstrating the potential of this approach. Project Encompass brings in a broad array of artists to work with classes in the elementary schools. This program, financed in its first year with a grant from the Alliance for Arts Education through the PDE, has been picked up in its second year by the school district in the amount of $4,000.

TASC (for Teachers; Artists; Students; Curriculum) is a Special Projects Act grant funded for $7,500 in 1977-78. It has four components: creative movement in physical education classes, artists in residence, creative drama for teachers of special students, and videotape reporting of these activities. Artists in residence come from the Pittsburgh Public Theatre, the Pittsburgh Symphony, Ballet, and Opera. The artists work with an interdisciplinary team in each junior high school composed of a science, mathematics, social studies, and language arts teacher. They work with the team to tie the arts into the subject matter being taught at the time.

The TASC Project has placed a dance specialist in the elementary and junior high schools to work with physical education teachers. Rick Beatty, an elementary physical education teacher, has found the inservice program very helpful. "Dance has widened my conceptions of creativity, and I have enlarged this area of the curriculum. It has enriched my teaching." He has found that, "It's letting a part of yourself you didn't know come into your teaching." Unfortunately not all of the physical education teachers have chosen to take advantage of the program.

There is also a CAPP Project (for Curriculum, Arts, Pupils, and Program) which is very similar to the TASC Project. In other words, the arts in general education program is not yet one program, but consists of many small projects. Dr. Cercone has been hired to bring consistency to this area.

The PDE has had considerable influence on this district. Dr. Geller has had support from them that reinforces his own beliefs. This has come not only in the form of grants, but also in visits and letters from McCarthy, who keeps tabs on the grants and compliments the staff when something is working. Cercone says, "Keeping in touch with our programs and people is very important. The state department keeps us informed about resources and workshops in which we can participate. They give us moral support. Our administrators listen to the people at the state level. In some cases, it is money; in others, it is a communications link."

A number of other school systems in the state are working through curriculum revision toward the concept of the arts in general education: the Upper St. Clair School District (Pittsburgh area), Mt. Lebanon, Mars Area School District (grades 1 through 5 only), Gettysburg School System, Conrad Weiser School District, Neshaminy (in Bucks County near Philadelphia), and Kane, to name those most familiar to the fine arts staff.

Of course, no state department of education can be 100 percent successful. Dr. Kenneth R. Raessler, music supervisor for the Williamsport Area Schools, says of the AIE Program of the PDE, "We're getting help in the synthesis of the arts, but no help in preserving the discreteness of the individual arts. When a principal or superintendent gets involved, they hear of the synthesis, and then they see a potential budget cut. What used to be several discrete areas can then be seen as one area. They then give authority to one arts educator to have authority over several, even though their expertise doesn't extend that far. The kind of leadership we need is in the preservation of discreteness."

Raessler admits to using the PDE's materials, "but only in the arts process area. The concept is a slow one to implement, because classroom teachers are not able to comprehend how to use the arts to enhance all of learning. I support the idea, but I worry about preserving our own identity."

He says, "What I need now in leadership from the state department of education is not necessarily what I needed five years ago or five years hence. They need to educate the administrators about the difference between the arts process and the educational value that can be derived from concentration on the pure art form. It seems to me that they are losing sight of this."

Raessler is adamant about the point. "The PDE needs to represent to the entire state, to all the constituency—school boards, administrators, classroom teachers, and others—both the arts in education concept *and* the worth of the discrete arts. They have gotten so involved in the former that they neglect the latter. We cannot be so involved in the arts in general education that we lose our image. Many times in order to achieve the balance that we want, we go overboard in one direction."

Kathleen Butera, Director of Educational Activities for the Pittsburgh Symphony, who has worked closely with arts in education programs in the area, was disturbed by the lack of

The state department gives us moral support. Our administrators listen to the people at the state level. In some cases it is money; in others it is a communications link.

171

communication she has witnessed between the PDE and her kind of community program. "As long as I solicit information, I get it, but they do not take any responsibility for the educational programs of non-profit community performing arts organizations. If nothing happens in the arts, it is the fault of all the components along the line—the state department, the IU's, the school systems, the teachers, and the community arts groups. Nobody seems to say, 'Wow, you are making this effort, let's see how we can work together.'" She says that one person from the AIE Program did attend a meeting, but that "there was no further contact or follow through. As long as I pursue it, I get a response and a good one. But they are not taking the initiative on the state level."

The Effect on Higher Education

It is one thing for a state department of education to influence school districts in a state, quite another for them to affect institutions of higher education. There is a built-in elite autonomy about colleges and universities that is difficult to penetrate. After all, by their own estimation, *they* are the preservers and the makers of civilization, not the state departments of education.

The record, then, of the Fine Arts Program in regard to these bastions of progress, is sketchier. And for good reason. "I really don't see," Toole says, "that the people in the PDE have any authority or leverage that they can exercise in the area of higher education. To begin with, the AIE Program is in the Office of Basic Education. They're not in the Office of Higher Education. That division in Pennsylvania is very clear cut, and the Office of Higher Education jealously guards its turf, not only with the PDE but also out in the field."

Toole notes that interest in teacher training is declining. "In a space of about five years, Bloomsburg State has gone from about 60 to 75 percent of their graduates being teacher trainees to less than 25 percent at present." While there aren't nearly enough good teachers at work, he says, "The message of the market being oversaturated has finally gotten home in higher education."

While the influence of the AIE Program upon teacher education programs in the state is difficult to assess, it is apparent that there has been some. At the University of Pittsburgh, for example, Horton Southworth, Chairperson, Teacher Development, and Barbara Fredette, Professor of Art, are working on a new masters curriculum for elementary teachers centered around the arts in basic education. Fredette has worked closely with the AIE staff at the PDE, has attended their workshops, and has helped them in the preparation of some of their publications. Her own arts-based workshops on campus are designed to persuade other faculty to adopt this new approach. Like most universities, they are slow to move to accommodate change because of the departmental academic games. They are sandbagged by the traditions. But Southworth and Fredette are nurturing the new concept in spite of the hazards of the skeptics, who are found in most schools of education.

It must be acknowledged, however, that direct efforts by the AIE Program to change college and university curricula have had limited impact. During the past five years, the AIE staff have sponsored a number of meetings involving school arts supervisors and coordinators and college arts education teachers and chairpersons that were designed to show college arts education people where public school programs are moving and how this implies a change in pre-service education in order to meet school needs.

Another root to altering higher education is through the influence of inservice education in the state. Teachers who graduate from state colleges and universities in Pennsylvania are granted a provisional certificate. Within five years they must accrue credits and receive administrative approval to make their certificate permanent. The AIE Program is trying to influence the 29 IU's to offer inservice programs in the arts that would count toward permanent certification. Probably 17 or 18 IU's are now offering such programs. Perhaps the colleges and universities in the state will make an attempt to involve themselves with these efforts and, in the process, meet the real needs of teachers in the field.

The Changing Role of State Departments

"State departments, as a rule, were particularly strong in the 60's," Carroll believes. "They were looked to for guidance, and, by taking a stand about the arts in basic education, many school districts simply followed their lead." The state departments legitimized what was going on through publications, technical assistance, and through funds to back up projects.

There is evidence that their role is changing. "My assessment," Carroll says, "is that we're getting in a back-to-local-control kind of posture. There is a big irritation, fear, and concern about government." He sees the distrust of the federal government being transferred to the state level. "People think that these sort of faceless folks are interfering in their way of life. And, therefore, they're fighting hard to make more and more decisions closer to home. It will be harder for state departments to influence the action."

While he sees local option being exercised more strongly each month, Carroll does not believe that the feistiness is all bad. "We're flexible enough that this local thing is almost encouraged in Pennsylvania. It can be a strength. It needs to be capitalized on. I think the arts can grow in a situation like this. But it's very different than in the 60's when departments of education had a lot more clout."

Toole agrees. A grand plan, developed under federal or state auspices, cannot be imposed from the top on down, he says. "It's not going to work." He sees the responsibility of the

The role of state departments is changing. We're getting in a back-to-local-control kind of posture. There is a big irritation, fear, and concern about government.

If staff are going to function out of a state department of education, a substantial amount of their time should be spent out in the field. Their work back in their cubbyhole is not productive.

state department as one of seizing opportunities "to foster creativity in the arts, if it searches out what it would consider to be lighthouse activities, programs, or projects and disseminates those examples rather widely." And when it finds these on the anemic side, it should support them any way that it can. "And sometimes it need only be moral support. It doesn't always have to be financial."

"As dissemination or diffusion agents, state department people can carve out a very useful role. And," Toole says, "I think to a considerable extent they have." He compares that role with the agricultural agent who "can foster and stimulate creative or innovative ways of dealing with agricultural problems. He knows about the guy across the ridge who's had the same kind of problem, and here's the way he dealt with it."

In sizing up the role of state department personnel, he says, "They're facilitating, they're suggestive, they're encouraging, they're supportive, they're not the designers and the grand planners. They're not regulatory. If you try to regulate or legislate the arts into existence, you're going to fail." What counts, he says, "is identifying and publicizing a successful event and doing everything you possibly can to foster and create a stimulating and receptive environment for the arts."

Financial problems are also a part of the changing situation that affects state departments. Toole notes that, "The department of education, at least in Pennsylvania, is experiencing some extremely difficult financial problems." One case in point, he says, is that travel is restrictive. "It's pretty difficult for people in the Department now to get out into the field. It would seem to me that, if staff are going to function out of the state department of education, whether it be in Pennsylvania or elsewhere, a substantial amount of their time should be spent in the field. Their work back in their cubbyhole is not as productive."

Toole's observations are borne out by the comments of the PDE's fine arts staff, one of whom complained that "there is a preoccupation with internal affairs within the Department of Education. As a result, a significant proportion of our time is taken up with meetings, status reports, memos, and other trivia which prevents us from attending the development of our arts initiatives and visiting schools." Another arts staff member acknowledged that they are doing less traveling, but said that "more accountability requires additional reports that can only be done in the office."

In general, the arts staff feels frustrated. They cannot assert sustained attention to their own projects, or develop curriculum materials like they used to. They are smothered in a bureaucratic maze and malaise.

What Remains to Be Done

It has become increasingly important not just to bring administrators, the classroom teachers, and the arts people along, but to reach the general public, as well. Carroll says "more and more, without their support, we're not going to keep these programs in the schools." He says, "Where school boards have tried to lay off arts teachers and have not, it's because the community has come in hard, and that's because those art teachers have built up a following, whether it be for band, camps, Christmas programs, or whatever. I think that this is one thing any state department ought to be concerned about—how to bring the general public along." What we really need, he says, "is to get people hooked on the importance of the arts as part of a basic education."

Carroll believes that concern for the quality of arts programs is also extremely important. "We have an awful lot of very pedantic arts programs, and, for whatever reason, the people teaching them have not kept alive in their art field. They have met so many frustrations. They are tired. The program tends to become routine. It does not capture the imagination of the students, and, by the way, that is the best way to get the public on your side. If students are really happy, they will go home and talk about the arts program. So, I suspect that the backup to getting general public support is to improve the quality of programs dramatically, where we can."

Staff of the AIE Program are painfully cognizant of the many problems they face in seeking to establish the arts in general education approach throughout the state. They mentioned a number of hurdles and constraints that must be overcome:

(1) *The Burden of Tradition.* "Tradition," Robert Revicki says, "burdens both the established visual arts and music programs from altering their mode of operation. This may be as much the expectations of administrators and the general community about what arts programs should be, as it is the reluctance of arts specialists to change. The community may not perceive that the relationship of the arts to the basics is valuable or that it will improve general learning."

(2) *The Migration of Teachers.* One reason that there is a dearth of model programs in the state is that the people who understand the concept often move away before any firmly rooted program can be established. According to McGeary, "People feel they have to move every few years, if they are going to be successful."

(3) *Reductions in Staff in Fine Arts at the PDE.* The AIE Program is now staffed by two persons. There used to be five. Gottschalk-Roehner resigned in July 1978, and her position has not yet been filled. Shifts in arts administrators within the staff have had an unsettling effect. The limited staff level curtails doing adequate follow-up and providing necessary technical assistance and other kinds of reinforcement. Overall, staff in the PDE has been reduced by about one-quarter due to the demands of the state legislature that staff for all state services be reduced. Fortunately, McGeary, Chief of the division that encompasses the program, has been able to devote a large measure of his time to activities in support of the arts in edu-

If students are really happy, they will go home and talk about the arts program. So I suspect that the backup to getting general public support is to improve dramatically, where we can, the quality of arts programs.

cation. Then, too, a graduate internship program has been established in cooperation with Pennsylvania colleges and universities. At the same time that these full-time, 16-week internships provide a unique opportunity for graduate students majoring in arts education to experience the functions of a state department of education, they also add manpower to the department to assist the AIE Program.

(4) *Inadequate Funding.* There simply isn't enough Title IV-C funding to go around. Only 5.5 percent of the state appropriation for the Pennsylvania Council on the Arts goes to the Artists-in-Schools Program. Funds for projects sponsored by the Alliance for Arts Education in the state are minimal. The lack of project funds limits the number of school districts that can launch arts in general education programs, since they depend upon project monies to innovate curricula. Many of the school districts in Pennsylvania are feeling the pinch of inflation and declining enrollments and have made cuts in their arts programs. Budgets for the arts within the PDE have been slashed. Colleges and universities in the state are also tightening their belts. Penn State, for example, attempted an "Arts Term" for their classroom teachers in which a quarter of the year was devoted to arts experiences in dance, drama, music, and visual arts. The program had to be terminated because of tightened budgets.

(5) *Lethargy.* "The toughest hurdle," Gottschalk-Roehner said recently, "is a lethargy that exists in many school districts on the part of teachers who are reluctant to become part of the planning process. It takes time to brain storm, to dig up resources, to evolve new ideas and curricular approaches. It is practically impossible to gather together in one place all the people you need to get moving. Teachers simply do not want to give the time to it."

(6) *Getting School Systems to Make the Commitment.* "This approach requires considerable commitment on the part of school districts," says Revicki. "It means inservice programs for administrators, classroom teachers, and arts specialists. It requires that community resources be brought in, and these, too, need orientation programs. Some say this approach shouldn't cost more money, that existing resources can be redeployed. However, it requires systems to support a drama and dance component, and this means bringing additional consultants into the schools."

(7) *Improving Relationships with Arts and Education Organizations.* McGeary feels strongly that the department needs to establish stronger relationships with arts education organizations, particularly in the areas of dance, theater, and visual arts. "These associations," he says, "could have taken a lot of pressure off the State Department of Education by keeping arts educators in touch with each other." He believes that organizations such as the Association for Supervision and Curriculum Development (ASCD) could have been encouraged to work cooperatively with the various arts education organizations.

176

"Some arts educators feel threats to their jobs, and this could have been averted with more contact and involvement with these groups."

(8) *The Effect of Teacher Negotiations.* Revicki observes that, "The bargaining unit for the school districts often prohibits any team effort. When the music or art teacher enters the classroom, the classroom teacher takes his contracted planning period. The students see this and get the idea that there is no relationship between their arts experiences and other areas of learning. The system itself, therefore, also promotes this disaffection within the classroom teacher as well."

(9) *Difficulties Dealing with the Secondary Level.* Most of the arts in general education programs that have begun are on the elementary level. The compartmentalization of courses at the secondary level makes it difficult to adopt the concept on a system-wide basis. Special efforts need to be made to reach these teachers.

(10) *The Limitations of Arts Specialists.* Revicki has found that, "The conceptions that arts specialists have of their art form are based upon their own experiences which are often very limited. They don't see the relationship, say, between musical expression and other life experiences. They divorce their art from life. Their preoccupation with technical skills closes their art form to personal responsiveness, creativeness, and the development of true artistic perception. This has the effect of impoverishing the arts specialists and, in turn, their students."

(11) *The Skepticism of Arts Educators.* "A good many arts educators are in a state of confusion," McGeary believes. "They don't know where their commitments lie. They take potshots, feel vulnerable, and are defensive. Their college education has, in the name of general education, neglected this focus. We want arts teachers to make choices, but they are not operating with any philosophical focus in mind. They are wandering around. Arts specialists should be the nucleus that can carry the ball, but the principals may have a commitment, and they wonder how to get the arts people working at it."

(12) *The Need for a Clear State Plan for the Arts.* McGeary states, "One of the things that must be done at the state level is to develop a sharper sense of what our plan should be. This includes a heightened understanding of learning theory, a concern for the philosophical aspects of the arts and general education, and a careful review of the people we wish to serve. We must get our own act together and learn how to administer, supervise, and otherwise assist arts education programs. Leadership management has been neglected and is causing us problems." During the past year efforts have been directed at reformulating and updating the state plan for the arts in education.

(13) *The Need to Maintain Cohesiveness as a Staff.* As the AIE staff has been cut and there have been shifts in position, it has become more difficult to sustain program momentum in a comprehensive way. The need for leadership and assistance in all the components of a comprehensive arts in education pro-

Some arts educators feel threats to their jobs, and this could have been averted with more contact and involvement with their professional associations.

The multitudinous efforts of the AIE staff to change arts programs in schools throughout the state through the adoption of the arts in general education have had considerable impact, although the process is just emerging from its formative period and must assert itself for a long time to come.

gram cannot be adequately provided. McGeary acknowledges that staff resources are very limited and that they "need a new surge of purpose to pull their potential into focus again."

Overview

Pennsylvania does have what many states call a "comprehensive arts education program." What the AIE Program calls its total "Arts in Education Program" consists of three components: arts in general education, which is the major focus of this case study; arts education, which encompasses the discrete arts; and specialized arts education, which focuses on arts for the handicapped and the talented. In each of these areas the AIE Program works on developing curricula, inservicing teachers and administrators, and making effective use of community resources.

The various grants from the JDR 3rd Fund gave emphasis to the arts in general education area, that part of the program that was most in need of development. So successful were these small seed grants and the determination of the staff, that the concentrated efforts from 1972 to present to advance this idea throughout the state as a new thrust in arts education have given greater emphasis to it than is evidenced in the other components. Balance, of course, is difficult to achieve while a staff is launching a new concept.

This may account for McGeary's strong belief that, if he had it all to do over again, "I would have developed the state plan more thoroughly and clearly." While he feels that "not having it has allowed us more flexibility," he admits that "having it would have given us more control, commitment, focus, and accountability within the department and the state program as a whole. There is danger in over-organizing to the point of stifling spontaneity, yet there is value in having things done. One is caught in the middle seeking the proper balance."

It seems clear that the multitudinous efforts of the AIE staff to change arts programs in schools throughout the state through the adoption of the arts in general education have had considerable impact, although the process is just emerging from its formative period and must assert itself for a long time to come. The way this concept has been spread from the PDE down to the local school level is akin to a revelation going through the rumor mill. What the PDE suggests and advocates is interpreted by the IU's and, in turn, reinterpreted at the district level. Ideas advanced by the state department of education are subjected to adaptation at the local school level and are adjusted by each teacher who chooses to amalgamate those concepts in the classroom. Progress and school change—presuming the state department is asserting a leadership role—cannot, therefore, be thought of in linear terms. It is not catechistic so much as catalytic. In other words, given the influence of the PDE and the Fund, what comes out at the school level may look quite different as the concept is adopted, adjusted, distilled, distorted, and even resisted and rejected.

The Arts in Education staff is aware of the relatively fragile role they play as one force within the complex of forces that control education and school change. They do not monitor the programs that emerge from their efforts. "One of the weaknesses of the movement," McGeary says, "is that we have not deliberately developed a sense of critique and evaluation." Perhaps, but what they have managed to do, and have done well, is to provide school systems with attractive new options in the arts and the ways to bring those options to affect improved education for every student in Pennsylvania.

CHAPTER EIGHT
Case Study:
Oklahoma–Winds of Change

Charles Fowler

"When Poteau (population 5,500) holds an art show, you know something is happening." That is the measured opinion of Donna Cobb, President (1977-78) of the Oklahoma Education Association (OEA). It wasn't any accident that during her administration the theme of the state convention of classroom teachers was "Forward to the Basics With the Arts."

"In terms of attendance," Cobb says, "OEA had been on the downhill for six or seven years with attendance around 6,000. Registration for this convention was 16,000." That represents almost one-half of the teachers in the state.

The convention is indicative of what is happening across the state of Oklahoma. With between 20 and 25 inservice mini-clinics designed to teach teachers how arts experiences of all kinds can be used to learn concepts in other curricular areas, the convention represents one more step in a carefully orchestrated plan to move the arts out into Oklahoma schools. "The net result," Cobb says of the convention, "is much new generated interest in the arts."

181

An "Okie" is not about to sit idly by, be left out, or out-paced, even in areas that challenge personal values and life style. Let them know that there is a national movement called the arts in basic education, and they will want a piece of the action.

This new energy for the arts emanates from the enterprising efforts of Peggy Long and Charles Mohr, the State Department of Education's Arts Coordinators. Sensing an opportunity to help the OEA and the cause of the arts in education, Long and Mohr met with Cobb right after she took office to suggest the theme. They then persuaded the Arts Council of Oklahoma City to hold its annual arts festival in connection with the convention and won the cooperation and participation of virtually all of Oklahoma City's arts enterprises as well.

Getting Started

What causes a state, especially one that is known for its tough frontier spirit, its rugged petroleum and cattle industries, and its raging football mania, to begin to turn around to favor the arts? Oklahoma as a state is 18th in land area and 27th in population (est. at 2.8 million). It produces nearly $2 billion annually in crops and livestock. Its 74,000 farms and ranches embrace more than 33 million acres. It is second only to Texas with its 2 million head of beef cows. A variety of mineral industries are active in 76 of its 77 counties and account for a yearly production valued at more than $1.2 billion. Oil and gas are produced in 71 counties. Oil derricks have even sprouted on the grounds of the State Capitol in Oklahoma City.

There is a quiet reserve among Oklahomans bred of a strong, conservative religious heritage—largely Southern Baptist. But the land also breeds a sense of openness, and rapid development has given the people a built-in tolerance for change.

What has all this to do with the arts? Much. Oklahoma is the 46th state to join the union (in 1907), making it one of the youngest and, consequently, most determined and competitive states in the country. An "Okie" is not about to sit idly by, be left out, or out-paced, even in areas that challenge personal values and lifestyle. Let them know that there is a national movement called the arts in basic education, and they will want a piece of the action.

How did the idea of comprehensive arts with its broadened role for the arts in basic education come to Oklahoma in the first place? Neither Long or Mohr brought the concept with them. Both attended college together, then taught in the same school prior to their tenure at the State Department of Education (SDE). Long joined the staff there in June of 1974, two years after Mohr. Initially, the $10,000 yearly grant of the Alliance for Arts Education was used to help finance this additional arts position within the SDE.

As is often the case, the idea manifested itself as much by accident as by design. The JDR 3rd Fund had been working with the Oklahoma City Public Schools and the Arts Council of Oklahoma City in their cosponsored program, "Opening Doors to Education."[1] Mary Frates, former Creative Education

Coordinator for the Arts Council of Oklahoma City, who worked with Opening Doors, was the catalyst for bringing the staff of the Fund together with Mohr and Long. Gene Wenner, then Assistant Director of the Fund, volunteered to help set up a structure and work with SDE administrators to establish an arts in basic education project in the state.

It was slow going at first. As far as the arts in basic education is concerned, Oklahoma was at ground zero. Wenner met with many of the administrators at the SDE to explain the program and seek their support. As Long recalls, not all these early forays met with ready success. One assistant superintendent in the SDE asked her, "How much business you going to do with that fast talker from the East?"

But, in spite of some resistance, Wenner succeeded in mobilizing the state department. Through his suggestions, an "Advisory Committee on Arts in Education" was established and a "Superintendent's Arts in Education Conference," sponsored by the SDE and the Alliance for Arts Education with the assistance of the Oklahoma Arts and Humanities Council, was held in May 1975. This was a working conference of 125 people—superintendents of schools, principals, arts specialists, artists, community people, representatives of higher education, classroom teachers, community people, students, etc.—designed to draw up a state plan for the arts. This was about the same time that the Fund brought the Coalition of States for the Arts in Education together, and Oklahoma was invited to belong.

In July 1975, a smaller task force from the Advisory Committee met for the purpose of completing the state plan. Wenner continued to provide technical assistance, visiting Oklahoma at least once every three months during 1975 and '76. Originally, the Advisory Committee supplied direction and was a mechanism for communication. At present, it functions in an auxiliary role to advocate and implement the plan.

We tried to break through the traditional insularity by asking questions like, "Do you believe the arts are for all children?" and "What is the climate for the arts in your community?"

Strategy

"Initially, we had to build awareness," Long recalls. "There was a charge by the Assistant Superintendent of Schools in the state for all the curriculum specialists to hold 30 one-day, two- and three-county workshops in the state from September 1975 to February 1976. Ours centered on the concept of a comprehensive arts in education program. We encouraged arts specialists, classroom teachers, and administrators to attend. These workshops brought many of the state's art people together for the first time.

"We tried to break through the traditional insularity by asking questions like, 'Do you believe the arts are for all children?' and 'What is the climate for the arts in your community?'.

---

[1]For a complete description of this program, see *Arts in Education Partners*, Nancy Shuker, Editor (New York: The JDR 3rd Fund, 1977), pp. 47-55.

We had to get them into process, get them into the planning, so that they could begin to see their own program in a broader context.

Then they were asked to react to a draft of a state plan for the arts. We presented three components—arts education, arts in basic education, and specialized arts education and asked them to look at their programs with this curriculum design in mind." (See Diagram 1)

Long admits that, "At first we tried demonstrating an integrated arts experience, but we saw there was little pay off in terms of real understanding of what a comprehensive arts program is. During the first several meetings, they beat us into the dust. Most of our resistance comes from arts specialists. They are not agreed that they should reach every student or that the arts are for everybody.

"We had to get them into *process*, get them into the planning, so that they could begin to see their own program in a broader context. As soon as we took this approach, they saw that their programs were centered on discrete arts with little attention to the other components. Then we asked the critical question: 'What do you have to do to bring balance to all three areas and reach all the students?' This was the beginning of the painful process of change.

"These workshops, with 50 people in each, reached 1,500 people across the state. They were the first step in getting people to look at arts programs in new ways. Later, after some reflection, many of these teachers came back to us saying, 'I really *do* see what you are talking about.'"

Building awareness, of course, has much to do with changing people's attitudes and values. A 1975 survey reveals that arts programs are provided in less than half the schools in Oklahoma, and these resources tend to focus on the talented few:[2]

Diagram 1

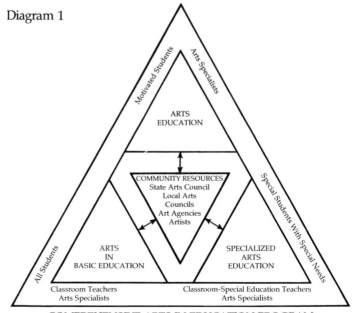

COMPREHENSIVE ARTS IN EDUCATION PROGRAM

[2]From the *Oklahoma Plan for Arts in Education* (Oklahoma City: Oklahoma State Department of Education, January 1976, revised), p. 2

Levels	Vocal Music	Instrumental Music	Visual Arts	Speech/ Drama
Elementary (1,126 schools)	51%	17%	17%	3%
Secondary (849 schools)	49%	43%	40%	54%

To make matters worse, the largely rural population of the state is scattered in numerous small school districts. Out of Oklahoma's 623 school systems, almost 400 have enrollments under 500, and there are 87 school districts that have 100 or less students. To complicate the situation, in the northeastern part of the state, the Cherokee population accounts for 90 percent of the students in the schools, and many do not speak English, when they first enroll. With 37 tribes, there are more Indians in Oklahoma than in any other state. They account for 12 percent of the school population.

Long and Mohr knew they had a difficult job on their hands. They had to sensitize teachers, administrators, and school board members throughout the state to the role the arts can play in motivating learning in all curriculum areas. And they had to persuade community arts councils and performing arts organizations to assume some responsibility within local arts education programs.

Demonstration Schools

To implement the state plan, Long and Mohr, in the Spring of 1976, invited applications from schools interested in establishing demonstration centers in the arts. They figured that by reaching just one percent of the schools in the state they could set up an effective networking system that potentially would reach 50 to 60 percent of the school population.

A group from the Advisory Committee selected five schools on the basis of their strong commitment to the arts. In June, the state arts coordinators held a five-day workshop for the Arts Planning Teams (APT) from these schools which consisted of the principal, arts specialists, classroom teachers, special education teachers, and some community or parental respresentatives. Members of the Advisory Committee were also invited. The 50 people who attended received training in group-process skills, planning, and problem identification and solving. Long and Mohr work as facilitators handling the staff development and networking activities themselves. Anything presentational is usually done by consultants.

A small amount of Title V funds was made available to the demonstration schools on a request basis. Maximum assistance was $1,200. Obviously, funding was not viewed as a primary motivation to get these programs rolling. "The worst thing you can do for a school system," Mohr says, "is to give them a chunk of money and tell them to go do a program. The best

> *The worst thing you can do for a school system is to give them a chunk of money and tell them to go do a program. The best thing you can do is to encourage them to plan and provide them with a focus.*

thing you can do is to encourage them to plan and provide them with a focus."

Surprisingly, not one of the demonstration sites submitted a request for these funds until January. "They were still engaged in the planning process and were being careful about their requests," Mohr recalls. "When the requests did come in, they were for funds to pay for artists, curriculum materials, and released time for teachers to attend workshops."

At the end of the first year in June 1977, another five-day evaluation workshop was held for the Arts Planning Teams from the five demonstration centers along with a planning workshop for teams from four new schools. The old schools shared information and strategies with the new schools. Demonstration sites increased to nine for the second year.

Role of the State Arts Council

Some of the success of the Oklahoma program can be attributed to the unusual arrangement that has developed between the SDE and the State Arts Council of Oklahoma (SACO). Even though the state legislature has never demonstrated strong support for the arts, it did take the unusual move to legislate a cooperative relationship betweeen SACO and the SDE.

In June 1977, the state legislature funneled $100,000 of funds for artist's residencies into the SDE budget. Funds were transferred from the SACO to the SDE, because the state legislature wanted "accountability." It seems that one of the poets took a book of poetry to school that had four-letter words in it. Parents protested. Then a visual artist in a rural school failed to wear a brassiere. The superintendent was offended. The matter was brought to the attention of the state legislature.

In response, the legislature issued a charge to the SDE and the SACO to develop guidelines for the program, to determine the roles of each agency, and to draw up regulations governing such matters as appropriate dress and behavior. In spite of the apparent strain, the two agencies have worked out a cooperative agreement that, at the least, assures proper preparation and follow-up to the residencies.

These funds, which are still administered by the SACO, support a five-day workshop in the summer to bring together artists and school sponsors to plan the year's residencies and to better understand the concept underlying the SDE's arts in basic education program. These funds support upwards of 50 artists a year—20 full-time and the rest half-time or less. They also pay for the arts coordinators who are attached to each of the demonstration schools.

Using artists in such a mainline educational role has caused some difficulties. Out of the six arts coordinators during the first year, four left; out of the five coordinators during the second year, one left. Nancy Meis, Program Director for Artists-in-Residence with the Council, says that the turnover "was due to false expectations. Some of the artists claimed that they didn't know the job before they took it."

To rectify this, the screening process has now been tightened. School personnel are involved, and they have formulated questions and formalized an interview process. A panel of five persons now screens these coordinators, and they are selected by teams of teachers and administrators from each school building. SDE funds are used to pay for regular meetings of the arts coordinators.

The collaboration between the two agencies is working. SACO personnel are present at all SDE inservice workshops attended by the arts coordinators, and demonstration center staff and SDE specialists and administrative staff plan together with the SACO staff. Ben DiSalvo, Executive Director of the SACO, acknowledges that, "For the success of Artists-in-Residence, we have to be as close as possible." He does admit that, "Artists have expressed some apprehension about 'diluting' the arts by using them to teach the basics. "But," he asks, "what is the difference in using the arts to teach the basics and using the arts with the aging to broaden their horizons and enhance the socialization process? In both cases we are building a base for the arts."

Artists have expressed some apprehension about "diluting" the arts by using them to teach the basics. But what is the difference in using the arts this way and using them with the aging to broaden horizons and enhance the socialization process? In both cases we are building a base for the arts.

Winning Administrative Support

Before any of the foregoing could be accomplished, broad support had to be established among the top administrators within the Oklahoma State Department of Education. One target was Dr. Leslie Fisher, State Superintendent for Public Instruction. His own education in the rural schools of Oklahoma had given him little or no arts background. He acknowledges now that, "Peggy (Long) persuaded me to inculcate the arts into education." With a playful grin he confesses, "When I told her I would support the arts, she relaxed her grip on my arm!"

But Fisher is proud of the developments in the arts that have taken place in just two years. "In spite of small budgets, we probably have made more progress in the arts than in any area of study in the schools. There was a void in the arts in the state. We worked with the administrative leaders. We asked them for help. This got things rolling. Then other school administrators followed along."

He gives considerable credit to the Fund: "There is nothing that has stimulated us as much as the JDR 3rd Fund. Without it, we would be about where we were. Their staff came here with a personal interest in what we were trying to do without asking anything in return. We needed this."

Fisher believes that one of the signs of change was the Oklahoma Education Association's convention. "This was probably the best teachers meeting ever held in the state. What made it outstanding was the genuine interest and involvement of classroom teachers in the arts. I've been attending these

It's a difficult concept to move into schools today because of the pressure for the basics and the lack of background in the arts among classroom teachers and administrators. At first this must be a selling job.

meetings for 35 years, and this is the one we will remember more than any other."

Both Long and Mohr have invited SDE administrators to participate in arts meetings whenever possible. The Director of Elementary Education, Leonard Bates, has attended a number of Coalition meetings. He credits these with "helping me to understand the arts." The SDE arts staff, he says "have given me articles to read, taken me to workshops, and shown me in-service programs. If administrators can see a program that works, they will be persuaded. That is the value of our demonstration schools."

He, too, gives "much credit to the JDR 3rd Fund." He says, "We were too fragmented and unorganized. We had no one in the SDE representing the arts six years ago. There was no coordination. The Fund gave us the leadership that got us started."

Bates, like Fisher, sees the OEA Convention as proof of the progress that has been made. "I was shocked, when they turned their meeting over to the arts. They used the arts to improve their convention. They capitalized on the enthusiasm."

Another key supporter is Dr. John Moseley, Director of Secondary Education for the state. "For any change to take place," he reasons, "there must be strong and committed people in leadership." Speaking of Long and Mohr, he says, "We hired the right arts people."

He, too, had to be won over. "My first involvement was through CEMREL's meeting at Oklahoma City University three or four years ago. That's where I became aware of the concept of the arts in basic education. Then, it was a matter of helping our arts coordinators find and use the resources that were already available."

Moseley recognizes the extent of the problem of introducing the idea of the arts in basic education into the schools. "It's a difficult concept to move into schools today because of the pressure for the basics and the lack of background in the arts among classroom teachers and administrators. At first, this must be a selling job."

Compared to several years ago, Moseley sees some important developments: arts for the handicapped, the arts in inservice education, and the visibility of arts in public schools and civic organizations. "All this is because of a coordinated effort. We see more cooperation between local and state arts councils. They involve us with their activities. The time has come to an end, when the schools can finance a complete program of all the arts for all the children. Schools must rely upon supplementary resources."

Another convert is J.D. Giddens, Assistant Superintendent for Instruction. "Our arts coordinators have talked with me. I met with Gene Wenner. I went to meetings in Chicago. I observed our demonstration schools. It all began to make sense. I bought the concept."

He acknowledges that, "When we were in school, these

programs were not available. We feel a bit cheated and want more for children today. We have altered our philosophy. I believe our basic courses can be taught better, when the arts are used in the teaching process."

The Influence of the SDE

Oklahoma is second only to Hawaii in the amount of state control of their schools. All schools must be accredited by the SDE in order to receive aid. As a consequence, the schools listen to the SDE and take direction from it.

The arts coordinators have benefited from this situation. Since the SDE is viewed largely as a regulatory agency by the schools, its curriculum program areas tend to be perceived as carrying similar authority. In this sense, the arts ride on the established prestige. When Long and Mohr, as representatives of the SDE, go out to the schools, the principals and superintendents generally listen.

In Oklahoma, the State Superintendent for Public Instruction is elected. Where this is not the case, as in Pennsylvania, the governor becomes the control agent in education with the effect of removing authority from those who know school management and who have real educational commitment. In the case of Oklahoma, Fisher is the titular superintendent of every school district in the state. The fact that he supports the arts and is verbal about it, gives strong inducement to the local districts.

Perhaps it is the youth of the state and its relatively small population that has kept the Oklahoma state bureaucracy of manageable proportions. This, too, has its good effect on the arts. There are less bureaucratic layers within the SDE than one finds in older more populated states which means more ready accessibility and more openness.

Then, too, the SDE can set up demonstration projects in the schools that are staffed in part by them and monitored from the central office. The schools accept a less autonomous role and seem to welcome and value the involvement and the thrust of the state agency. Where bureaucracies are larger and older, this doesn't seem to be the case.

One other factor within the SDE has worked in favor of the arts, at least in the past. There has been no budget within the department for programmatic activities specifically in the arts. This lack of funds to carry out actions and programs has caused the arts coordinators to use every possible resource within and outside the SDE. In this sense, the lack of budget has forced cooperation between various programs and agencies. The arts have not been able to "go it alone." The interactions and transactions that have resulted have, in effect, brought wide support to the arts, because of the numbers of people and agencies that have had to become involved.

However, the lack of immediately accessible funds to start and sustain programs has of necessity diverted the energies of 189

When we were in school, these programs were not available. We feel a bit cheated and want more for children today. We have altered our philosophy. I believe our basic courses can be taught better when the arts are used in the teaching process.

the SDE's arts coordinators from program content to fund raising. Moseley recognizes that, "We have overloaded Peg (Long) and Charles (Mohr). We grew so fast in so short a time that demands have escalated. Their days run into nights and weekends."

Jack Strahorn, Assistant Superintendent for Federal Programs, who is in charge of distributing federal education dollars, says, "I help Peggy because she is a hard worker, and she believes in what she is doing. She gets along well with people."

Others within the department feel the same way and have worked closely with the arts area to help develop innovative programs. Dr. Charles Sandmann, Director of Federal Programs, sees a need for state monies to support integrated arts programs throughout Oklahoma. "Too many schools," he says, "especially rural schools, leave something wanting educationally. These children go through life with no exposure to the arts. My own son has missed the arts. I have a gut level feeling we are not fulfilling the need, and I am supportive to make things happen."

At the same time, Sandmann is cautious about pressing for the arts to be in the center of the curriculum. "I'm not sure I want to see everything revolve around the arts. Career education and economics are also pressing to be at the core. 'My way is the right way. You're going to dance my tune.' I'm not certain this is the way to go."

Sandmann is an avid supporter of community education, which he feels "has great potential for the arts." There are now some 24 communities in Oklahoma that are involved. "Community education programs open the schools up to serve both students and parents. When communities are asked what they want from such programs, they invariably come up with requests for the arts." Sandmann believes these programs can reach more people than the integration concept.

This points out that considerable support has been generated from various funding sources within the SDE, but, more importantly, it demonstrates that awareness has now reached a level where people are beginning to seek some of their own solutions. There is now activity on many fronts. Enough momentum has been produced to keep the idea alive.

To ease the work load and extend the expertise of the arts staff, the Department has hired Becki Weiner, a visual arts specialist, for the 1978-79 school year to complement the work of Long (theater) and Mohr (music). The Fund's Administrative Fellowship program has supplied additional assistance. During the 1977-78 school year, Dr. Robert Lee Kidd III, a JDR 3rd Fellow, worked closely with the demonstration schools, their staffs, and the arts coordinators, as has Karen Kinnett, JDR 3rd Fund Fellow during the 1978-79 school year.

Because of the rapid growth and expansion of the Arts in Education Program in Oklahoma, it was made an independent unit or section within the organizational structure of the SDE as of July 1, 1979. With this status will go a small budget for fiscal year 1980. Long will serve as administrator of the program with Mohr and Weiner as arts in education coordinators. Also cooperating as part of the staff is Sharon McColl, a former JDR 3rd Fund Administrative Fellow for the state of Michigan. She serves as coordinator of the project on the Arts for the Gifted and Talented in cooperation with the Coalition of States for the Arts in Education.

Progress in the Schools

The public schools are the watermark for measuring the effectiveness of a state department of education. Some outstanding changes have taken place in Oklahoma schools in arts education from 1976 to present, as a direct result of the efforts of the SDE, particularly in the demonstration schools.

While there were only five demonstration schools during the first year of the project, the elementary network will be expanded during the fourth year to include 13 satellite schools in five districts. The middle/junior high school network will expand to six demonstration schools and one satellite school. Satellite schools will receive staff development, networking, and technical assistance from the SDE and will work closely with the demonstration schools in their districts. A total of 27 demonstration and satellite schools will be working in the Arts in Education Program during the 1980 school year.

These schools, which are developing as showcases for the comprehensive plan, especially emphasize the use of the arts in basic education. Classroom teachers in these schools are learning through the help of the arts coordinators, the resources of visiting artists, and inservice training workshops to overcome their anxieties and insecurities about the arts and to explore them as aids to all learning.

The demonstration schools vary from the new, affluent suburban "open" school to the old, rural-town traditional. Wiley Post Elementary School exemplifies the former. There, the 940 students receive a substantial program of art and music. The modern, bright, carpeted facilities were created to foster the open school approach. The faculty is young and high-spirited.

James Burnett, Principal of the school, is what every arts person wants for an administrator. He was a band and orchestra director for 14 years and for 11 years played trombone in the Oklahoma Symphony. He says of elementary school children, "Those who have a poor self concept are the ones who don't want to progress or learn. They are really crippled. The arts help children get in touch with their feelings and express themselves."

Test scores show children in this school to be one or two years above grade level. The arts in basic education program, according to Burnett, "is reinforcing our philosophy and providing another channel to voice it." Sandy Wisley, Vice Principal, sees the integrated arts as being "a creative, fun, and exciting way to teach the basics," although she does not see it 191

Those who have a poor self concept are the ones who don't want to progress or learn. They are really crippled. The arts help children get in touch with their feelings and express themselves.

I think the approach strengthens the music program because it creates more involvement in music on the part of both teachers and students. Why should music stop at the music room?

as helping the arts. "Children do not see the integrated arts as arts," she says. "When the children drew a large heart with valves and the blood system, they saw it as a science lesson, not an arts lesson."

During the first year of the Arts in Education Program, a planning team was formed that included several classroom teachers, the arts specialists, the physical education teacher, and the principal. Prior to school opening, the team attended a workshop conducted by the SDE. When school started, the entire faculty was retrained. With the help of visiting artists—a movement specialist, a poet, an Indian artist who did pottery, weaving, and painting, a painter, a flamenco guitarist, and two pantomimists—they attempted to expose the children to as many arts as possible to show them that the arts are more than just visual arts and music.

Wisley says, "In the second year, the concentration was on integration. The teachers felt more comfortable trying to use the arts themselves this year, after watching artists last year." Resource people were again brought in with the help of CETA funds, this time five different artists who call themselves "ART, Inc." This group, sponsored by the SDE and the Arts Council of Oklahoma City, came to the school three different times, performing for and working with the students, and providing inservice workshops for the teachers.

Nelda Rawlings, a classroom teacher who represents the fifth and sixth grade levels on the Arts in Education Planning Team, noted some of the problems: "To plan and assemble materials takes extra time. At first the teachers were frightened. They felt insecure, because of their lack of background in the arts. To understand the concept of the arts used as process is difficult." Perhaps the most helpful device the SDE used was to hire substitutes for teachers who attend workshops. Then the teachers who attend share what they have learned with the other teachers upon their return.

Karen Kinnett, the Arts Coordinator for Wiley Post during the 1977-78 school year, believes that, "The children are becoming aesthetic individuals. I'm not certain the program will result in more people going to the symphony, but these children are developing a better self concept, and this will affect their whole lives."

Kinnett works with children in four other schools—one a junior high—to demonstrate the integration of the arts into basic education, so that teachers can see how children respond. She says, "The idea is to ignite the teachers' interest, so that they will want training." She talks to the arts specialists and encourages them to attend workshops, and she also visits with principals to open them to the possibilities of the arts in general education.

It was the music specialist at Wiley Post, Kathlyn Reynolds, who was instrumental in bringing the concept to the school. "I think the approach strengthens the music program," she says, "because it creates more involvement in music on the part of both teachers and students. Why should music stop at the music room?" Speaking of music teachers in general, she declares, "We've been too narrow. 'Open the book and sing a song.' I try to bring in poetry, movement, and instruments." To illustrate, she asks, "Why does Indian music sound like it does and not like rock? We learn the sign language and listen to an Indian flute maker tell about this music."

Russell Dougherty Elementary School in the Edmond School District, or "Rusty Dirty" as it has been called, contrasts sharply with Wiley Post. This is an old building with the typical blackboards and rows of seats and desks. Most of the faculty have been there for many years. The curriculum is the traditional basics with some music and art. Edmond is a town of about 17,000 just to the north of Oklahoma City.

How did such a school become a demonstration center for the arts in basic education? It all stemmed from an SDE-sponsored workshop that their special education teacher and a music teacher attended. They expressed an interest in the idea to Joan Wernersbach, their principal. In turn, Wernersbach got interested and asked her superintendent if she should get involved. He said, yes, but maintained that she would have to get all the teachers interested and supportive to make the idea work.

Wernersbach felt that there was considerable potential for creativity among the teachers, but that it was dormant. She found several teachers who were interested in the concept, and they attended a workshop where artists worked directly with them. The music teacher, who had been there for 12 years, led the way and eventually became the in-school coordinator. A core group of nine faculty became the arts planning team.

The principal succeeded in getting parents involved as well. The president of the Booster Club, a group similar to a Parent-Teachers Association, attended all the workshops. Another mother took over the job of public relations for the project. Eventually the Booster Club raised $2,500 "to be used during the 1978/1979 school year for the continuation of the Arts in Education Program which has been so successful this year."[3] It also requested that the board of education allocate an equivalent amount to support the program.

Through this program, the whole school has been transformed. The walls have been brightened with murals. The faculty has become more energetic, assertive, and creative. The curriculum has been charged with excitement. Wernersbach says, "If teachers are developing themselves, then they are being more effective with their students. Everybody has been stimulated to some degree, some more than others."

The Superintendent of Schools in Edmond, George Rowley, has a positive response to the program: "Parental support, student attitudes, and teacher response has changed. Parental complaints have been reduced to just about zero." He says, "When the arts program is strong, you can see it on the students' faces. I feel good, when I hear something fine is hap-

To plan and assemble materials takes extra time. At first the teachers were frightened. They felt insecure because of their lack of background in the arts. To understand the concept of the arts used as process, is difficult.

---

[3] A letter to the principal from the co-presidents of the Russell Dougherty Booster Club, May 12, 1978.

The most logical approach to getting the arts into rural schools is through inservice education. We must rely upon the classroom teacher.

pening in the schools." In order to command administrative support for such efforts, he believes that, "If a principal and teachers can show that what they are doing is beneficial to students, then a superintendent is going to respond favorably."

Reaching the Rural Areas

One of the most difficult problems in Oklahoma, as in other western states, is how to move the arts into the rural schools. The SDE has made special efforts to bring the concept of comprehensive arts to the smallest as well as the largest school systems throughout the state. This is a costly and complex task, and there are no easy answers as to how to accomplish the mission successfully.

One means that has been tried is a touring arts group. The Players, sponsored by SACO, toured for 13 weeks giving assemblies, classroom presentations, and workshops in various arts. "We were sharing our art form with people who had never seen a live performance or knew what one was," recalls Beth Shumway, a dancer with the group. Performing in Yarbrough, a town that isn't even on the map with a school that enrolls about 100 children, kindergarden through twelfth grade, "was like being an ambassador in a semi-foreign country," Shumway says. "They don't even have movie theaters in these towns."

SDE administrators agree that the most logical approach to getting the arts into rural schools is through inservice education. Dr. John Moseley, Director of Secondary Education, says, "In rural schools we must rely upon the classroom teacher. However, we must provide them with assistance." He suggests itinerant artists and arts specialists, but, he says, "even this is costly."

Perhaps the most impressive realization of what can be done is a Title IV-C Project, "Arts Resource Team Services," operating on about $100,000 a year, in the extreme southeastern corner of the state. The project, which is going into its third year, covers 77 schools in seven counties in an area that is sparsely populated and marked by poverty. The largest city in these counties is McAlester with under 20,000 population. All other towns are 10,000 or less. Apathy toward the schools is rampant. Only about two of the schools even have a Parent-Teachers Association.

This project has provided the schools with arts resource specialists who function as arts coordinators and resource teachers. Melinda Lucas, whose code name on her CB radio is "Hopalong," is one of these specialists. She is assigned to a three-county area and hopalong she does, traveling about 1,000 miles each week to visit the various small schools in her region.

Lucas has organized four arts tours in her first two years, bringing artists from the University of Oklahoma in Norman to give performances and workshops for students and teachers. "To get the arts into the rural area," she says, "you have to pack them up and truck them around." She makes guides for

194

the teachers, so that they can tie these arts experiences into their classroom work through preparation and follow-up. Expenses for the tours are paid by the grant. The schools feed the artists and arrange for housing them in the community.

Persuasion is Lucas' main stock in trade. She succeeded in getting several schools to pay for a visiting poet. In addition to the tours, she arranges for visiting artists of all kinds to spend time in these schools. She also holds workshops in the arts for classroom teachers. But there are problems. "Have you ever tried to listen to Mozart in a gym?" she asks. "The people live in this great open countryside, but they don't think of environment. Can you imagine taking a square block of Harlem and putting it in one of the cow pastures?"

The project itself has suffered because of the turnover in the arts resource specialists. Lucas is the only one of five that has lasted during each of the first two years. But there have been successes. In Ft. Towson School District (population 430) an arts team has been organized to get the arts into the schools. They hired a vocal music teacher for the 1977-78 school year and an art teacher for 1978-79. Doye Day, Superintendent of Schools, remarks that, "After this school has been here for some 90 years, we finally had some school songs." He says, "The seeds are planted for incorporating the arts into the subject matter, but a limited number of teachers have used it."

The entire faculty traveled 30 miles to attend a four-hour arts workshop, with one hour devoted to drama, one to music, one to visual arts, and one integrating all the arts. "It was well-organized and efficiently run, and they made it comfortable for us to participate," Day says.

Prior to this workshop, the faculty was released an hour early one day for an awareness workshop conducted by Lucas. She then did a series of three workshops for the elementary teachers and has conducted a number of demonstration classes. For six weeks, a visiting folk artist taught the teachers and students guitar, banjo, dulcimer, and other folk arts. "Now," Day says, "we are adding the local ethnic arts to the curriculum—weaving, basket making, pottery, and bead work." Arts and crafts programs are being added to the adult education program at night and on weekends. "We have community support," Day says. Another visiting artist taught oil painting. "I started doing oils myself," Day reveals. "I've now painted four 'masterpieces' and am working on my fifth!"

David Gentry, the high school principal in Ft. Towson, speaks with genuine enthusiasm about the effects of the new arts activities. "There is more school spirit. The kids have rallied around it. We have added a creative writing class this coming year. Speech and drama were added last year. This is the first year that the whole eighth grade class sang a song of their choice at their graduation exercises. Students have begun to participate better. Two years ago, the only school outlet was basketball before and after school."

Lucas' work with the administrators and teachers and her entourage of visiting artists have literally turned the school 195

Have you ever tried to listen to Mozart in a gym? The people live in this great open countryside, but they don't think of environment.

around. The administrators acknowledge what a difference having an arts resource person has made. "Have you ever tried to say 'no' to Melinda?" Day asks with a wry smile. They have been sold on the arts, and they know it. A teacher in Idabel, another of Lucas' school districts, says: "Melinda, you come by just often enough to give us the shot in the arm we need."

But it seems obvious that few people can do what Lucas does. She confronts stone walls every day and has been remarkably successful at eradicating them. She has learned to be as astute at visual arts, dance, and theater as at music, which is her major subject of expertise. Being originally from the area has helped. She understands the people and knows how to talk their language. Yet much remains to be done, not only in her three counties, but in all the rural schools of the state. There simply aren't enough Lucases to go around and not enough funds to support them.

Evaluation

During the spring of 1978, nine status review teams visited school demonstration centers and systematically evaluated these programs. The teams, appointed by the SDE's arts co-ordinators, were composed of as many as 16 people. They spent one full day observing the strengths of the programs, assessing needs, and studying the involvement of the school staff—the faculty, arts specialists, administrators, and the arts coordinator. They looked at school management—the work of the Arts Planning Team, the use of community resources, and the commitment of the school district to the program. They commented upon the extent the project was being docu-mented, the kind of in-school evaluation that was being used, and the efforts at public relations. The schools were also asked to profile themselves.

Joe Bob Weaver, a math specialist in the SDE who served on one of the status review teams, notes that, "The role of the principal in asserting leadership is crucial. Some could be stron-ger in getting the in-school arts planning team together and moving." He observed that, "Some teachers are reluctant to try anything new. They make it tough on those who do. They throw a bucket of cold water over the innovators."

"Where the program worked," Weaver says, "I saw ex-citement among students and teachers. The affective area was being taken advantage of. One of the strong points is the integration that ensues in place of isolation. This approach might preclude arts people becoming so involved in their own bailiwick that they negate everything else." He sees the process as helping math. "There is a natural affinity between math and the arts. It is important," he maintains, "to show how math is applied to other areas such as geometric design and perspec-tive."

Status reviews were compiled and presented to each school. The purpose of the review is to provide a mechanism for self study to help the schools determine their own progress. The results establish the feasibility of each school's continued participation as a demonstration center.

In addition to this yearly assessment, there is an elaborate attempt to develop a system for on-going evaluation. Dr. Gladys Dronberger, Assistant Administrator for Planning, Research, and Evaluation with the SDE, has worked closely with the Arts in Education Project to develop and test possible approaches that might be used to assess the effect of these programs on students, administrators, and teachers. She has developed a number of attitudinal instruments based upon Robert Stake's approach.[4]

Dronberger admits, "As far as I'm concerned, we are just starting. We're measuring student, teacher, and administrative change. We've developed instruments for students to evaluate their experience with an artist in schools, and for teachers and principals to measure what they think makes a good artist in residence. Refining instrumentation and cutting it down to manageable size is our problem at present."

She believes that, "The program needs a full-time evaluator, control groups, and closer attention to achievement test scores to determine if an ingestion of the arts has an effect on vandalism, student and faculty absenteeism, and failure. Unfortunately," she says, "people would rather be involved with doing the project than be bothered with evaluation."

Much remains to be done in the area of assessment, if concrete proof can be assembled to prove conclusively what are now vague and totally subjective notions about the educational effect of these efforts. Some hard data is needed to sell the approach to non-believers. Such information is one more way to persuade the skeptics—those reluctant and resistent teachers and administrators who lack any personal knowledge of the arts.

The program needs a full-time evaluator, control groups, and closer attention to achievement test scores. Unfortunately, people would rather be involved with doing the project than be bothered with evaluation.

Problems

Like any attempt to change schools on such a vast scale, the project has faced a number of problems:

(1) *Demonstration School Failures.* Of the five demonstration schools set up during the 1975-76 school year, two dropped out during the second year.[5] In both cases the problem boiled down to a lack of communication. In one of these situations, the arts planning team had opposition from the rest of the faculty. A group of older, traditional teachers were not represented on the team. They were not certain that "entertainment," as they called it, has any place in the classroom.

[4]Robert Stake, *Evaluating the Arts in Education: A Responsive Approach* (Columbus, Ohio: Charles E. Merrill Publishing Company, 1975).

[5]During the second year, four more schools were added making a total of eight elementary and one junior high. At the end of the year, six elementary schools and one junior high were left. Five additional junior highs were added during the third year.

197

The first grade teacher who was chairman of the arts planning team explained that, "While some teachers felt left out, others felt put down. The latter group have always used the arts in their classrooms. They said, in effect, 'I've been doing this for years, now you come along and tell me to do it your way.' They resented being told to do what they felt they were already doing. The project became divisive." Apparently, the principal of the school felt the arts team was intimidating the other faculty.

The turnover of arts coordinators did not help. This caused a lack of continuity and expectations. One of these arts coordinators was heavy-handed and, rather than acting as a facilitator and demonstrator, attempted to usurp the administration of the project from the teachers. The teachers resisted being supervised. Then, too, the school adopted a new reading series and many teachers felt bogged down. They were under considerable pressure, some of it induced by their own peers. They felt they couldn't afford the extra time the arts require.

The arts planning team itself did not function cohesively. The music teacher, who was a member of the team, never attended the meetings. Three or four of the seven members usually went, but they failed to carry decisions to the entire faculty for their approval.

The status review team visited the school in May 1978, and they were objective in noting what they saw. The faculty did not take kindly to what they perceived as negative criticism. The faculty voted 13 to 3 to end the project. Even most of the arts planning team voted the program down along with the rest of the faculty.

According to the arts coordinator who worked with this program in its final days, there was a need for more staff development prior to the beginning of the project. The SDE has now tightened its screening process to assure that there is strong in-school commitment prior to designating a school as a demonstration site.

In the case of the other school that dropped out of the project, the principal there did not get involved until too late. In this situation, an upper-level administrator attempted to implement the program without asking principals to participate in workshops where their understanding and commitment could have been developed. Consequently, the program was implemented haphazardly and sporadically, and it received a poor ranking in the status review, so poor that they voluntarily withdrew from the program.

(2) *Improving the Arts Coordinators.* In one school where an artist/coordinator did not work out, the principal described the situation this way: "The arts coordinator was killing our enthusiasm. He didn't schedule himself properly and would fail to show up. He scheduled visiting artists poorly. He didn't work with teachers well. He didn't prepare. As an introvert, he didn't feel comfortable with kids. His concept of elementary art and control were inadequate." To be successful in this role, artists need to understand education. Fortunately, the in-school arts

planning teams now are part of the screening process for selecting their arts coordinator, and the SDE has scheduled two pre-school workshops, one in June another in August, to orient the coordinators. Additional meetings are held throughout the year.

Of the six arts coordinators selected for the school year beginning in September 1979, two are classroom teachers who have some arts training, one was an arts coordinator the year before, another is Melinda Lucas from the Region X arts project discussed earlier, and both of the other two have had public school teaching, although they are practicing artists. The selection process was a more careful one that sought people with coordinating skills. Administrators and teachers from the demonstration districts made the final selection. The background of these six arts coordinators is more comprehensive than before, and they have a clear understanding of the school environment.

In order to assure that the coordinators and others connected with the program get off to a firm start, a two-day workshop was held in June 1979 for orientation and planning. This will be followed by a five-day planning workshop in early August for arts planning teams, arts coordinators, principals, and district-level coordinators from the 26 demonstration and satellite schools. Obviously, much progress has been made in making certain that coordinators deliver quality services.

(3) *Moving into the Secondary Schools.* So far, the arts in basic education program has concentrated on the elementary school level. With the exception of one junior high school, all the demonstration schools during the first two years were elementary. However, another five demonstration sites were added during the 1978-79 school year making a separate network of six elementary and six junior high schools. What will these secondary-school programs look like?

Long says, "We anticipate a project approach, where arts people will work on a particular curriculum unit of study in conjunction with individual subject-matter areas." Because of the structure of the curriculum and the autonomy of the various subject matters, getting the arts in these classrooms is difficult. These schools will not have arts coordinators like the elementary demonstration schools. But they will have access to the Artists-in-Residence Program, community resources, and technical assistance from the SDE. Each school will have an arts planning team, and these have met prior to school opening.

"Our hope," Long says, "is that principals will begin to view the arts specialist as a resource person and free up some time for planning, demonstration, and other activities. We're talking about more effective use of the time of these specialists and not having them just concentrate on the most talented students holding festivals, attending contests, or entering exhibits. Where schools are committed to students being involved in the process of the arts, schedules and curricula in the arts will change. Arts specialists must redefine their role in the schools themselves."

(4) *The Replication of Model Programs.* Long and Mohr ex-

Our hope is that principals will begin to view the arts specialist as a resource person and free up some time for planning, demonstration, and other activities. We're talking about more effective use of the time of these specialists and not having them just concentrate on the most talented students.

If you set up a quality program that focuses on improving general education, administrators and classroom teachers will respond to invitations to attend arts conferences and workshops.

press some uncertainty as to how model programs can be replicated in new districts. The networking process is a constant and long-term concern. They continue to hold workshops and inservice programs and have brought people from the demonstration schools out to other schools to work with teachers and administrators. The SDE has produced a number of publications to advance the idea and have plans to produce more. At the same time, Long says, "We've never said that this program should touch every school. It is up to each individual school to make the commitment, because we are talking about total school change. This doesn't mean we do not try to sensitize schools to the possibilities. We are not interested in imposing this approach on school systems."

(5) *Effective Use of Artists.* Both Long and Mohr are interested in making artists' residencies more effective. This is going to take additional cooperative planning with the State Arts Council of Oklahoma. Schools, too, need further assistance in order to reap the full benefit of visiting artists.

(6) *Improving the Quality of Arts Experiences.* Even in the demonstration schools, there is a need to upgrade the quality of the arts experiences. These are often early attempts by classroom teachers that, in some cases, are aesthetically and artistically naive. Greater depth can only come through more study and better arts experiences on the part of the teachers. Inservice workshops must continue to educate the teachers in the various arts so that their understanding is increased dramatically.

(7) *Improving Arts Offerings in College and University Teacher Education Programs.* While the SDE has sponsored meetings of college and university personnel, much remains to be done. Long and Mohr have met with the dean of education at the University of Oklahoma, and he is trying to make changes. A meeting with their methods teachers resulted in a comprehensive arts course designed initially for graduate students. All of the deans of education, some heads of fine arts departments, and many methods teachers were brought together by the SDE to introduce them to the concept. "Pockets of change are happening in some post-secondary institutions depending on the people," Mohr says.

In Cameron State University the visual arts department is sponsoring a program of arts for children. Students at the university inservice teachers and prepare children for the encounters with the arts and also follow up the experience in the schools.

Oklahoma City University has a CEMREL Demonstration Center, and teachers around the state have been encouraged to use the facility.

In February of 1979, two workshops were held for methods teachers in arts and in education from the twenty state universities in Oklahoma that prepare teachers. Thirty-five teachers from 11 universities attended the one-day workshops, where the arts in education philosophy was presented through a slide/tape show and a panel of teachers and administrators from the demonstration schools. The response was enthusiastic.

Because of their interest in continuing this kind of dialogue and exchange, a "Higher Education Council for the Arts in Education" will be formed next year with two representatives from each university. The Council will examine the implications of arts in education on teacher preparation programs and determine the role of arts courses in this preparation. The year will be culminated with a statewide conference in the spring of 1980. This project will be coordinated through the Oklahoma Alliance for Arts Education with funding from the national AAE office.

Overview

There is no question that what is happening in the state of Oklahoma is extraordinary. Through the tireless efforts of Long and Mohr and the cooperative help they have enlisted from innumerable sources, the arts are assuming new status in basic education. As Long says, "If you set up a quality program that focuses on improving general education, administrators and classroom teachers will respond to invitations to attend conferences and workshops."

Administrators around the state who know the approach speak highly of it. Ron Jarvis, Principal of Western Hills Elementary School in Lawton, one of the demonstration schools, says unhesitatingly, "School attitudes and discipline have improved. We have developed more pride and appreciation of other people." Rod Mastin, Principal of Pioneer Park Elementary School in Lawton, a school that has adopted the program, notes that, "Every year I've had broken windows and break-ins. Not this year. What students learn to appreciate, they don't destroy. Students are enjoying school more. This is a way to increase attendance and develop pride in the school."

Through careful planning at the state department level, school board members, curriculum coordinators, and many other key educational people have been won over as supporters of the comprehensive approach. Persuasion has been unrelenting and by no means accidental. Long and Mohr use three words to describe their approach: *awareness*, referring to building understanding; *intentionality*, meaning that little happens that isn't planned for; and *collaboration*, implying the establishment of commitment and involvement. Drawing upon a line from *The Little Prince*, Fisher says, "You have to 'gentle' them with the arts."

Of course, ingrained attitudes and values die hard, and much remains to be accomplished in Oklahoma. Many administrators and classroom teachers do not readily see the relationship between the arts and learning experiences. But in a very brief time, the gains already made throughout the state are nothing short of remarkable.

Every year I've had broken windows and break-ins. Not this year. What students learn to appreciate, they don't destroy. Students are enjoying school more. This is a way to increase attendance and develop pride in the school.

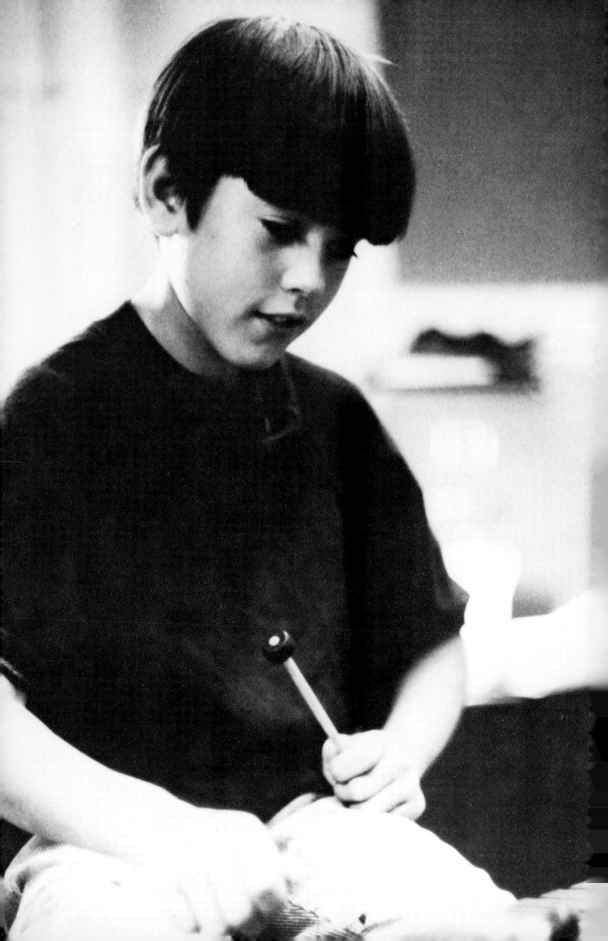

CHAPTER NINE
The Unfinished Task

Kathryn Bloom

Over the past 12 years the JDR 3rd Fund's Arts in Education Program has been in the vanguard of the arts in education movement, but it has by no means operated in isolation from or independent of other major national efforts. Beginning in the early Sixties a number of developments have served to encourage a favorable climate and more positive attitudes toward the values of the arts in education of every child. Among them are the following:

1. In 1963, the U.S. Office of Education established the Arts and Humanities Program, the first program at the federal level created specifically to meet the needs of the arts in education.

2. In 1965, the Elementary and Secondary Education Act was passed. During the next three or four years, hundreds of millions of dollars underwrote the costs of arts programs, mainly of a cultural enrichment nature, in school systems nationally.

3. In 1967, the first steps were taken to establish the Arts   203

The arts are increasingly being given parity with other subjects of instruction and comprehensive arts in education programs are being supported by tax levy and other public and private funds.

in Education Program of the JDR 3rd Fund. Pilot and related projects were begun in 1968 and 1969.

4. Two years later the U.S. Office of Education established and underwrote most of the costs for Project IMPACT (Interdisciplinary Model Programs in the Arts for Children and Teachers), a two-year arts in education project located in five schools and school systems nationally. This project, which had notable success and captured considerable attention among educators, attempted to place the arts at the core of general education.

5. In 1967, CEMREL's Aesthetic Education Program began to develop a series of carefully planned and field-tested instructional units in various arts disciplines for use in the elementary schools. More recently, CEMREL has established a number of Aesthetic Learning Centers that provide a variety of services to the school systems in which they are located.

6. In 1965, the National Arts and Humanities Foundation Act was passed. This created the National Endowment for the Arts and the National Endowment for the Humanities, both of which have supported educational programs in the arts. Of particular significance nationally is the Arts Endowment's Artists-in-Schools Program, started in 1968, which has placed artists and performers in school systems in all 50 states and five special jursidictions.

7. In 1972, the Alliance for Arts Education was established under the aegis of the John F. Kennedy Center for the Performing Arts and the U.S. Office of Education, and AAE has continued to administer a national and local program for the arts in education. Also operating under the umbrella of the Kennedy Center is the National Committee, Arts for the Handicapped, with Office of Education support.

8. For several years, the U.S. Office of Education has awarded planning grants of up to $10,000 to state education departments and school systems for planning and development of arts education programs. While these grants have not been large, they have had a catalytic effect in stimulating broad national interest. Beginning in the 1979-80 school year, this program introduced "saturation" grants of up to $50,000 for projects in selected urban, suburban, and rural school districts.

9. When federal support was first given to arts in education efforts, the four professional associations representing education in the visual arts, music, theater, and dance banded together to support activities initiated within the individual associations, as well as cooperating with the U.S. Office of Education and the Alliance for Arts Education. More recently, a larger umbrella organization has been formed, the Assembly of National Arts Education Associations, which is concerned primarily with advocacy, policymaking, and legislation.

10. In 1977, *Coming to Our Senses*, a panel report on the significance of the arts for American education chaired by David Rockefeller, Jr., was published. It surveyed the status of the arts in education and made a large number of recommendations. The report continues to play a significant role in increas-

ing public awareness and providing an impetus for advocacy. In direct response to the report, the organization Arts, Education and Americans, Inc. was formed to continue these efforts nationally.

11. The Gifted and Talented Program and the Emergency School Aid Act administered by the U.S. Office of Education, as well as CETA (the Comprehensive Employment and Training Act of the U.S. Department of Labor) have played an important role in advancing the arts in education concept. Currently, the Educational Testing Service is planning a program, entitled National Arts Awards, to provide recognition for artistically gifted students in the nation's schools.

As the arts begin to demonstrate their value in meeting broad educational goals, they also begin to make a much stronger case for their own intrinsic value to schooling.

The contribution to the field of the JDR 3rd Fund's Arts in Education Program must of course be viewed in this larger context. It is clear that no one program, by itself, could create the kind of favorable climate that exists today, a climate that seems to encourage maintenance of on-going efforts and the initiation of new activities. Within this context, however, it is important to mention some of the aspects of the Fund's work which appear to have been significant and influential:

1. The fact that arts in education pilot projects were established eleven years ago helped move an idea that had been around for some time from rhetoric and theory to operating reality in school systems and state education agencies. These agencies have served as reference points and sources of information to a very broad public.

2. With the emergence of an acceptable rationale and an organized approach to program planning and development, more policy decisions have been made in favor of the arts. The arts are increasingly being given parity with other subjects of instruction and comprehensive arts in education programs are being supported by tax levy and other public and private funds. In addition, these programs seem to be demonstrating a remarkable staying power in times of social stress and financial crisis.

3. As the arts begin to demonstrate their value in meeting broad educational goals, they also begin to make a much stronger case for their own intrinsic value to schooling.

4. Demonstration projects in school systems have proved to be the means for developing and refining rather sophisticated programs. State education departments have proved to offer one mechanism for extending the concept to a very large number of school systems. Networking and collaboration appear to be key strategies in this process.

While the future of the arts in education movement looks relatively bright, in our judgment there are still some nagging questions that remain to be addressed. Some of them are:

1. There is the eternal and difficult problem of quality versus quantity. As programs multiply in number, does this necessarily mean that quality will suffer?

2. How will needs for training be addressed? What are the 205

most effective approaches for classroom teachers? For specialists? For administrators? For artists and arts organization personnel? Who should or will take on this task?

3. In order for teachers in any field to be employed by school systems as full-time salaried faculty members, they must meet certification requirements that are mandated on a state-by-state basis. Very few state education departments have certification requirements in any disciplines of the arts except art and music. Establishing certification requirements is a lengthy and difficult process. Will state departments move in this direction? Who will spur them? Help them?

4. Just what does the term "interdisciplinary" mean in the arts in education concept? Who will define it and suggest effective practices for the elementary, secondary, and college levels?

5. The installation of "comprehensive arts in education programs" prompts the need for, among other things, change in the content of teaching. Many people believe that a program is not "comprehensive" unless there is a scope and sequence for arts instruction. This could be interpreted to mean that every student, kindergarten through twelfth grade, should receive continuous and sequential instruction, grade by grade, in art, music, theater, dance, filmmaking, and all other art forms. This would be equivalent to (and as impractical as) insisting that every student receive thirteen years of continuous and sequential instruction in mathematics or chemistry. Where are the individuals and institutions that will come to grips with this issue and explore its implications?

6. Experience shows that arts councils at the state and local levels can coordinate the educational programs and services to schools offered by their constituent cultural institutions. Such coordination can be cost-effective, avoid duplication of efforts, and result in important benefits to all parties. Are arts councils ready to assume this responsibility?

7. The programmatic work that has been done over the last 15 or so years has never been adequately documented. The published material on the arts in education, especially on the operational level, is inadequate. The information and material that do exist literally cry out for research and evaluation efforts that will scrutinize and assess the impact of these programs on schooling, on the community, and on all the practitioners. Who will undertake this awesome but essential task?

8. While there is more money available to support the arts in education, the sum is still insufficient and often undependable to insure the dissemination and adoption of the concept on a broader national scale. Who will take the lead and the long-term responsibility for identifying and seeing that funds are made available, regularly and over time? Is this a task for national agencies? State? Local? All?

These few examples help to illustrate the challenge to be faced and are intended to stimulate further questions and initiatives. From the viewpoint of the JDR 3rd Fund, finding answers to these questions is the unfinished task that lies ahead.

APPENDIX A
Grants and Related Support Provided by the JDR 3rd Fund's Arts in Education Program, 1968-1979

Beginning in fiscal year 1968 and continuing for each succeeding fiscal year, allocations for support of the activities of the Arts in Education Programs have been $500,000 a year for a total of almost $5,500,000 by the end of fiscal year 1979.

During the Program's first steps and the several years that followed, grants were appropriated to support arts in education projects and programs, since school districts and state departments were being invited to try out an idea that had never been tested before. However, great care was taken to insure substantial financial involvement by the grantee institutions, as well as a commitment to assume the support of successful undertakings at the end of grant periods.

When the landmark decision was made in 1973 that the New York City/JDR 3rd Fund Arts in General Education Program should have parity with other subjects of study and therefore should be supported with board of education and other public and private funds, the Fund began to use this same approach with other school districts and state education departments. Gradually, grantmaking for a program here and a project there was phased out. Instead, dissemination monies, which could be used at the director's discretion, were employed to support the activities of the League of Cities and the Ad Hoc Coalition of States. Grants, when they were made, were for efforts that would benefit either or both networks, not just one or two member institutions. An example of the latter are the appropriations made for the JDR 3rd Administrative Fellowship Training Program which enabled each school district and state department in the two networks to appoint fellows during the 1977-78 and 1978-79 school years.

Funds appropriated and expended for grants from fiscal year 1968 through 1979 totaled $2,571,069. Dissemination (discretionary) funds appropriated and expended in this same eleven-year period total $453,812. These sums together total $3,024,881. Approximately 60 percent of allocations were used for administrative costs. However, since the Fund was an operating foundation, the Program's staff members played an active role as consultants and technical experts. This staff time, considered in the nature of grants, substantially reduces actual operating costs.

GRANTS AND RELATED SUPPORT
PROVIDED BY
THE ARTS IN EDUCATION PROGRAM
1968-1979

Grant to the School District of University City, Missouri for support of the Arts in General Education Project. This was the first pilot project supported by the JDR 3rd Fund to test the feasibility of making all the arts integral to the education of every child in an entire school system. $346,400 for a five-year period from May 1, 1968 to June 30, 1973.

Grant to the St. Louis Art Museum to develop educational services to complement the University City Arts in General Education Project. $14,000 for a one-year period from August 15, 1968 to August 14, 1969.

Grant to CEMREL (Central Midwestern Regional Educational Laboratory), St. Louis, Missouri, to evaluate the University City Arts in General Education Project. $110,200 for a three-year period from July 1, 1969 to June 30, 1972.

Grant to The Museum of Modern Art to assist with planning and developmental work to create the Children's Art Caravan, a mobile version of the Children's Art Carnival. $35,000 for a year and a half during the period from June 1, 1963 to March 31, 1972.

Grant to the Bank Street College of Education to support the project, The Development of An Integrated Program of the Arts and Humanities for Children in an Urban Community, carried on in Public School 51 in New York City. This was the second pilot project supported by the JDR 3rd Fund. Approximately $150,000 for a three-year period from September 1, 1968 to August 31, 1971. A second grant of $23,000 to Bank Street College to evaluate the pilot project during a one-year period from September 4, 1969 to September 4, 1970.

Grant to the Bank Street College of Education to support the project, Development of Arts Leadership Teams, an In-Service Training Program for Integrating the Arts into the School Curriculum. This project was an outgrowth of the pilot project at Public School 51. $46,000 for an eighteen-month period from September 15, 1971 to March 31, 1973.

Grant to the Mineola, Long Island, Public Schools for the project, The Improvement and Integration of the Fine Arts Program into the Curriculum of the Mineola Public Schools. This was the third pilot project supported by the Fund. $361,250 for a five-year period from July 1, 1969 to June 30, 1974.

Grant to the Union Free School District No. 5 (Town of Rye), Port Chester, New York for the project, Developing the Program and Facility for a High School with Special Emphasis in the Arts and Humanities for All its Students. Approximately $113,600 for a three-year period from August 1, 1969 to July 31, 1972.

Grant to Educational System for the Seventies to support a project, Arts Curriculum Development Project for ES'70. In-kind services in the amount of approximately $31,500 were provided to ES'70 for office space, supplies, and equipment for a one-year period from October 15, 1969 to October 14, 1970.

Grant to the College Entrance Examination Board to inaugurate Advanced Placement in Studio Art, Art History, and Music. $200,000 for a two and one-half year period from March 1, 1970 to August 31, 1972.

Grant of $7,500 to New York University to support a graduate internship in the JDR 3rd Fund office. $7,500 for a one-year period from September 1, 1969 to August 31, 1970.

Grant to Carnegie-Mellon University for a graduate internship at CEMREL in St. Louis to assist with the University City Arts in General Education Project. $6,000 for a one-year period from June 1, 1970 to May 31, 1971.

Grant to the Lane Intermediate Education District, Eugene, Oregon to support A Program for the Improvement of Art Education in the Elementary Schools of Lane County. $16,000 for a one-year period from May 15, 1970 to May 14, 1971.

Grant to the University of Oregon to continue the project in the Elementary Schools of Lane County. $12,000 for a one-year period from July 1, 1971 to June 30, 1972.

Grant to John Adams High School, Portland, Oregon for developing the arts in general education in an experimental high school. $54,500 for approximately three years during a period from February 15, 1971 to June 30, 1974.

Grant to the Baldwin School of Puerto Rico to develop an integrated arts curriculum. $36,000 for a year and one-half from February 1, 1972 to June 30, 1973.

Grant to the Jefferson County Public Schools, Lakewood, Colorado to incorporate the arts in general education into an interdisciplinary curriculum. Approximately $282,500 for a five-year period from October 15, 1971 to August 31, 1976.

Grant to the New York City Board of Education—Community District 2 to assist in the development of a new experimental elementary school, Public School 3-M in which the arts were to be made central to the school curriculum. Approximately $50,750 for a two-year period from September 1, 1971 to August 31, 1973.

Grant to the Arts Council of Oklahoma City to implement the Creative Education Program and, particularly, Opening Doors, in the Oklahoma City Public Schools. $113,400 for a four and one-half year period from February 1, 1972 to July 31, 1976.

Grant to assist the New York State Department of Education to implement Project SEARCH, which was initiated to establish an integrated humanities and arts program in six public school districts and one parochial school. $194,000 during approximately five years from June 1, 1972 to April 30, 1977.

Grant to the Pennsylvania Department of Education to assist with the planning and implementation of a state-wide arts in basic education program. $62,000 during a three and one-half year period from June 1, 1972 to October 14, 1976.

Grant jointly to the Asia Society and CEMREL for a pilot project to develop teaching materials in Asian arts for classroom use. $17,000 for a six-month period from February 1, 1973 to July 31, 1973.

Grant to the Education Development Center, Newton, Massachusetts to plan to develop educational television programming based on concepts common to science, technology, mathematics, and the arts which led to the educational television series, "The Infinity Factory." $13,700 for a three-month period from February 1, 1973 to April 30, 1973.

Grant to the Research Division of the Institute for the Development of Educational Activities, Los Angeles, California to support A Study of the Arts in Precollegiate Education. Approximately $80,200 for a four-year period from September 1, 1973 to August 31, 1974.

Grant to the Ridgewood, New Jersey, Public Schools to develop a project in aesthetic education. $12,000 for a three-month period from June 1, 1973 to August 31, 1973.

Grant to the Boston Metropolitan Cultural Alliance to assist in planning for an arts in education program for the Boston Public Schools. $12,500 for a one-year period from October 15, 1973 to October 14, 1974.

Grant to the National Association of State Boards of Education to conduct a Survey of Arts in Education Policies of State Boards of Education. $5,500 for a six-month period from October 15, 1977 to April 15, 1977.

Grants to each of the six school districts in the League of Cities and the nine state education departments in the Ad Hoc Coalition of States for the Arts in Education to support the JDR 3rd Fund Administrative Fellowship Training Program. $5,000 each, or a total of $75,000 was appropriated for five-month fellowships beginning January 3, 1978 and ending August 31, 1978, and $6,000 each, or a total of $90,000 was awarded for fellowships ranging up to one year beginning July 1, 1978 and ending September 1, 1979.

APPENDIX B
Considerations for School Systems Contemplating a Comprehensive Arts in General Education Program

Jane Remer

During its 12-year history, the JDR 3rd Fund's Arts in Education Program worked on a relatively modest annual budget with a number of carefully-selected school systems, state departments of education, and others concerned with quality education. The Fund's main purpose was to explore ways in which all the arts can become a vital part of the daily teaching and learning process of all children and youth in entire schools and school systems.

The Fund's earlier experience was mainly with small school districts, most of which are maintaining their programs today. From this experience, many answers to the questions, "why the arts in general education?" and "how do you make them an integral part of the life of a school and one of the priorities of the district?" have emerged. The lessons learned have been invaluable, and the knowledge gained has been applied to the Fund's subsequent programmatic efforts.

Recently, the Fund has concentrated on the coordination of two national networks: The Ad Hoc Coalition of States for the Arts in Education and the League of Cities for the Arts in Education. This paper is concerned with the League, its programs, and the way those programs were organized and implemented.

The League of Cities was formed in April 1976 with members representing school districts in Hartford, Little Rock, Minneapolis, New York City, Seattle, and Winston-Salem. These six school systems, each of which had a two- to four-year-old partnership with the Fund, decided to form a network to share information and exchange ideas on ways to develop comprehensive arts in general education programs in their own locales. Members felt that a common effort would accelerate individual progress and also provide a bank of knowledge, information, and experience to other school systems contemplating similar efforts.

The members of the League share a common goal and are following a similar course to reach it. The process, originated in New York City, has been adapted to suit the needs and conditions in the other sites. In these programs, the arts are considered worthwhile in and of themselves, as tools for living and learning, and as vehicles for the process of school change and development.

The Fund has received numerous requests for information about the programs now underway in the League. What people seem to want is a rationale for the arts, a definition of a comprehensive arts in general education program, and some guidelines for establishing similar programs in their own communities.

A rationale for the arts in general education and a definition of comprehensive programs are fairly well-established (and can be found in the Appendices along with other resource and reference materials). Telling people how these programs work, however, is more difficult. But they do work, and it is in keeping with the League's Mission Statement to share what it has learned.

This paper attempts to reflect a composite of the Fund's experience with the League. Its main focus is on "how to" rather than "why," and it stresses processes and strategies that have been found to be effective in different urban settings. It is hoped that the League's approach will have meaning for other people and relevance to other school districts that are interested in "all the arts for all the children" and in school- and system-wide change.

Some Outcomes That Can Be Anticipated

When the arts and the arts process are linked with a systematic and orderly process for school change and development, the following outcomes can be observed:

• Learning in the "basics" is not jeopardized; it tends to be strengthened.

- Attitudes toward school and schooling improve, as does attendance for both students and teachers.
- Morale climbs, and the sense of personal isolation diminishes. People feel better about themselves, start to work together, and come up with creative solutions to traditionally difficult problems.
- Better and more varied programs in the arts and in arts-enlivened curricular areas tend to attract certain segments of the population who are wary of public education.
- Arts in general education programs tend to stimulate increased interest, support, and involvement of the local and general community in its schools, and vice versa. This is especially true of parents as well as arts and cultural organizations.
- The model process for comprehensive school and system change through networking and collaboration (which is the basis for the League's arts in general education programs) seems to have relevance for similar efforts in career, environmental, and special education.
- Financial, material, and human resources are used in more effective ways; existing resources that were untapped or unrecognized are marshalled to support on-going programs.

The Program and the Process

The basic conviction that underlies all League programs is that all the arts are integral to the education of all children, because they can make an important contribution to the daily schooling process, kindergarten through high school, throughout entire school systems.

The hypothesis is that the quality of education and equality of educational opportunity can improve when:

1. The arts are related to each other and to other disciplines;

2. Quality programs in all the arts are available to all the children;

3. The community's artists and its arts and cultural resources are used regularly in and out of the school building;

4. Special needs of special children (the gifted and talented, the handicapped, the bilingual) are met by the arts and through participation in creative activities; and

5. The arts are used to create learning situations that help reduce personal and racial isolation and increase self-esteem.

This hypothesis is both fluid and flexible. The above five points often appear as the main objectives or characteristics of League programs in proposals for funding or other descriptive materials.

The strategies being devised to test this hypothesis are derived from a theory of educational change that regards the individual school as the most effective social unit for self-renewal and change, because it is the smallest, yet most complete setting in which formal schooling takes place on a contin- 217 uum. According to this theory, the principal can be both a creative educational leader and an effective social engineer, when he or she works closely with staff, children, parents, and community on programs that gradually and systematically translate the school's educational philosophy into daily reality. It is assumed that, when those who have a stake in the consequences reach important decisions through a continuing round of dialogue, decision-making, action, and evaluation of issues and problems, benefits can accrue to the total school community and especially the children.

Schools, however, cannot go it alone if they wish to make fundamental, comprehensive, and enduring changes in their structure and operation. They need the support of other schools, the school district, the community, and other local, state, and national resources. The means for securing this support is through collaborative action.

Thus, a network of schools committed to the same philosophical approach is formed. This network is supported by a "hub" (a person or a team of people) that coordinates its activities, seeks out and secures needed resources, and provides technical and consulting assistance.

Once a group of schools successfully demonstrates the effectiveness of a new idea or approach, other schools in the system can be encouraged to visit them to determine whether they wish to follow a similar course. Eventually, given proper support and recognition, a significant number, or a "critical mass" of improved schools develops. These schools are now theoretically in a position to help "tip" or influence the rest of the system in beneficial ways. At the very least, schooling will have improved in a significant number of buildings for a significant number of children. At best, model programs, practices, and processes will be available for inspection and adaptation, in whole or in part, by the remainder of the system.

The League experience is too brief to make any definitive observations about the "critical mass" portion of this change theory. Besides, in school systems that range in size from 30 to over 900 school buildings, the notion of "mass" is relative. Time alone will tell whether and to what degree the model process now being developed has an impact upon a large segment or even the entire population of a school system. Meanwhile, we do know that with networking and collaboration individual school change and development through the arts can and does occur, under certain conditions.

Under Certain Conditions

Experience with the League (and with other comprehensive arts in education programs during the past decade) has begun to reveal the circumstances under which programs of this nature develop, thrive, and survive. Following are a series of questions which might be considered before a school system decides to embark on a program. It is also useful to refer to them periodically during the planning, development, and expansion process in order to determine the rate and nature of progress being made.

1. Are the school system and the community relatively stable and yet resilient enough to respond to change?

2. Is there (or is there likely to be) evidence of continuing top-level leadership and support for the concept of a comprehensive arts in general education program?

3. What support is there likely to be from among parents, the arts and education communities, volunteer and civic groups, unions, professional associations, business and industry, local and state legislators?

4. Is the notion of partnership—to plan, implement, fund—accepted by those who will be involved?

5. Have there been discussions with administrators, supervisors, principals, teachers, arts specialists, artists, heads of arts organizations and agencies, etc. in order to make clear that the arts in general education is a comprehensive educational approach, not a special arts program, a curriculum development program, a cultural enrichment series, or a remedial effort?

6. Have potential sources of planning and development funds been explored at the local, state, and federal level? Is it clearly understood that "outside" funds are used mainly for special programmatic or developmental purposes and that the regular school budget will support the main costs of program administration and operation?

Getting Started

Initiating an arts in general education program may (and probably should) take as long as a year or two, depending on the size and complexity of the school system, the proposed network, and the obstacles encountered.

Ideally, the initiative for starting the program comes from the school district. It can, however, also come from a variety of other sources: a Junior League, a private foundation, a state or community arts council, and/or a group of concerned citizens. Regardless of its point of origin, community groups should understand from the beginning that the school system is legally responsible for the education of children and must have the final say in decisions that affect this process.

While the school system must be involved from the outset, the superintendent may choose to delegate some of the initial research and planning responsibilities to committees or task forces.

Some of the strategies that have been employed (sequentially or simultaneously) by League sites during the planning phase have been to:

• **Form a planning committee** consisting of key professionals and practitioners from the school system, the arts com- 219 munity, colleges, and civic organizations. The planning group's task is to design a comprehensive program. It should:

1. Examine the rationale, definition, and concept of the arts in general education and their application to local conditions.

2. Study the local (and if desirable, national) scene for promising programs and practices.

3. Identify potential resources—human, material, and financial—in and out of the school system.

4. Prepare a proposed comprehensive plan with specific program objectives and activities.

5. Suggest the size, composition, and structure of a network and determine whether it should consist of one tier of "demonstration" schools or include additional tiers of "cooperating" or "satellite" schools.

6. Suggest the size and composition of a coordinating "hub" and define its administrative organization and responsibilities.

7. Check out the proposed plan with potential participants.

8. Report results to key decision-makers in the school system and the community.

9. Formalize acceptance of the plan and announce intentions publicly.

• **Form an advisory committee (optional).** The original planning committee can usually be converted into a consultative body. Define responsibilities, roles, and functions.

• **Identify the personnel for program management.** Coordination may be provided by a single person working in consultation with others or by a multi-disciplinary team. The coordinator(s) should have decision-making power, and should have knowledge of the arts, curriculum, and instruction and how the schools and the system operate. In most situations, a team seems to work better than a single person, since many diverse talents and abilities (not to mention time and energy) are required to coordinate a comprehensive, interdisciplinary program.

• **Inform all schools in the system of the opportunity to volunteer for the program** (by letter of invitation, by public event, by the media). Include a description of the proposed program, the commitments of the district (and partners), and guidelines and criteria for participation. Outline the required commitments from the school and request proposals for participation.

• **Form a task force (or ask the planning/advisory committee) to visit the schools**, talk with administrators, staff, and parents and verify eligibility for participation.

• **Identify schools and announce participants.** Describe the configuration of the network (one, two, or more tiers) and the rationale for its formation. The network should be small enough to manage and large enough to notice.

• **Form the network:** Hold planning meetings to discuss and clarify the concept and the program. Chart an immediate and long-range course based on needs and concerns as identified by network principals and their staffs. Teachers may also be included providing size is not a problem, the tasks are appropriate, and their role is an active and not a passive one.

- **Review existing resources** and allocate or reallocate them based on needs as identified by principals and their staffs and verified by the program coordinator(s). These decisions should be made in consultation with the schools.
- **Visit the schools to help them get started.** The coordinator(s) should meet periodically with each principal and staff to discuss the school development process and how the arts can facilitate it.
- **Meet with artists, arts and cultural resource organizations, and arts agencies** to define program purposes and needs. The coordinator(s) should examine existing programs, suggest new approaches to be planned jointly with the schools, and set up planning meetings.

The Network and The Hub

Too often, the terms "network" and "networking" are either misunderstood or not fully translated into action. There is a tendency to think that, once a group of schools is identified and officially formed into a network, that is all that needs to be done. The network exists—on paper. Occasionally principals (and their staffs) show up at meetings or events to engage in some activity that has been planned for them (usually without their prior knowledge or consent). This is not the concept of networking that underlies the League's programs.

The network is a living, functioning delivery system. It is a forum for exchange of ideas, problem-solving, and information-sharing. It is a "floating place" where heads of schools chart their own destiny, set their own agenda, and chair their own meetings. It meets regularly, in school or elsewhere, plans with resource personnel, consultants from local and national arts and education organizations, partners, sponsors, and other participants in the program.

The network is the very heart of the change process. It is a source of support and an effective mechanism for communication for the individual network schools which are generally geographically separate. It should ultimately be a source of support and technical assistance to other "non-network" schools that need advice and guidance regarding the arts in education. Like any heart, it must beat regularly to keep the body of the program alive and vital.

And a word about the "hub": Whether coordination is provided by a single person or a team of people, the hub's main function is to facilitate program planning and development.

The word "facilitate" is crucial. Too often in education the traditional program director or manager is expected to act as a supervisor or "inspector general." While there are many situ-   221 ations that do require leadership and quick decisions, the hub's main role is to help the schools help themselves. It should provide technical and consulting assistance and liaison between the schools and other resources. Its other chief function is to seek, individually or in concert with other organizations and partners, money from all possible sources so that time for planning and development, or "walk-around" time (the hardest to come by), can be assured.

When the hub and the network are fully-functioning and strong, comprehensive arts in education programs can survive almost anything, including changes in top leadership, budget crises, strikes, and the like.

Building the Program at the Grass Roots Level: School Development Through the Arts

In arts in general education programs, each network school forms a planning committee. Depending on the size of the school, the planning committee, led by the principal, can consist of the entire faculty or a core group, all of whom volunteer for the task. Parents, artists, and other community representatives should also be represented.

The four basic questions for each school are:

1. How can the arts and the creative process be integrated into the daily classroom experience of every child in this building?

2. How can our school develop and change through the arts?

3. How can the school meet the five main objectives outlined in the system's plan to which it has made a commitment—strengthen and expand study in the arts; promote interdisciplinary teaching and learning; use community resources more effectively; meet the special needs of special children; and reduce personal and racial isolation?

4. How will the school meet its own objectives, such as: increased attendance, higher morale, reduced vandalism, better attitudes toward learning, greater community and parental involvement, maintaining racial and ethnic balance, and better integration of staff and students?

The League is employing the following strategies to answer these questions:

• Monthly meetings of demonstration school principals and program coordinator(s) to discuss issues, meet with consultants in the arts and education and define, redefine, and evaluate plans and programs. These meetings may take place at a school, at the central office, or elsewhere. They should be mandatory (part of the commitment each principal makes when volunteering to join the network).

• Site visits by network principals (and staff) to each school within the network (and in the case of the League, to other sites) to observe what is happening, talk with administration and staff, and explore a particular issue or problem in depth. These meetings are conducted by the host school principal or site coordinator(s) and follow his/her agenda. The program coordinator(s), central administrators, partners, and other resource personnel participate.

- Half- or full-day school planning meetings in which the entire school staff assembles to define and solve issues and problems related to the arts in education.
- Network retreats or all-day planning and development conferences.
- School/community events, fund raising affairs, show-cases, festivals, performances, exhibits.
- Staff and curriculum development activities, in and out of school (on school time, after school, for credit or not.)
- Meetings with artists, arts and cultural organizations, and other resource personnel to jointly plan and develop programs, services, and events.
- Artist residencies: short and long term; individuals and resource teams.
- Evaluation efforts (questionnaires, reports, interviews, standardized tests, narrative histories, etc.).
- Documentation and dissemination activities (conferences, seminars, workshops, reports, portfolios, video-tapes, film, exhibits, manuals, articles for school and local newspaper, etc.).

School development is a long-term process that must be nurtured at the individual school level, through the network and through the efforts of the program coordinator(s).

This approach runs counter to the way in which most school systems and other bureaucracies generally operate. Here, authority and often decision-making power are decentralized, whereas normally they are vested in a few chief administrators. This notion is often difficult to accept, let alone translate into practice. It requires an unusual amount of trust and confidence on the part of the school system's administration and the willingness to encourage independence rather than dependence on the traditional power structure.

Mid-Course Corrections

As programs move "off the page" into operation, they develop a life of their own. Changes occur and, in domino fashion, these changes precipitate others of which some are desirable and some are not. It is essential for decision-makers to be responsive to the flow of current events in order to make the appropriate adjustments.

- **Establishing and Maintaining Balance Among Program Components.** Frequently, the first year or so of operation will focus on one or two of the five main objectives. While obviously all aims cannot be realized immediately, and one does have to start somewhere, extreme care must be exercised so that pro- 223 grams do not become "unbalanced" or one-dimensional. (See Appendix C for a definition of a comprehensive arts in general education program.)

• **Reorganizing the Hub.** The hub often changes as programs develop. A single coordinator may find that it is difficult, if not impossible, to manage all the complex aspects of a comprehensive program without additional help. If the hub is a team, its personnel may not adequately reflect the variety of talents and abilities required. Staff turnover may result in leadership gaps. Should these events occur, they should be recognized as a good opportunity to reorganize the hub and to redefine administrative roles and responsibilities.

• **Reorganizing the Network.** Most networks in the school districts comprising the League have remained relatively stable. Inevitably, however, principals may retire, move to other schools, or fail to follow through on their original commitments. Some may feel, after a year or so, that the program makes too heavy a demand on their time. Others may be disappointed in what they perceive as a lack of special recognition, extra resources, or financial support.

In addition to network membership, other questions of an organizational or practical nature may arise: Was the original group of schools too small, just right, too large? Were the number of tiers and the number of schools in each manageable, and did they make programmatic sense? Has the concept of the arts in general education been internalized and given adequate time and support to flourish?

If the strength of the network appears to be in jeopardy, it is often both wise and necessary to consider reorganization. Guidelines and criteria for membership can be updated and the original schools given a fresh chance to declare their continuing commitment or to opt out. New schools may be added, and/or schools may move from one tier to another. In all cases, participation should continue to be voluntary, and membership policy should now be formulated in consultation with the network principals.

Extending the Concept, Enlarging the Network— Or Both

At some point, generally after about two years of school-based operation, the question of expansion is inevitably raised. Key decision-makers are encouraged by signs of the program's effectiveness and staying power, and they continue or increase their support.

Other schools in the system are beginning to want "a piece of the action." The word has gotten out, with some evidence to support it, that the arts in general education concept offers schools another (and perhaps more fruitful) way to go. And there now exists a substantial amount of experience that can be shared with others both verbally and in writing. The question now is: How can the concept be extended to other schools?

Extending the concept can be looked at in several ways: feeding new schools into "open slots" in the original network; enlarging the original network; setting up new and related networks; or a combination of all three.

The following are some of the ways that are being explored by League sites:

• A school system, seeing the value and effectiveness of the idea in a few demonstration schools, declares the arts in general education a priority for all its elementary schools and encourages principals and teachers to join the program in a series of sub- or mini-networks, all coordinated by the central office. Increased staff and administrative time is allocated, and the demonstration network provides consulting and training services for the new schools. Manuals and resource books based on actual experience are provided as references.

• In systems that have districts or areas, "mini" arts in general education networks are set up within geographical boundaries using the original demonstration schools as reference points and their staffs as resource personnel. The same planning process is undergone, and schools still volunteer and compete for participation. Main administrative support is provided by the district office with supplementary assistance coming from the central office and the hub.

The central office sets up other networks using the arts in general education model process and interrelates the arts with the particular area of study; e.g., career, environmental, and special education. Arts in general education principals, staff, and management, plus central board or district supervisors assist in this process through leadership, staff, and curriculum development workshops and conferences. Manuals and other publications are used as references. These "new" networks have functional relationships with the arts in general education network.

• School systems under a desegregation mandate create magnet schools, some of which focus on the arts and the arts in general education. These schools form their own network, are often staffed by former "demonstration school" principals, and are under the supervision of the coordinator or team from the central board.

• Title IV-C grants are used to adapt and test the arts in education concept in other schools and sites in those states that have declared the arts in general education a priority and eligible for funding. In this case, the state education department, in concert with the local school district, takes responsibility for state-wide coordination and supervision, and the original demonstration site provides information and consulting expertise.

The above are organized and formal ways in which other schools can become involved in the arts in education. The following are informal and often accidental means:

• Principals move to new schools and take their philosophy and experience with them.

- Principals and staff from non-network schools meet principals and staff from demonstration schools sharing certain arts resources. Ideas and information are exchanged and certain arts in general education practices are put into effect.
- Volunteer organizations (such as the Junior League) and civic groups (such as the New York Urban Coalition) that have been involved with the arts in general education programs share their experience with other schools and organizations.
- Heads of schools in programs such as the Principal-as-Leader Program, which subscribes to an educational change theory similar to that upon which arts in general education programs are based, pick up on the idea either through formal and informal meetings, conferences, and other means of communication.
- State and local arts councils that have been intimately involved as partners or sponsors of arts in general education programs spread the word to their constituency and to other schools and school systems.
- National programs, such as the National Endowment for the Arts' Artists-in-Schools Program, the National Endowment for the Humanities, the Special Projects Act of the Emergency School Aid Act, the Office of Education/Kennedy Center's Alliance for Arts Education Program, and the National Institute of Education help to initiate or support the concept of the arts in education through competitive grants and categorical aid.

Some Concerns Shared by the League of Cities

There are several issues that concern the League of Cities and others engaged in building and maintaining arts in general education programs. Some have been raised or implied in previous sections. Others include the following:

- quality versus quantity;
- process versus product;
- interdisciplinary teaching and learning (by a team? one person? both? how? what? when? where?); and
- leadership and staff turnover.

In addition, what are the appropriate roles and functions of:

- artists in schools;
- arts organizations in and out of schools;
- arts specialists;
- parents, volunteers, other resource personnel;
- colleges and universities (especially with regard to teacher training, research, and evaluation); and
- partners and sponsors?

In due course, and undoubtedly through cooperative effort on a national scale, partial solutions and even answers may be worked out as programs mature in the League of Cities and elsewhere around the country.

For further information regarding individual programs, please contact the arts in education program coordinators.

Hartford Public Schools
Central Administrative Offices
249 High Street
Hartford, Connecticut 06103

Little Rock Public Schools
Department of Instruction
West Markham and Izard
   Streets
Little Rock, Arkansas 72201

Minneapolis Public Schools
807 Northeast Broadway
Minneapolis, Minnesota
   55413

Center for School Develop-
   ment
New York City Board of
   Education
131 Livingston Street
Brooklyn, New York 11201

Seattle Public Schools
Administrative and Service
   Center
815 Fourth Avenue North
Seattle, Washington 98109

Winston-Salem/Forsyth
   County Schools
Post Office Box 2513
Winston-Salem, North Car-
   olina 27102

State Education Departments

State education departments can play a major role in disseminating information about and supporting the idea of the arts in general education on a state-wide basis. They can declare the arts a priority in the education of every child in the state and design comprehensive plans that assure, among other things, adequate technical and consulting assistance.

Through state-wide and local networks, leadership training institutes, staff and curriculum development workshops, certification procedures, mandates, publications, conferences, and resource people, state education departments can provide leadership to a very broad audience. They can also make money available from a variety of state and federally funded programs and assist in the difficult task of research and evaluation.

Ad Hoc Coalition of States for the Arts in Education

Further information about state-wide priorities and programs for the arts in education, as well as demonstration programs in schools and school districts in the states that are members of the Coalition, can be secured by contacting the following offices:

Fine Arts Specialist
Arizona Department of Ed-
   ucation
1535 West Jefferson
Phoenix, Arizona 85007

Fine Arts Consultant
California State Department
   of Education
721 Capitol Mall
Sacramento, California 95814 227

State Arts Consultant
Division of Curriculum
Indiana Department of
   Public Instruction
Room 229, State House
Indianapolis, Indiana 46204

Arts in Education Specialist
Massachusetts Department
   of Education
31 St. James Avenue
Boston, Massachusetts
   02116

Fine Arts Specialist
Michigan Department of
   Education
Box 30008
Lansing, Michigan 48909

Director
Division of Humanities and
   Arts Education
New York State Education
   Department
Albany, New York 12234

Administrator
Arts in Education Program
Oklahoma State Depart-
   ment of Education
2500 North Lincoln Boule-
   vard
Oklahoma City, Oklahoma
   73105

Chief
Division of General Education
Bureau of Curriculum Ser-
   vices
Pennsylvania Department
   of Education
Harrisburg, Pennsylvania
   17126

Supervisor Arts Education
Division of Instructional
   Programs
Washington Department of
   Public Instruction
Old Capitol Building
Olympia, Washington
   98504

APPENDIX C
A Glossary of Terms Used in Comprehensive Arts in General Education Programs

Jane Remer

Certain key concepts or ideas are embedded in the language of comprehensive arts in general education programs. This terminology turns up again and again in position papers, publications, reports, discussions, meetings, and conferences. The following are definitions or descriptions of the terms most frequently used.

Comprehensive Arts in General Education Program. A comprehensive arts in general (or basic) education program is a long-range school development effort designed to improve the quality of education for all children by incorporating all the arts in the daily teaching and learning process, kindergarten through high school. In these programs, the arts are seen as tools for learning in all subjects, media for expression and self-discovery, and important areas of study in their own right. These programs have also been recognized as an impetus for total school change using the arts as a vehicle for staff, curriculum, and leadership development.

For a program to be truly comprehensive, it should include the visual, performing, literary, environmental, industrial, household, and folk arts. It should develop conceptual, thematic, and functional relationships among the arts and between the arts and all other subjects. It should identify and regularly use all the appropriate arts and cultural resources in the school and the community in ways that increase an understanding of the arts and establish connections between the creative process and the learning process. In addition, it should use the arts and the arts process to meet the special needs of special children (including the gifted, talented, handicapped, and bilingual) and to help reduce personal and racial isolation. All participants, including artists, educators, administrators, parents, and other resource personnel, should assist in program planning, execution, and assessment.

Such comprehensive school development efforts are based on the belief that educational change through the arts is both possible and desirable and that a school's commitment to the arts can result in programs that are consistent with the goals of the school and the school system and beneficial to all children. Comprehensive arts in general education programs bring all the arts to all the children in a school, not necessarily all schools, all at once, but perhaps eventually, depending on the pace and scope of change desired.

Change. Change in education means change in people's attitudes, perceptions, values, and behavior. It is often a lonely, difficult, and long-term business. To be comprehensive, enduring, and constructive, it should be carefully planned for and responsive to the needs of children. The idea of change can be threatening, and its positive implications are often not fully understood until (and unless) the process is undergone by all those whom it will or is intended to affect. (For a full description of the change theory underlying the League's arts in general education programs, see Appendix B.)

Choice. Participation in a comprehensive program is based upon people's voluntary decisions to become engaged in light of the benefits that may accrue. This notion applies equally to school administrators, staff, the community, artists, and resource people. It helps to insure that programs will be "grass roots" oriented rather than imposed upon the unwilling or uninformed from the "top down."

Collaboration. Programs are built on the premise that the whole can be greater than the sum of its parts when concerned individuals define their similarities and differences, negotiate, and come to consensus on those issues where purposes coincide or overlap. The main focus, however, is on quality education for children.

Demonstration. Programs, schools, and people can work together to establish tangible evidence (both the process and the product) that the arts can make a difference in the quality of education for all children, in school life and in human relations.

In order to test the validity and impact of a "new" idea, one must work from strength and commitment. If schools are expected to be the prime movers in a program, then they must be able to give evidence of past support and present commitment to the program's overall goals and objectives. Arts in general education programs are not currently viewed as "turn-around" or "remedial" efforts intended to solve social inequities that go far beyond the province or responsibility of school systems.

Existing Structures, Resources, and Circumstances. Programs are built on or in recognition of existing structures, resources, and circumstances. While the purpose is to promote improvement, and therefore, change, the process is a gradual (and time-consuming) one which recognizes the strengths and weaknesses of the "status quo" and attempts to chart a course using the former and minimizing the latter.

Model Process. Schools and schools systems can develop the instructional methodology and content and specific strategies for change that work best in their own settings. There are certain general guidelines, criteria, strategies, program components, and a definition of what constitutes the "whole picture" which are common to all, but the method of "getting there" varies from place to place. It is the process that becomes the model, not the product.

Networking. Networking—the regular and voluntary coming together of people with common or overlapping concerns to discuss issues, share problems, and generate new ideas—is an essential strategy in the planning and development of comprehensive arts in general education programs, because it provides a non-threatening, cost-effective mechanism for mutual support, professional growth, and concerted action.

Arts in general education networks operate laterally, peer-to-peer, as distinct from vertically, top-down. They rely on what John Goodlad has termed the "DDAE" process: a continuing round of Dialogue, Decision-making, Action, and Evaluation. Decisions are generally reached through negotiation and consensus, and individual needs are weighed against practical, political, and financial realities that affect the group as a whole.

To function effectively, all networks need a "hub" or organizing center. The hub usually consists of a team that provides leadership and support services to members. It coordinates activities, maintains communication among program participants, identifies, secures, and "brokers" resources, and acts as a liaison between the schools and the community.

Networks within school districts often exist among administrators, demonstration school principals, teachers, students, artists, and arts organizations. Nationally, six school districts have formed the League of Cities for the Arts in Education and nine state education departments have formed the Coalition of States for the same purpose.

231

Ownership. All program participants have a stake in their own destiny, and therefore must have a say in it, especially the professional staff in the schools. It is primarily they who will plan and design their own arts in general education program.

Planning. Adequate time for advance and on-going planning is built into each program at a ratio of approximately ten to one: ten parts preparation to one part action. This work is done jointly by all those who will be involved in or affected by program implementation. Continuing assessment and "mid-course" corrections are made.

School development. The process by which a school unit, under the leadership of its principal, defines its guiding philosophical principles, examines its existing mode of operation, its staff talent, its building and community resources, and determines where the gaps are and how to close them—this is school development. Such a change process is gradual and long-term. It should involve the whole school community at some point or another. The school development process is supported and accelerated by networking and collaboration among those who have similar concerns, information, and answers to share.

School people know that, when the total school environment is systematically improved over time, a better climate for living and learning results. The arts are beginning to be perceived as natural allies in this process because they can serve as both the substance and the vehicle for environmental change and school development.

When a school integrates all the arts into the daily teaching and learning process, revised class scheduling, new and improved staffing patterns, teaching approaches, and curriculum materials generally result. New and better use of unusual talents and resources in the school and the community are additional outcomes.

Time. Programs and people must be given plenty of time to explore, falter, and grow; to discover for themselves what works, what doesn't, and why—and most importantly, how to "fix it." All too often, expectations for new programs, especially those that are comprehensive and complex, are unrealistic. Premature judgments, demands for accountability and performance tend to destroy an effort that is on the verge of becoming solid and stable. There is no magic formula, but three or four years is not enough to establish the full potential of a comprehensive arts in general education program that will serve all the children in an entire school, let alone an entire school district.

APPENDIX D
A Rationale for the Arts in Education

Kathryn Bloom
and Jane Remer

Many educators, as well as persons directly concerned with the arts, share the conviction that the arts are a means for expressing and interpreting human behavior and experience. It follows, therefore, that the education of children is incomplete if the arts are not part of the daily teaching and learning process. Arts in education programs are designed to make all of the arts integral to the general, or basic, education of every child in entire school systems. Work with these programs demonstrates that changes take place in schools so that they become humane environments in which the arts are valued as tools for learning as well as for their own intrinsic sake. Experience further indicates that the arts are useful to educators in meeting some of their main goals—that is, providing a great variety of educational opportunities, distinguished by quality, for all children.

The following are specific ways that the arts can contribute to the general, or basic, education of every child:

1. The arts provide a medium for personal expression, a deep need experienced by children and adults alike. Children's

involvement in the arts can be a strong motivating force for improved communication through speaking and writing as well as through drawing or singing.

2. The arts focus attention and energy on personal observation and self-awareness. They can make children and adults more aware of their environment and help them develop a stronger sense of themselves and a greater confidence in their own abilities. Through increased self-knowledge, children are more likely to be able to command and integrate their mental, physical, and emotional faculties and cope with the world around them.

3. The arts are a universal human phenomenon and means of communication. Involvement in them, both as participant and observer, can promote a deeper understanding and acceptance of the similarities and differences among races, religions, and cultural traditions.

4. The arts involve the elements of sound, movement, color, mass, energy, space, line, shape, and language. These elements, singly or in combination, are common to the concepts underlying many subjects in the curriculum. For example, exploring solutions to problems in mathematics and science through the arts can increase the understanding of the process and the value of both.

5. The arts embody and chronicle the cultural, aesthetic, and social development of the world's peoples. Through the arts, children can become more aware of their own cultural heritage in a broad historical context. Arts institutions, cultural organizations, and artists have a vital role to play in the education of children, both in schools and in the community.

6. The arts are a tangible expression of human creativity and, as such, reflect peoples' perceptions of their world. Through the arts, children and adults can become more aware of their own creative and human potential.

7. The various fields of the arts offer a wide range of career choices to young people. Arts in education programs provide opportunities for students to explore the possibility of becoming a professional actor, dancer, musician, painter, photographer, architect, or teacher. There are also many lesser known opportunities in arts-related technical areas such as lighting engineer, costumer in a theater, or a specialist in designing and installing exhibitions in museums. Other opportunities lie in administrative and educational work in arts organizations such as museums, performing arts groups, and arts councils.

8. The arts can contribute substantially to special education. Educational programs emphasizing the arts and the creative process are being developed for students with learning disabilities, such as the retarded and handicapped. These programs are conceived as alternative approaches to learning for youngsters who may have problems in adjusting to more traditional classroom situations. The infusion of the arts into the general education of all children also encourages the identification of talented youngsters whose special abilities may otherwise go unnoticed or unrecognized.

9. The arts, as a means for personal and creative involvement by children and teachers, are a source of pleasure and mental stimulation. Learning as a pleasant, rewarding activity is a new experience for many young people and can be very important in encouraging positive attitudes toward schooling.

10. The arts are useful tools for everyday living. An understanding of the arts provides people with a broader range of choices about the environment in which they live, the lifestyle they develop, and the way they spend their leisure time.

APPENDIX E
Ten Characteristics of School Systems that Have Developed Effective Arts in General Education Programs

Jane Remer

As has been stated frequently by one eminent educator, reading, writing, and arithmetic do not, in themselves, constitute an education; rather, they are the tools that one needs to become educated. The arts are also important tools for education. Quality education can result when the arts are incorporated in the teaching and learning process.

When an entire school system embarks on an arts in general education project, certain kinds of changes take place in the schools and in the community. While not all the characteristics of change described here appear in every situation, they do identify main features that are common to most of the school systems with which the Fund has been associated.

1. **A Commitment to Quality Education for All Children.** The school system has a commitment to improving the quality of education for all children and has established a mechanism for systematic change and innovation.

2. **A Commitment to Quality Education through the Arts.** A significant number of chief school officials, administrators, 237

teachers, and parents subscribe to the belief that teaching and learning through the arts improves the quality of education for all children. They regard education as a creative living and learning process and feel that the arts provide a powerful motivation for this process. They have found that, by incorporating the arts into all aspects of schooling, children develop positive attitudes towards learning, a stronger sense of themselves, and a keener awareness of the world around them.

3. **The Creative Use of Existing Human, Financial, and Physical Resources.** The school system allocates a significant amount of time, effort, and money to the planning and development of arts in education programs. Local public funds provide the permanent base of support for school programs; private funds are used mainly for research and development purposes. Existing facilities in the schools and the community are fully utilized.

4. **A Coherent, Collaborative Approach to Program Planning and Development.** Programs are planned, developed, operated, and assessed by those who participate in them. Consequently, these programs relate to the actual strengths and needs of individual schools and make use of the appropriate resources in the schools and community. Professional consultants in the arts and education are involved in the planning and development process.

5. **An Organic Program Design.** Though they will vary from school to school, effective arts in general education programs have at least three related points of emphasis in common:

(a.) Strong programs in all the arts for all children;

(b.) Interdisciplinary teaching and learning; and

(c.) Effective and regular use of community cultural resources, including services provided by artists and arts institutions.

6. **A Continuing Curriculum and Staff Development Effort.** Program planning and development occur simultaneously with curriculum and staff development workshops, seminars, and meetings. These activities encourage the development of new learnings, skills, teaching strategies, and materials that are appropriate to the content and structure of new programs. The instructional staff, including teachers, artists, and community volunteers, has access to new or existing arts resource materials and can test them out in actual classroom situations.

7. **On-going Internal and External Documentation and Evaluation.** Evaluation of the school's efforts in program planning and development are continuous, largely internal, and address questions of effectiveness in terms of the goals and objectives the school has set for itself. Judgments about quality and achievement are made by those best in the position to render and make use of them, and modifications are made as soon as they are needed. Educational research and evaluation consultants or outside agencies are used to help determine the effectiveness of overall program goals and outcomes.

8. **An Effective Communications Network.** A conscious and systematic effort is made to share information about the

school's new arts programs, and problems and prospects are discussed within the school, with other schools and cultural institutions, and with community advisory groups. As a result of this network, other schools wishing to move in similar directions are encouraged to do so more effectively.

9. **A Broadened and Humanistic Concept of Schooling.** In the course of incorporating all the arts into an entire school system, the concept of schooling broadens, and teaching and learning become more humanistic. School buildings and classrooms are transformed into attractive living and working environments; the content of the curriculum is significantly altered; teachers develop new capabilities and patterns of instruction; and a working partnership is formed between the schools and the community.

10. **An Increased Commitment to and Understanding of the Change Process in Education.** The process of educational change is often slow and difficult. It calls for imaginative leadership and cooperative working arrangements among many different sectors of the community. It also requires patience, fortitude, and broad public awareness and commitment. School systems that have developed effective arts in general education programs have not only improved the quality of teaching and learning in their schools but also developed a greater understanding of the change process. This process is generally most effective when the individual school is viewed as a social unit and the most powerful agent for progressive change in education.

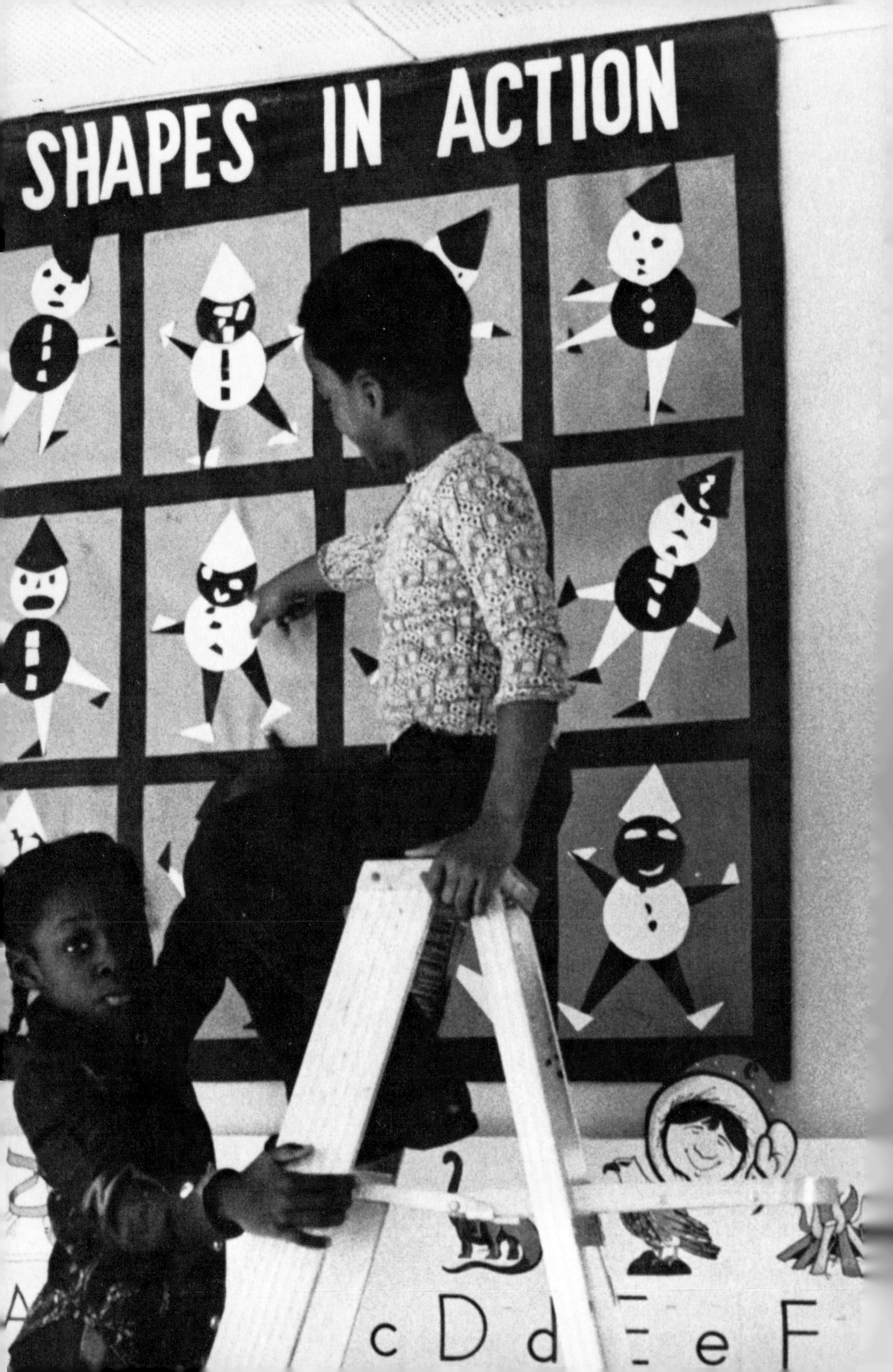
SHAPES IN ACTION
c D d e F

APPENDIX F
Community Arts Programs and Educational Effectiveness in the Schools

Kathryn Bloom

I. **HIGHEST LEVEL OF
    EDUCATIONAL EFFECTIVENESS:**[1]

   A. **The form, content, and structure of the program grow
out of a cooperative effort** by school personnel (teachers, curriculum specialists, administrators), artists and arts organization
representatives, and are related to and supportive of the content
of teaching and learning in the schools.
   B. **Programs are planned as an on-going series of related
educational events.**
   C. **The program includes the participation of artists who
serve as resources to teachers and students** in a variety of direct
teaching and learning activities. These include creative experi-

---

[1]This material is excerpted from a program paper, *An Emerging Pattern for
Educational Change: The Arts in General Education* (New York, New York: The
JDR 3rd Fund, 1973).   241

ences or demonstrations of the techniques, skills, and talents indigenous to their particular profession.

D. Preparatory and follow-up curriculum materials planned specifically for the program are provided to the schools. These materials result from work done jointly by school representatives, artists, and arts organization educational staff. Related visual and written materials and resources such as slides, recordings, tapes, films, reproductions, and teacher's guides are available in the schools and used by teachers in classrooms.

E. In-service training is available to teachers in order that they have a general understanding of the arts organization, its purposes, its resources, and the nature of its services in terms of curriculum development.

F. Orientation and training are available to artists and arts organization educators, so they have an understanding of the nature of schools, the content of the educational program, and the learning characteristics of students at different age levels.

G. As a result of the foregoing, the arts event becomes part of the process of teaching and learning, not just a "field trip," time off from school work, or another assembly program.

II. MIDDLE LEVEL OF EDUCATIONAL EFFECTIVENESS:

A. The content of the program is planned by arts organization educators with some help from school personnel, but is not focused on the content of school studies.

B. Programs are isolated and sporadic events.

C. Contact with artists is limited.

D. Some preparatory materials are provided to the schools for the arts events. Few related materials are available in the schools.

E. No inservice training is available to teachers. Often they have no more information about the arts event or organization than the children they accompany.

F. No training is available to artists or arts organization educators. They assume an automatic interest or curiosity on the part of teachers and children. Capability to work with different age groups is learned on the job by trial and error.

G. The arts event is of some value to children and teachers but remains separate from the larger educational program of the schools.

III. LOW LEVEL OF EDUCATIONAL EFFECTIVENESS:

A. The content of the program is accidentally determined by the fact that the arts organization has a special event it feels has some significance for the schools, and the schools decide to send all fifth grade classes and their teachers to it.

B. Programs are single, isolated, unrelated events or activities.

C. Artists are not involved as resources to teachers and students in the program.

D. No preparatory or follow-up materials are available.

E. No inservice training is available for teachers.

F. Arts organization representatives do not work with teachers and students, since their regular responsibilities make very heavy demands on their time, or the schools have not made appointments for their classes in advance.

G. Educationally, the arts event is of dubious value to students and teachers.

BIBLIOGRAPHY

All the Arts for All the Children: A Report on the Arts in General Education, New York City, 1974-77. New York City Board of Education.

A New Wind Blowing: Arts in Education in Oklahoma Schools. Oklahoma City, Oklahoma: Oklahoma State Department of Education, 1978.

The Art Museum as Educator. A study by the Council on Museums and Education in the Visual Arts. Berkeley, California: the University of California Press, 1978.

The Arts As Perception: A Way of Learning. Albany, New York: Project SEARCH, the State Education Department, 1978.

Arts in Education Symposium: Revised Case Studies. New York: the Association of Junior Leagues, 1977.

The Arts in General Education. An entire issue of the *Music Educators Journal.* Vol. 64, No. 5 (January 1978).

Bentzen, Mary M. *Changing Schools: The Magic Feather Principle.* I/D/E/A Reports on Schooling. A Charles F. Kettering Foundation Program. New York: McGraw-Hill, 1974.

245

Bloom, Kathryn. *The Arts in Education Program: Progress and Prospects*. New York: The JDR 3rd Fund, 1976.

Bloom, Kathryn. *Arts Organizations and their Services to Schools: Patrons or Partners?* New York: The JDR 3rd Fund, 1974.

Cohen, Elaine Pear, and Ruth Straus Gainer. *Art: Another Language for Learning*. New York: Citation Press, 1976.

Coming to Our Senses: The Significance of the Arts for American Education. A report by the Arts, Education and Americans Panel. New York: McGraw-Hill, 1977.

Comprehensive Arts Planning: Ad Hoc Coalition of States for the Arts in Education. New York: The JDR 3rd Fund, 1975.

Dobbs, Stephen M. (editor). *Arts Education and Back to Basics*. National Art Education Association Publication. Reston, Virginia: 1979.

The Ecology of Education: The Arts. An entire issue of *The National Elementary Principal*. Vol. 55, No. 3 (January/February 1976).

Eddy, Junius. *Arts Education 1977—In Prose and Print: An Overview of Nine Significant Publications Affecting the Arts in American Education*. Washington, D.C.: The Arts and Humanities Program, Office of Education, U.S. Department of Health, Education, and Welfare, 1978. GPO Publication No. 260-934/2044.

Eddy, Junius. *It Begins with Craft: Report of a Conference on Performance in an Arts in Education Program*. Washington, D.C.: The John F. Kennedy Center for the Performing Arts, 1968.

Eddy, Junius. *Seattle's Arts for Learning Project*. An Evaluative Report. Seattle, Washington: The Seattle Public Schools, 1978.

Fowler, Charles B. *The Arts Process in Basic Education*. Harrisburg, Pennsylvania: Pennsylvania Department of Education, 1973.

Fowler, Charles B. *Dance as Education*. Washington, D.C.: the National Dance Association, an Association of the American Alliance for Health, Physical Education, Recreation, and Dance, 1977.

Gary, Charles L. (editor). *Try a New Face*. Washington, D.C.: Office of Education, U.S. Department of Health, Education, and Welfare, 1979. HEW Publication No. (OE) 79-7305.

Goodlad, John I. *The Dynamics of Educational Change*. I/D/E/A Reports on Schooling. A Charles F. Kettering Foundation Program. New York: McGraw-Hill, 1975.

Laybourne, Kit (editor). *Doing the Media—A Portfolio of Activities and Resources*. New York: The Center for Understanding Media, 1972.

Madeja, Stanley S. *Aesthetic Education: A Social and Individual Need*. St. Louis, Missouri: CEMREL, Inc., 1973.

Madeja, Stanley S. *All the Arts for Every Child*. New York: The JDR 3rd Fund, 1973.

Madeja, Stanley S. (editor). *Arts and Aesthetics: An Agenda for the Future*. St. Louis, Missouri: CEMREL, Inc., 1977.

Madeja, Stanley S. (editor). *The Arts, Cognition, and Basic Skills.* St. Louis, Missouri: CEMREL, Inc., 1978.

Murphy, Judith, and Lonna Jones. *Research in Arts Education: A Federal Chapter.* Washington, D.C.: Office of Education, U.S. Department of Health, Education, and Welfare, 1978. HEW Publication No. (OE) 76-02000.

Newsom, Barbara Y., and Adele Z. Silver. *The Art Museum as Educator: A Collection of Studies as Guides to Practice and Policy.* Berkeley, California: University of California Press, 1977.

Remer, Jane. *The Identification Process for Schools Participating in the New York City Arts in General Education Project Network.* New York: The JDR 3rd Fund, 1975.

Remer, Jane. *The League of Cities for the Arts in Education.* New York: The JDR 3rd Fund, 1977.

Remer, Jane. *Networks, the Arts and School Change.* New York: The JDR 3rd Fund, 1975.

RITA: Reading Improvement Through the Arts. Albany, New York: The New York State Education Department, Division of Federal Educational Opportunity Programs Title I ESEA and the Division of Humanities and Arts Education, 1979.

Shapiro, Stephen R., Richard Place, and Richard Scheidenhelm. *Artists in the Classroom.* Hartford, Connecticut: Connecticut Commission on the Arts, 1973.

Shuker, Nancy (editor). *Arts in Education Partners: Schools and Their Communities.* Jointly sponsored by the Junior League of Oklahoma City, the Arts Council of Oklahoma City, Oklahoma City Public Schools, the Association of Junior Leagues, and The JDR 3rd Fund, 1977. Available from ACA Publications, 570 Seventh Avenue, New York, New York 10018.

Smith, Ralph A. *Aesthetic Concepts and Education.* Urbana, Illinois: University of Illinois Press, 1970.

Stake, Robert E. *Evaluating the Arts in Education: A Responsive Approach.* Columbus, Ohio: Charles E. Merrill Publishing Company, 1975.

Toward an Aesthetic Education. Reston, Virginia: the Music Educators National Conference and CEMREL, Inc., 1970.

Tye, Kenneth A., and Jerrold M. Novotney. *Schools in Transition: The Practitioner as Change Agent.* I/D/E/A Reports on Schooling. A Charles F. Kettering Foundation Program. New York: McGraw-Hill, 1975.

Weinstein, Gerald, and Mario D. Fantini. *Toward Humanistic Education, A Curriculum of Affect.* New York: Praeger University Series, 1970.

The JDR 3rd Fund

The JDR 3rd Fund was founded in 1963 by John D. Rockefeller 3rd to carry out a program of cultural exchange with Asia. In 1968, the trustees expanded the scope of the Fund to include an Arts in Education Program devoted to the goal of making all of the arts integral to the education of every child in elementary and secondary schools. More recently, the Fund undertook a third program concerned with the role and quality of the private, non-profit sector in American life. In addition, the Fund has from time to time sponsored a few projects in other areas such as the National Committee for the Bicentennial Era.

TRUSTEES OF THE JDR 3RD FUND

*deceased

John Spencer 1967-1969
    Dean of the College
    Middlebury College
Phillips Talbot 1964-1979
    President
    The Asia Society
Kenneth T. Young, Jr.* 1963-1972
    Former Senior Visiting Fellow
    Council on Foreign Relations

OFFICERS OF THE JDR 3RD FUND

Mrs. John D. Rockefeller 3rd
President
Porter McKeever
Vice President
Patricia E. Lucas
Secretary
David G. Fernald
Treasurer
George J. Pipino
Assistant Treasurer

ARTS IN EDUCATION
PROGRAM STAFF, 1968-1979

Kathryn Bloom
    Director 1968-1979
Richard Grove
    Associate Director 1968-1970
Jerome J. Hausman
    Consultant 1968-1975
Jack Morrison
    Associate Director 1970-1975
Gene C. Wenner
    Program Associate 1971-1975
    Assistant Director 1976-1978
Jane Remer
    Program Associate 1973-1975
    Assistant Director 1976-1978
    Associate Director 1978-1979
Dorothy O'Hara
    Secretary to the Director 1972-1979
Karen S. Kane
    Secretary 1968-1977
Dolores Bock
    Secretary 1972-1978
Camy Calve
    Secretary 1978-1979 249